ABSOLUTE BEGINNER'S GUIDE

 TO

Microsoft®
Office Word 2003

Laura Acklen

 800 East 96th Street,
Indianapolis, Indiana 46240

Absolute Beginner's Guide to Microsoft® Office Word 2003

International Standard Book Number: 0-7897-2970-9

Library of Congress Catalog Card Number: 2003103658

Printed in the United States of America

First Printing: December 2003

06   05   04   03   4   3   2   1

Trademarks

All terms mentioned in this book that are known to be trademarks or service marks have been appropriately capitalized. Que Publishing cannot attest to the accuracy of this information. Use of a term in this book should not be regarded as affecting the validity of any trademark or service mark.

Warning and Disclaimer

Every effort has been made to make this book as complete and as accurate as possible, but no warranty or fitness is implied. The information provided is on an "as is" basis. The author and the publisher shall have neither liability nor responsibility to any person or entity with respect to any loss or damages arising from the information contained in this book.

Bulk Sales

Que Publishing offers excellent discounts on this book when ordered in quantity for bulk purchases or special sales. For more information, please contact

U.S. Corporate and Government Sales
1-800-382-3419
corpsales@pearsontechgroup.com

For sales outside of the U.S., please contact

International Sales
1-317-428-3341
international@pearsontechgroup.com

Associate Publisher
Greg Wiegand

Acquisitions Editor
Stephanie J. McComb

Development Editor
Christy Miller Kuziensky

Managing Editor
Charlotte Clapp

Project Editor
Dan Knott

Copy Editor
Chuck Hutchinson

Indexer
Mandie Frank

Proofreader
Kathy Bidwell

Technical Editor
Bill Rodgers

Publishing Coordinator
Sharry Lee Gregory

Interior Designer
Ann Jones

Cover Designer
Dan Armstrong

Page Layout
Michelle Mitchell

Graphics
Tammy Graham
Tara Lipscomb

Contents at a Glance

Table of Contents

About the Author

Laura Acklen has been involved in the development of a number of academic and corporate training series. She worked on the development team for the Que Education and Training Essentials books and wrote the Windows 3.1, Windows 95, Word for Windows 95, and Word for Windows 6.0 student manuals. Laura wrote Que Publishing's *First Look at Windows 95*. She is also the author of Sams *Teach Yourself Office 2000 in 10 Minutes*, and the co-author of DDC Publishing's *Upgrading to Office 2000* in the One-Day series. Laura is a Microsoft Office User Specialist in all levels of Microsoft Word 2000. Most recently, she conducted MOUS Certification courses for DDC Publishing in major cities all over Texas.

Dedication

To my dear friends at Deep Eddy Pool, for creating the friendly oasis that I regularly slip away to.

Acknowledgments

Once again, I'm happy to be working with Stephanie McComb, Senior Acquisitions Editor at Que Publishing. I've already informed her that she may not ever leave this business because I want to do all my books with her.

I want to express my sincere appreciation for the efforts of the editing team: Christy Miller Kuziensky, for hanging in there through a really tough development edit; Chuck Hutchinson, for his kind suggestions and for making those "easy" corrections for me; Dan Knott, for making me laugh while we worked on author review; Sharry Lee Gregory, for staying on top of all the important details (like author payments).

I would especially like to thank Bill Rodgers, the Technical Editor on this book. Bill did an excellent review. He took the time to make helpful suggestions, and he did so in a very nice way. He also stepped in and helped with Chapter 17, "Working with XML," and for that I am very grateful.

We Want to Hear from You!

As the reader of this book, *you* are our most important critic and commentator. We value your opinion and want to know what we're doing right, what we could do better, what areas you'd like to see us publish in, and any other words of wisdom you're willing to pass our way.

As an associate publisher for Que Publishing, I welcome your comments. You can email or write me directly to let me know what you did or didn't like about this book—as well as what we can do to make our books better.

Please note that I cannot help you with technical problems related to the topic of this book. We do have a User Services group, however, where I will forward specific technical questions related to the book.

When you write, please be sure to include this book's title and author as well as your name, email address, and phone number. I will carefully review your comments and share them with the author and editors who worked on the book.

Email: feedback@quepublishing.com

Mail: Greg Wiegand
            Associate Publisher
            Que Publishing
            800 East 96th Street
            Indianapolis, IN 46240 USA

For more information about this book or another Que Publishing title, visit our Web site at www.quepublishing.com. Type the ISBN (excluding hyphens) or the title of a book in the Search field to find the page you're looking for.

INTRODUCTION

If you are new to Word 2003 or to word processing in general, the *Absolute Beginner's Guide to Microsoft Office Word 2003* is the book for you. With clear, concise explanations and easy-to-use numbered steps, we will help you to quickly learn everything you need to get the most out of the Word 2003 application. We try to make you feel as though you have someone sitting next to you, explaining what a feature is and why you would want to use it, and giving you step-by-step instructions on how to make it work.

We assume that you have no previous experience in Word 2003, so you will start from the beginning and work up to some pretty advanced features. We do assume that you know how to use Windows, so if you're new to computers, you might consider picking up a copy of Que Publishing's *Absolute Beginner's Guide to Windows XP* (ISBN: 0-7897-2856-7) by Shelley O'Hara.

This latest version of Word offers some exciting new features and enhancements to make your work quicker and easier. The new task pane puts many common features at your fingertips. You'll see how this task pane morphs into different task panes depending on what you are working on at the time. For example, if you Alt+click a word or phrase, you activate the Research task pane that lets you search for information in the built-in writing tools and online resources.

You may be upgrading to Word 2003 from a previous version. If so, you'll really like the "New to Word 2003" designations so you can quickly zero in on the newest features. You should be aware that when you upgrade, Microsoft strongly suggests that you let the install program remove the previous version to avoid potential conflicts.

Some Key Terms

To use Word, you need to know the basic terminology used for common mouse actions:

- **Point**—Move the mouse on the desk to move the pointer onscreen. The tip of the arrow should be on the item to which you are pointing.
- **Click**—Press and release the left mouse button once. You use a click to select commands and toolbar buttons, as well as perform other tasks.
- **Double-click**—Press and release the left mouse button twice in rapid succession.

- **Right-click**—Press and release the right mouse button once. You can right-click to display a shortcut menu just about anywhere in the program.

- **Drag and drop**—Hold down the mouse button and drag the pointer across the screen. Release the mouse button. Dragging is most often used for selecting and moving text and objects.

Points to Keep in Mind

You can customize Word so that it is set up the way you like to work. For consistency, though, this book makes some assumptions about how you use your computer. When working through steps and especially when viewing the figures in this book, keep in mind the following distinctions:

- Word offers you several different methods to perform the same task. For example, for commands, you can select a command from a menu, use a shortcut key, use a toolbar button, or select from the shortcut menu. This book usually mentions one or two methods (the most common for that particular task) and then includes other methods in a tip.

- Your Word screen might not look identical to the one used in this book's figures. For instance, if you use the ruler, you see that. (Most of the figures in this book don't show the ruler.) Don't let these differences distract you; the figures might look different from what you see on your computer, but Word 2003 works the same way.

- Your computer setup is most likely different from the one used in the book. Therefore, you will see different programs listed on your Start menu, different fonts in your font list, different folders and documents, and so on. Again, don't be distracted by the differences.

How to Use This Book

This book is divided into six parts, each part focusing on a different theme. The book builds on the skills you need, starting with the basics of formatting and then moving to more complex topics such as templates and macros. You can read the book straight through, look up topics when you have a question, or browse through the contents, reading information that interests you. Here is a quick breakdown of the parts.

Part I, "Learning the Basics," covers the essentials for creating and editing documents. Everything you need to know to create, edit, spell check, print, and apply basic formatting is in this section. Chapter 1 covers creating and saving documents and ways to get Help when you need it. Chapter 2 focuses on locating and opening documents. In Chapter 3, you learn editing techniques and ways to preview documents before printing. Chapter 4 covers basic formatting techniques and methods for working in the Reveal Formatting task pane. Chapter 5 explains how to use the writing tools.

Part II, "Making It Look Nice," explains how to apply formatting to paragraphs (Chapter 6) and pages (Chapter 7). Chapter 8 covers the use of styles for consistency and flexibility when you format your documents.

Part III, "Organizing Information," focuses on ways to organize information. Chapter 9 shows you how to use the Tables feature to organize and format information in columns. Chapter 10 shows you how to quickly create bulleted and numbered lists, as well as how to organize information in an outline format.

Part IV, "Adding Visuals," explains how to add graphics and other elements to improve the appearance of your documents. Chapter 11 shows you how to add pictures, text boxes, and AutoShapes to your documents. Chapter 12 discusses working with data from other sources, including how to use Object Linking and Embedding (OLE) to link to information created in different applications.

Part V, "Automating Your Work," covers the tools that you can use to automate repetitive tasks. In Chapter 13, you learn how to use the Merge feature to generate documents, such as form letters with envelopes and labels. Chapter 14 shows you how to use templates to automate the creation of frequently used documents. In Chapter 15, you learn how to use Word's tools to collaborate on documents. Chapter 16 discusses how to create and play macros, which are capable of automating virtually every process in Word. In Chapter 17, you learn how to save documents in XML format and how to work with XML tags.

Part VI contains two chapters and two appendixes that are provided for you on the book's Web site (www.quepublishing.com). Chapter 18 explains how to create and manipulate charts, diagrams, and equations. In Chapter 19, you learn how to create fill-in-the-blank forms complete with check boxes, drop-down lists, and text boxes. Appendix A explains how to recover from a system crash. In Appendix B, you learn how to download updates and how to install additional options for Word 2003. In the index, page numbers preceded by "PDF:" are for Chapters 18 and 19 and Appendixes A and B.

We hope you enjoy your Word learning experience!

Where to Find More Help

After you learn the concepts that are covered in this *Absolute Beginner's Guide*, you may want to explore some of the more advanced features in the program. I highly recommend Que Publishing's *Special Edition Using Microsoft Office Word 2003* (ISBN: 0-7897-2958-X) by Bill Camarda for in-depth coverage of the same features that were covered in this book and additional coverage on features for intermediate and advanced users.

Word has an extensive built-in Help system and, for the first time, you can search for help topics and articles on Microsoft's Office Web site, which is constantly being updated. Chapter 1, "Getting Comfortable with Word," has information on using Word's Help features.

Microsoft offers technical support to registered users of the program. See the Microsoft Help and Support page at `http://support.microsoft.com/` for more information on telephone support and submitting a request for online help.

You can also get peer-to-peer support on the Microsoft Word newsgroups. On the Microsoft Help and Support Web page, click the Newsgroups tab for links to subscribe to the Word newsgroups (select Office and then Word). At present, there are 23 different newsgroups, divided into feature categories, not product versions.

Conventions Used in This Book

You will find cautions, tips, and notes scattered throughout this book. Don't skip over them; they contain some important tidbits to help you along the way.

tip

A *tip* is a piece of advice—a little trick, actually—that helps you use software or your computer more effectively. Tips can also help you maneuver around problems or limitations.

caution

A *caution* tells you to beware of a potentially dangerous act or situation. In some cases, ignoring cautions could cause you significant problems, so pay particular attention to them!

A *note* is designed to provide information that is generally useful but not necessarily essential for what you're doing at the moment. Some are similar to extended tips—interesting, but not essential.

There are some other helpful conventions in the book to make your learning experience as smooth as possible. Text that you are going to type looks like this: `type a filename`. Buttons you click, menu commands you select, keys you press, and other action-related items are in **bold** in the text to help you locate instructions as you are reading. New terms being defined in the text are in *italic*. The letter of a menu command, check box, button, or other interface element that is the Windows "hotkey" for that feature is underlined for those of you who prefer to stick with keyboard shortcuts rather than the mouse for navigating the interface. Keep these conventions in mind as you read through the text.

PART

I

Learning the Basics

IN THIS CHAPTER

- Starting Word and recognizing different parts of the screen.

- Discovering what a toolbar is, why you want to use it, and how to switch to another toolbar.

- Using the task pane to open recently edited documents and get help when you need it.

- Using the built-in and online Help system to learn more about the vast collection of features in Word.

- Saving documents in the native Word format and in other formats so you can share documents with others.

GETTING COMFORTABLE WITH WORD

If you've used a previous version of Word, you may be tempted to skip this chapter. Don't. It is chock full of tips and tricks to help you get the most out of the Word interface. The rest of the book will make a lot more sense if you have a solid foundation to build on. This chapter provides the basic information that you need to skip to any other chapter in the book.

One thing you haven't seen yet is the task pane. The task pane is a significant addition to the Word 2003 interface, and although it's fairly user-friendly, you'll get a lot more out of it if you know how to use it correctly. As you work through this book, you'll see that the task pane is hooked to a variety of Word features.

What Is Word?

This may be the first time you've ever used Word or any other word processing program. Hold on to your hat because you are about to learn how to use a program that can handle almost any task you can imagine. From writing simple letters and memos to generating a mass mailing to producing high-quality presentation materials, Word can do all this and more.

Starting Word

The fastest way to start Word is to double-click the *shortcut* on the desktop. If you don't have the shortcut, you can use the Start menu instead:

1. Click the **Start** button.
2. Point to **All Programs**.
3. Click **Microsoft Office Word 2003**.

If you don't see Microsoft Office Word 2003 on the Programs menu, locate the Microsoft Office folder and open it. You should see a Microsoft Word entry. If not, the program hasn't been installed on your system yet. Insert the Office 2003 CD in the CD drive. If the Setup program doesn't start in a minute or two, choose **Start**, **Run**, browse to the CD drive, and then double-click setup.exe to start the Setup program.

Getting Acquainted with the Word Interface

You may be new to Word, but if you've used any other Windows program, you'll recognize most of the screen elements. The screen always contains a title bar, menu bar, toolbar, and control buttons. You'll find that the nice thing about a Windows program is that after you learn one application, you have a head start on the next one.

When you start Word, a blank document appears (see Figure 1.1), which means you can start typing immediately. The insertion point shows you where the text will appear.

In addition to the common Windows application elements, Word 2003 also has some unique features to help you get your work done faster. For example, the task pane is a new feature in Word 2003 and the most prominent element on the screen (see Figure 1.1). The task pane is covered in detail later in this chapter.

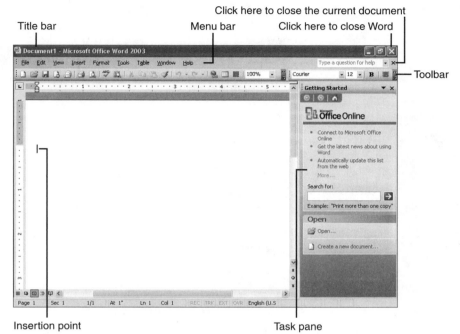

FIGURE 1.1

The Word screen has the same elements that you have seen in other Windows applications.

Title bar

Menu bar

Click here to close the current document

Click here to close Word

Toolbar

Insertion point

Task pane

Working with Toolbars

The toolbar line on the Word screen actually contains two toolbars: the Standard toolbar, which contains buttons for frequently used features such as Open, Save, and Print; and the Formatting toolbar, which contains buttons for common formatting tasks such as Font, Bold, and Bullets. You can choose from 21 different toolbars, including toolbars for working with graphics, reviewing documents, editing tables, and creating merge files.

Follow these steps to see a list of toolbars:

1. Right-click anywhere on the toolbar to open the toolbar list (see Figure 1.2). If a check mark appears next to the name, it means the toolbar is already on. You'll see that the Standard and Formatting toolbars already have check marks next to them.

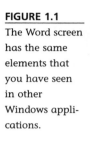

tip

The Standard and Formatting toolbars share a single line to reduce the amount of space they take up on the screen, but you can separate them if you like. To separate the toolbars, choose **Tools**, **Customize**, or right-click a toolbar and choose **Customize**. In the Options tab, place a check mark in the **Show Standard and Formatting toolbars on two rows** check box. One advantage to placing each toolbar on a line by itself is that you create room for more buttons.

FIGURE 1.2

Right-click a toolbar to open the toolbar list, where you can switch to another toolbar or turn off the toolbar(s).

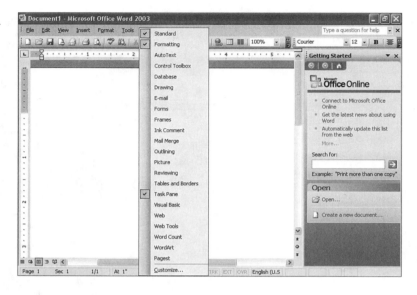

2. Click the toolbar you want to turn on. Clicking an *unchecked* toolbar name turns it on; clicking a *checked* toolbar name turns it off.

3. Click anywhere in the document to clear the toolbar list.

Using the Task Pane

The task pane, one of the new features in Word 2003, is designed to make it easier for you to select recently used documents, create new documents, and get help when you need it. Positioned on the right side of the screen, the task pane is out of the way but still accessible.

When you open Word, the Getting Started task pane lists your most recently opened documents (see Figure 1.3). An open icon is placed next to the More command; clicking it displays the Open dialog box where you can browse for documents. The upper section of the task pane enables you to search Microsoft online resources for answers to your questions. This page of the task pane is the Home page. You can get back to it later by clicking the house icon at the top of the task pane.

tip

If the Getting Started task pane isn't displayed on your screen, you can press F1 to display the Assistance task pane and then click the house icon to switch to the Getting Started task pane.

FIGURE 1.3

The Home page of the task pane gives you quick access to recently opened documents and support options.

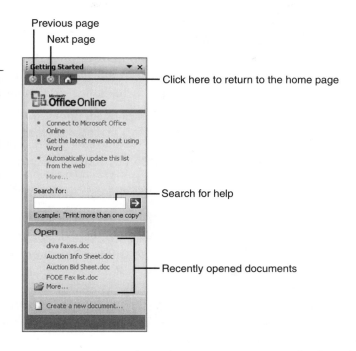

Previous page
Next page

Click here to return to the home page

Search for help

Recently opened documents

As you open pages in the task pane, you can move back to the previous page or on to the next page by using the arrow buttons at the top of the pane.

If you prefer to have more room on your screen, you can close the task pane by simply clicking the Close button in the upper-right corner of the task pane.

Getting Assistance

Word 2003 offers an amazing amount of support to get you up and running as quickly as possible. Even if you're not sure *exactly* what you're looking for, you can still find the help you need. And after you've found the information, you can go right back to what you were doing and continue working.

Unlike previous versions of Word, this latest version is geared toward more online interaction. In

tip

Sometimes all you need is a little push in the right direction to get you going. If you're trying to figure out which toolbar button is which, try this technique: You can display the name of a toolbar button by pointing to it with the mouse and pausing. A ScreenTip appears and either tells you the name or provides a brief description of the button.

addition to the usual help topics that are built in to the program, other support resources are available online. Therefore, you must have Internet access to take advantage of these additional resources.

Not everyone has Internet access, however, so I want to cover the resources that are included with Word first; then I'll address the additional support options available online. When you initially access the help topics, you are searching the static help information included with the software and the updatable information stored on Microsoft Office Online. What does this mean? That even if you do not have an active Internet connection, you can still find the information you need.

Accessing Help Topics

The book you're reading right now is the absolute best resource for a beginner. The second best resource is the help topics, which contain information on virtually every feature in the program. You can access the help topics in two ways: by searching through the Index or browsing through the Table of Contents.

To access the help topics, press **F1**, or choose **Help**, **Microsoft Word Help**. If the task pane is already open, the Assistance pane appears. Otherwise, the task pane opens with the Assistance pane displayed (see Figure 1.4). The Assistance pane is the launching pad for the support resources that are available to you.

Searching by Keywords

There are two ways to take advantage of the built-in help topics. You can search through the help index, or you can look through a table of contents. Searching by keyword is great when you want to search for a particular subject and get a list of help topics to choose from.

To search through the help topics, follow these steps:

1. Type a keyword (or just the first few letters) in the Search text box (see Figure 1.4).

2. Either press **Enter** or click the green arrow to search the help topics. A list of topics that contain the keyword is displayed (see Figure 1.5).

3. Click one of the topics to open it in a new window (see Figure 1.6). You can now click any of the help topics in the Search Results pane to display them in the Microsoft Word Help dialog box.

FIGURE 1.4

The Assistance pane of the task pane groups all the support options together in one place.

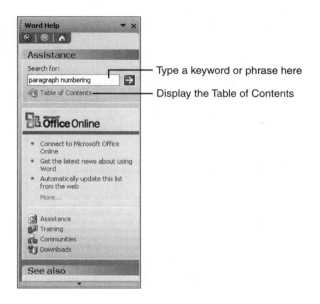

Type a keyword or phrase here

Display the Table of Contents

When a search returns too many help topics to look through, try refining your search to be more specific. Consider searching for more specific keywords or phrases. You can also type a question in your own words because Word's help is designed to work with natural language phrases. Simply type the new keywords or phrase in the Search text box. Furthermore, you can limit the scope of the search by selecting from the drop-down list in the Search section of the Search Results pane. For example, you may choose to search only the offline Help information.

Searching the Table of Contents

The Table of Contents section is more task-oriented, so you'll find the features are organized into projects. Because the topics are organized by task, you don't have to know exactly what feature you are looking for. If you want to change the margins or learn how to insert an image, this is the right place to search.

note

If you have an active Internet connection, you search Microsoft Office Online each time you use the help topics. Searching the whole system will take longer for the search results to come up than if you were searching through the help files on your local system.

FIGURE 1.5
If a lengthy list of help topics is returned, you may want to refine your search a bit.

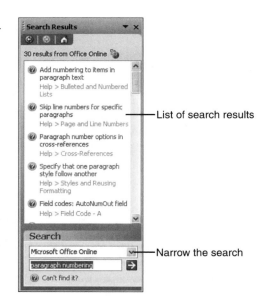

List of search results

Narrow the search

The selected help topic is shown here

Select one of these help topics

FIGURE 1.6
When you click a help topic, the information is displayed in a new window.

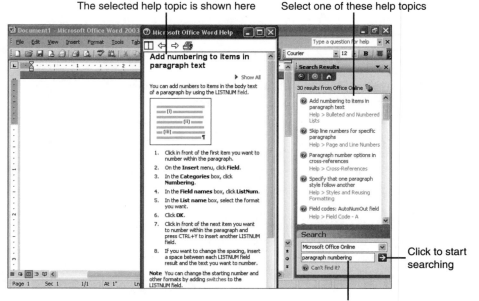

Click to start searching

Type a new keyword or phrase here

To look through the Table of Contents, follow these steps:

1. Click the Table of Contents link to display a list of headings (see Figure 1.7).
2. Click a book icon to open a category.
3. Help topics have question mark icons next to them. Click one of these icons to display a help topic.

Getting Help on the Web

Microsoft is leading a trend toward placing more and more support resources online. Why would the company do this, you ask? Consider how much easier it is to keep the information current and how much more cost effective it is to take advantage of the Internet as a distribution tool. The cost of printing user manuals has led many software companies to put electronic versions of their manuals on the installation CD.

> **tip**
>
> When you're searching through the help topics, you will find yourself in the Search Results task pane. You can't look through the Table of Contents in this pane, so you need to switch back to the Help task pane. Click the down arrow next to the Close button (upper-right corner) on the task pane. This opens a list of task panes to choose from. Select **Help**. Using this drop-down list, you can switch back and forth between different task panes.

FIGURE 1.7

The Contents tab of the Microsoft Word Help pane organizes help topics using a book-and-chapter model.

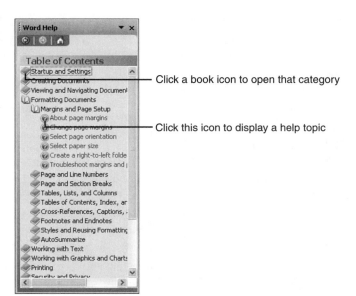

Click a book icon to open that category

Click this icon to display a help topic

Microsoft is taking this approach one step further by creating a huge storehouse of user guides, tutorials, and research tools on its Web site. It continually updates the site, so you are always getting the most up-to-date information. As tutorials and demos are designed, they are placed on the site and are instantly available. When you think about this new way of providing information, the advantages of current information (and lots more of it) outweigh the disadvantage of not receiving printed materials.

The Assistance page of the task pane provides several links where you can find help online. I'll cover the high points here, and you can explore the others on your own.

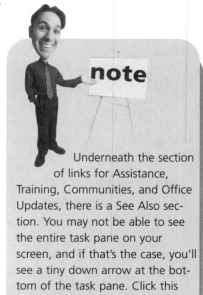

Getting Assistance with Word

Microsoft offers a nice collection of articles on how to use Word. Click the **Get the latest news about using Microsoft Word** link on the Assistance page (refer to Figure 1.4) to display the Word Assistance page on Microsoft Office Online (see Figure 1.8). Select a category to open another window with a list of articles. Select an article and go!

If you click the Assistance link on the task pane, you can browse through a list of articles for Word, Outlook, Excel, PowerPoint, Access, FrontPage, Publisher, Project, Visio, and InfoPath.

note

Underneath the section of links for Assistance, Training, Communities, and Office Updates, there is a See Also section. You may not be able to see the entire task pane on your screen, and if that's the case, you'll see a tiny down arrow at the bottom of the task pane. Click this down arrow to scroll down through the task pane to review the other links for What's New, Contact Us, Accessibility Help, and Online Content Settings. When you scroll down through the task pane, you'll see a tiny up arrow at the top of the task pane. Click this arrow to scroll back up.

Using Online Training

Microsoft Office Online has a Training section with training courses on Word, Outlook, Excel, Access, and PowerPoint, to name a few. Click the **Training** link (on the Assistance task pane or on the Office Online Web site) and then select Word from the Training Home page. You'll see a list of courses that you can take. Notice that the length of the course is shown along with a rating based on feedback from others who have taken this course (see Figure 1.9).

When you start a course, you'll see a brief overview with a list of goals. You'll hear a short narrative if you have your speakers turned on. After you complete a course, you have an opportunity to provide feedback. Take a minute and answer these questions. They really help people who come along after you.

FIGURE 1.8

The Assistance section of Microsoft Office Online provides links to dozens of articles on using Word.

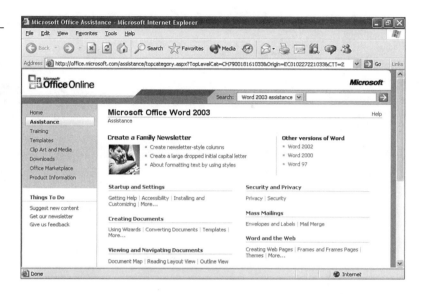

FIGURE 1.9

Several courses are available to take you step by step through a task.

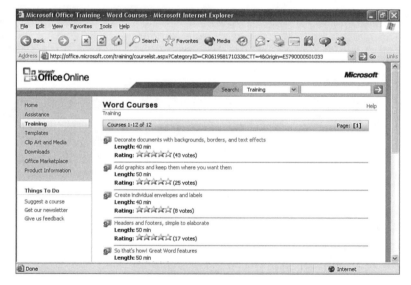

Using the Research Resources

Most word processing programs have a dictionary, thesaurus, and grammar checker. New in Word 2003, the Research feature expands this offering to include online reference books, research sites, business and financial sites, and any other resources that your company sets up. Let me give you an example of a simple use; then I'll spark your interest with something a little more complex.

Say you are writing an article on a technical topic and want to make sure you're using the correct terminology and spelling. Use the Research feature to check your work.

To use the Research resources, do the following:

- Select a word or phrase. Right-click the selection and then choose **Look Up**. The Research task pane opens and displays the results of your search (see Figure 1.10).

- Hold down the **Alt** key and click a word in your document to display the Research task pane.

note

The layout of the pages on the Office Online site may change, and as a result, they may look different from the pages shown in the figures. Don't let the differences throw you. In most cases, the options are still there, but they may be in a different place. The method to access these pages should remain the same.

FIGURE 1.10

The Research pane allows you to research online resources without leaving Word.

Start searching

Specify what to search here

Add or remove resources here

Alt-click a word to look it up

Selected text

By default, Research uses all the online research books for the search. If you don't find what you're looking for, you can choose to search through the research sites, the financial and business sites, or any specific book or site. Simply click the drop-down list arrow under the green arrow and choose what you want to search.

To take this example further, suppose your company has a huge database of product information on an intranet. A system administrator could set up this database as a Research resource. You could then search for a particular product and copy the relevant details directly into your document.

Saving Documents

Electronic copies of documents have virtually replaced paper copies, so even if you don't think you'll ever work with a document again, saving it on disk is a good idea so that you can keep a record of it. Hard drive space is cheap compared to the time required for you to re-create the document later.

Keep in mind that because fewer paper copies are kept, the electronic copies need more protection. Regularly backing up your important files is extremely important.

Saving a Document in Word Format

Until you save your document, it is stored in memory, which is a temporary location. Memory is considered a temporary storage location because when you turn off your computer, the memory space is cleared. If the power is interrupted, or if your system locks up, you may lose everything that you haven't saved.

Follow these steps to save a document:

1. Click the **Save** button on the Standard toolbar or choose **File, Save** (**Ctrl+S**).

    ■ If you've already named this document, it will seem as though nothing has happened. Because the document has already been named, Word saves the changes without any intervention from you.

    ■ If you haven't named the document yet, the Save As dialog box appears (see Figure 1.11).

This is where the file will be saved.

FIGURE 1.11

The Save As dialog box enables you to save a new document or an existing document under a new name.

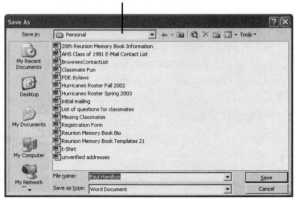

2. Type a filename and press **Enter** (or click the **Save** button).

   ■ Filenames can be up to 255 characters in length and can contain letters, numbers, and spaces. Some symbols can be used, but not others, so to avoid problems, stick with hyphens (-) and underscores (_).

   ■ When you type a filename without selecting a location, the document is saved in the default folder, which is the folder that Word is currently pointing to. You'll learn how to search for a file you saved but could not find afterward in the next chapter. If this has happened to you, don't sweat it; it happens to the best of us.

BACKING UP YOUR WORK AUTOMATICALLY

Word has an AutoRecover feature that automatically makes a copy of your document while you work. If your system stops responding and you can't save the document normally, you can open the AutoRecover copy when you restart Word. The AutoRecover feature is already turned on and set to make an AutoRecover copy every 10 minutes. You can adjust the interval in the Save tab of the Options dialog box. Choose **Tools**, **Options** and click the **Save** tab. You can adjust the backup interval by typing a new value in the **Save AutoRecover info every** text box or by clicking the spinner arrows next to the text box. See Appendix A (at www.quepublishing.com), "Recovering from a System Crash," for more information on recovering documents after a system failure.

Saving to a Different File Format

Microsoft Word is the dominant word processing program on the market, but others are available. You can freely share your Word documents with someone who uses a completely different program, such as WordPerfect, or someone who uses a different version of Microsoft Word by simply saving the document in a different format. Word has a nice collection of conversion files, or *filters*, as they are sometimes called. You can save documents in all the frequently used formats including WordPerfect, previous versions of Word, Rich Text Format (RTF), Web Page (HTML), XML, and Plain Text (*.txt).

To save a file in a different format, follow these steps:

1. Choose **File**, **Save As**.
2. In the Save As dialog box, click the **Save as type** drop-down list arrow to open the list of file types.
3. Scroll through the list to locate the file format that you want to use (see Figure 1.12). As you can see, Word can save to many different file formats.
4. Select the format from the **Save as type** drop-down list.
5. If necessary, type a filename and select a location for the file.
6. Click **Save**.

note

If you have files that were created with the Microsoft Works program, you can open those files in Word. Open them in Works and save them to Rich Text Format (*.rtf). You can then open the RTF files directly into Word 2003.

FIGURE 1.12

The Save As dialog box enables you to save a document to a different file format.

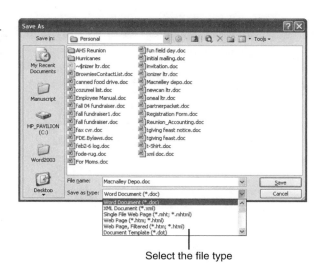

Select the file type

Exiting Word

The fastest way to exit Word is to click the application's Close button, which is represented as an X icon. Two Close buttons appear in the upper-right corner. This can be a little confusing. The top one is the application Close button; the bottom one is the document Close button.

To exit Word, follow these steps:

1. Click the application Close button. Before you close the program, Word prompts you to save any unsaved changes (in every open document window).

2. If necessary, give filenames to any documents that you have not yet saved and named.

THE ABSOLUTE MINIMUM

After reading this chapter, you now know how to

- Start Word with a desktop shortcut or through the Start menu.
- Use the essential elements on the screen and learn what they do.
- Switch to a different toolbar and turn the toolbars off and on.
- Use the new task pane to open recently used documents and access Help.
- Use Word's built-in and online help resources to get you up to speed on using Word's features.
- Save documents in Word format or in a different file format, such as WordPerfect, RTF, or HTML.
- Exit Word and save unsaved open documents.

In the next chapter, you'll learn how to locate and open documents using the tools in the Open dialog box.

IN THIS CHAPTER

- Using the tools in the Open dialog box to navigate through the drives and folders on your system (and/or network).

- Searching for a file when you can't remember its name or where it is located.

- Organizing your files into folders so you can locate them later.

- Learning how to move, copy, rename, and delete files within the file management dialog boxes.

- Converting files from different formats so you can work with documents created in other programs.

2

FINDING AND OPENING DOCUMENTS

One of the fundamental advantages of using a word processing program is the ability to leverage the time you spend creating one document when it's time to create another. Let me give you an example. Suppose you send out a company memo several times a week. Instead of creating a new memo each time, you probably open an existing memo, make some changes to it, and save it as a new memo. Rather than spend 30 minutes or more creating a memo from scratch, you spend only a few minutes filling in the current information.

Learning how to use Word's file management tools is very important. You'll be surprised at how much time you will spend navigating through the folders on your system to locate and open existing documents.

Becoming Familiar with the Open Dialog Box

When you're ready to open a file, you'll use the Open dialog box. This is one of the "file management" dialog boxes in Word. Others are the Save As, Insert File, and Insert Picture dialog boxes. It's important to spend a few minutes becoming familiar with file management dialog boxes because you will use them not only to locate files, but also to organize your files and folders. After you use Word for a while, you'll see that you spend a lot of time in these dialog boxes.

To display the Open dialog box, click the **Open** button or choose **File**, **Open (Ctrl+O)**. The Open dialog box appears (see Figure 2.1).

Opening a File

When you open the Open dialog box, Word automatically displays the contents of the default or the most recently used folder. The section "Navigating Through Drives and Folders" covers switching to a different drive and/or folder.

Different types of files have different file icons. The icon for a Word document has blue W on a white page. Files in Portable Document Format (PDF) have a window with icons in it over a white page. Application files usually have a smaller version of the icon that appears on the desktop. The icons can help you zero in on the file you want.

To open a file, follow these steps:

1. Click the file you want to open.

2. Click **Open**. You can also double-click the file to select and open it at the same time.

> **tip**
>
> Word maintains a list of the last few documents that you've opened. They are shown at the bottom of the File menu. To choose one of these documents, open the **File** menu and then either click the filename or press the underlined number next to the filename. Word then opens the file into a new document window, and you are ready to go.
>
> By default, four files are shown. You can increase the number of recently used files shown in the list. Choose **Tools**, **Options** and then click the **General** tab. In the **Recently used file list** text box, either type a new value or click the spinner arrows to change the value. Click **OK**.

Customizing the View

There are several different ways to display files and folders in the Open dialog box. The way you display them could be personal preference, or a different view could make it easier to locate a file. Whatever the reason, switching to a different view is a snap using the View button.

You can click the **View** button to cycle through the different views, or you can click the **drop-down arrow** to the right of the View button to choose from the following options:

FIGURE 2.1

Use Word's Open dialog box to locate and open documents.

Folder icon   Current folder   Views button

List of files in current folder

File icon

- **Thumbnails**—Displays thumbnail size images of picture files, and in some cases, documents. Otherwise, a large icon on a white page identifies the type of file.

- **Tiles**—Displays the files and folders in two columns with large icons. The type and size of the document are also shown.

- **Icons**—Displays the folders and files with an identifying icon. Only the folder or filename is shown.

- **List**—Displays the names of the folders and files with small icons.

- **Details**—Displays the names of the folders and files with small icons. The size, type, and modification date and time are also shown (see Figure 2.2).

- **Properties**—Displays the properties for a selected file in the right pane.

- **Preview**—Displays a preview of a selected file in the right pane.

- **WebView**—Displays a preview of HTML documents that will be posted on the Web.

List of files in Details view

FIGURE 2.2

The Details view provides a lot of information about the files and folders.

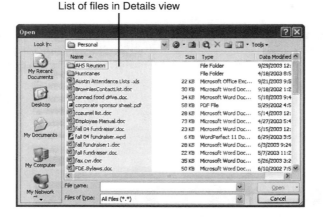

You can enlarge the Open dialog box and display more files and folders at one time. This capability is especially helpful when you're using the Details view. Point to a side or corner of the dialog box and wait for the two-sided arrow to appear. Then click and drag the dialog box border. Release the mouse button when you're satisfied with the new size. If you click and drag a corner, you'll maintain the aspect ratio as you resize the dialog box.

tip

In Word, you can open multiple documents at one time. How many? The number depends on your system resources. When I tested this feature, I was able to open more than 40 documents at once. To select more than one document, click the first document and then hold down the **Ctrl** key as you click the others. When you're finished selecting files, click **Open**.

Arranging the File List

The Details view provides an added advantage: You can sort the file list by the creation or modification date, size, or type. For example, you might arrange the file list by the modification date to locate a file that you edited on a specific date (see Figure 2.3).

To rearrange the file list, follow these steps:

1. Click a column heading that you want to sort by, such as **Type**.

2. Click the column heading again to arrange the list in reverse order.

Click one of the column headings to sort the list

FIGURE 2.3
Arranging the
file list by date
or type can help
you locate a
specific file.

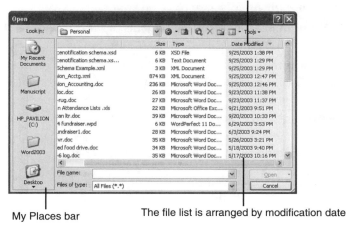

My Places bar   The file list is arranged by modification date

Adding Shortcuts to the My Places Bar

You probably have a handful of documents that
you use often. If you're lucky, they are stored in
the default directory so you can get to them
quickly. More often than not, though, they are
in another folder and perhaps even on another
drive. As you'll see in the next section, locating
files can take a few seconds of navigating, especially if you have to look through drives on a
network. Rather than navigate through the
same folders to locate the files, you can add
shortcuts to the folders (or drives) to the My
Places bar so that you can get to those documents
quickly.

You can take advantage of the My Places bar in
several ways. The following buttons are there by
default:

> **tip**
>
> The procedure seems
> straightforward enough, but
> I still do a double-take
> whenever I want to get my
> list back "the way it was"
> before I started sorting by
> date. The default arrange-
> ment is by name, so to revert to
> the original, click the Name col-
> umn heading. Click once to
> arrange from *A–Z*; click twice to
> arrange from *Z–A*.

- **My Recent Documents**—Takes you to a list of the most recently used documents. This list, which is stored in a folder on your system, actually contains
  shortcuts to the documents, not the documents themselves, so don't worry
  that your documents have been moved. You can quickly open a recent document by double-clicking one of the shortcuts in the list, or by selecting the
  shortcut and then choosing **Open**.

- **Desktop**—Displays the contents of your desktop. If you have created a shortcut to a document, folder, or drive on your desktop, you can select it here.
- **My Documents**—Displays the contents of the My Documents folder on your system.
- **My Computer**—Displays a list of drives and shared network folders on your system. The list matches the one you see when you start Windows Explorer or My Computer.
- **My Network Places**—Displays the network resources available on your system. Here again, this list matches the one you see when you open My Network Places from the Windows Explorer or My Computer.

In addition to these buttons, you can also add your own buttons for frequently used folders or drives.

To add a folder or drive to the My Places bar, do the following:

1. Select a folder or drive.
2. Click the **Tools** button on the dialog box's toolbar.
3. Choose **Add to My Places**.

When you add a folder or drive to the My Places bar, a button is added to the bottom of the bar, so you may have to scroll down to see it. The drive button has a drive icon on it; the folder button has a folder icon. Use the tiny arrows at the top and bottom to scroll up and down on the My Places bar.

> **tip**
>
> You can remove items that you add to the My Places bar if you change your mind, or if you simply don't use that drive or folder as much anymore. You can also rearrange the buttons on the bar.
>
> Right-click a button on the My Places bar and then choose **Remove** to take it off the bar. Choose **Move Up** to move the button up, or choose **Move Down** to move the button down.

Navigating Through Drives and Folders

At first, you may choose to save all your documents in the same folder because keeping everything in one place is often easier when you are just starting out. However, the more documents you create, the more difficult it may become to locate the one you want. The "Organizing Files in Folders" section later in this chapter covers file management strategies to help you organize your files.

You can easily move around the drives or folders on your system by using the tools in the file management dialog boxes (that is, Open, Save As, Insert File). Use these techniques to look through the drives and folders:

- Double-click a **folder icon** to open the folder and display the list of files and folders in that folder.

- Click the **History** button and choose a recently viewed folder or drive.

- Click the **Up One Level** button to move up a level in the folder list or move back to the previous folder.

- Click the **Look in** drop-down list arrow and choose another folder, drive, or location (see Figure 2.4).

note

When you navigate to a different folder in the Open dialog box, that folder then becomes the new default folder. The next time you open the Open dialog box, you'll see the list of files in that same folder.

Select a recently-opened folder ─┐

Click to move up a level in the folder list

FIGURE 2.4

Using buttons on the toolbar, you can quickly jump to a different drive or folder.

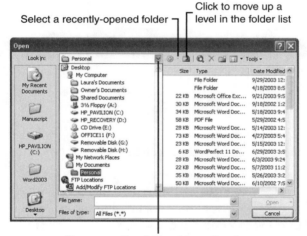

Choose another folder, drive or location from the Look in drop-down list

Searching for a File

The hard drives being installed in new computers are absolutely huge. You can store thousands and thousands of files on a single drive. Even with the best file management system, however, locating a single file can sometimes be daunting. Learning how to use the tools that help you locate files is one of the most important skills you can master. Word has a nice collection of tools to help you locate files so you don't have to start another program to do a search.

Listing Files by Type

When you have many different types of files in a folder, limiting the number of files in the list can be a big help. One way to accomplish this is to display only a specific type of file in the list. For example, if you display only Word documents in the list, you can more easily find the file you are looking for.

By default, the file type is set to **All Files (*.*)**, so you will see every file saved in that folder, whether or not you can work with that file in Word.

To display only a particular type of file, follow these steps:

1. Click the **Files of type** drop-down list arrow to display the list of file types (see Figure 2.5).

FIGURE 2.5

After you select a particular file type, only those files are shown in the file list.

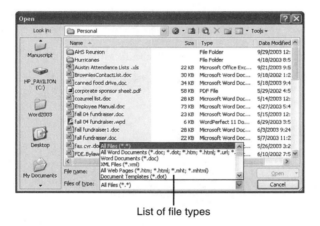

List of file types

2. Choose the type of file you want displayed in the list, such as Word Documents or WordPerfect 5.x/6.x.

3. When you are ready to see all the files again, select **All Files (*.*)** from the **Files of type** drop-down list.

Searching by File Properties

Say you can't remember the exact filename or exactly where your document is stored. You might remember a partial filename or maybe something about the contents. It could be a client's name, a project name, a technical term, or a phone number—all you need is a single piece of information that can be found in the file. You can then take that information and use it to search for the file.

Follow these steps to search for files by filename:

1. Type the filename or a portion of the filename in the **File name** text box.

2. Press **Enter** to display the list of files that match (see Figure 2.6).

A new file list is created

FIGURE 2.6

When you search for files, Word builds a new list of files that fit the search criteria.

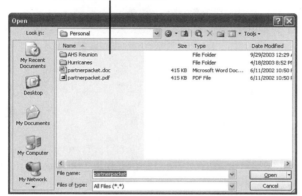

3. When you are ready to switch back to the full list of files, or if you want to start another search, remove the text in the File name text box and then press **Enter**.

To search for files by content, do the following:

1. Click the **Tools** button on the toolbar and then choose **Search** to display the File Search dialog box (see Figure 2.7).

2. Type the text you want to search for in the **Search text** text box.

3. (optional) Open the **Search in** list box and select the location that you want to search in.

4. (optional) Open the **Results should be** list box and choose the type of file you want to search.

5. Choose **Search**. Word searches for the file(s) and displays a list of files that contain the search text in the window.

FIGURE 2.7
The Basic tab of
the File Search
dialog box
allows you to
search for text
in a file.

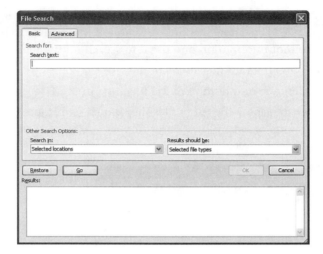

Organizing Files in Folders

Creating an efficient system for organizing your files is very important. You may
have already experienced the frustration of spending hours on a document, only to
have trouble finding it the next day. Even the very best documents won't do you any
good if you can't find them later.

The nice thing about Word is that you can perform all your file management tasks
from within the program. You don't have to start Windows Explorer to create new
folders and move files around. Also, you can work with virtually any file on your
system, not just Word files.

Creating New Folders

Setting up an electronic filing system is just like setting up a filing system for your
printed documents. Just as you would take out a manila folder and attach a label to
it, you can create a folder on your hard disk and give it a name. Organizing files
into folders by account, subject, project, or client helps you to locate the files you
need quickly and easily.

To create a new folder, do the following:

1. In a Word file management dialog box, such as the Open or Save As dialog
   box, open the drive or folder where you want to create the new folder.

2. Click the **Create New Folder** button on the toolbar, or right-click in the file
   list and choose **New, Folder**. A new folder icon appears in the file list with
   the temporary name New Folder (see Figure 2.8).

FIGURE 2.8

When you cre-
ate a new folder,
you replace the
temporary
name New
Folder with your
folder name.

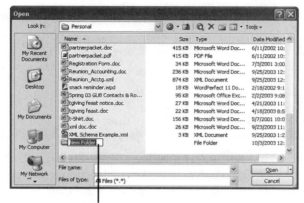

Type the name here

3. Type a name for the folder. Because the temporary name New Folder is selected, the name that you type automatically replaces it.

4. Either press **Enter** or click in the file list when you are finished.

Moving and Copying Files

If you accidentally save a file to the wrong folder, it's not a disaster. You can always move it to another folder later. Just be sure to *move* the file rather than *copy* it because you don't want two copies in two different places. Otherwise, things can get pretty confusing when you're trying to figure out which copy is the most recent.

To move files, follow these steps:

1. Select the file(s) that you want to move.

2. Right-click a selected file and choose **Cut**.

3. Navigate to the folder where you want to store the files.

4. Right-click in the file list and choose **Paste**.

There are also good reasons why you would want to copy a file rather than move it. Backups come to mind. If you've been working on an important document all day, it's a good idea to make a copy of the file onto a floppy disk or CD when you're fin-ished. You'll sleep better at night knowing that you have a backup copy. Likewise, if you want to share a file with a co-worker on your network, you should copy the file to his or her folder on the network. This way, you still have your original, and your co-worker has a copy that he or she can freely edit.

To copy files, do the following:

1. Select the file(s) that you want to copy.

2. Right-click a selected file and choose **Copy**.

3. Switch to the folder where you want to store the files.

4. Right-click in the file list and choose **Paste**.

Remember, if you want to move or copy more than one file, you just need to click the first file to select it. Then hold down the **Ctrl** key and click the others. Continue to hold down the Ctrl key until you are finished selecting the other files.

The instructions to move and copy files work on folders, too, so if you want to work with all the files in a folder, you don't have to select them all. Just select the folder and work with it instead.

Renaming Files

When you save a file (or create a folder), you try to give it a descriptive name. Later, however, that name may no longer seem appropriate. The situation could be as simple as a misspelling in the name, or a case in which the content of the file changes and the name needs to reflect that change. Regardless of the reason, you can quickly rename a file or folder in just four easy steps.

To rename a file or folder, do the following:

1. Click the file or folder that you want to rename.

2. Wait a second and click the file or folder name again. An outline appears around the file or folder name, and the name is selected (see Figure 2.9).

3. Edit the name as necessary.

4. Either press **Enter** or click in the file list when you are finished.

tip

Clicking, pausing, and clicking again can be a little tricky, especially if you accidentally move the mouse between clicks or click too quickly. You may find it easier to right-click a selected file and choose **Rename** to rename a file.

Deleting Files and Folders

If you decide that you no longer need a file or folder, you can delete it. Before you delete a folder, open it and make sure that it doesn't contain any folders or files that you need to keep. Deleting a folder automatically deletes the contents.

FIGURE 2.9

When an out-
line appears
around the file-
name, and the
text is selected,
you can edit the
name.

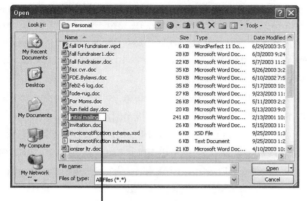

An outline appears around the name.

Follow these steps to delete a file or folder:

1. Select the file(s) or folder(s).
2. Click the **Delete** button, or right-click the
   selected file(s) or folder(s) and then choose
   Delete.

Mistakes can happen to anyone, which is why
we all love the Undo Delete feature. If you accidentally delete a file or folder, you can quickly
restore it. Right-click in the file list and then
choose **Undo Delete**. You can also press **Ctrl+Z**,
which, by the way, is the universal keystroke for
undoing actions.

caution

The **Ctrl+Z** keyboard
shortcut works only on
the last item you
deleted. If you've
deleted more than one
item, you should open the Recycle
Bin and restore the previously
deleted files.

Converting Documents on Open

You might also be surprised at how many Word users are still using older versions of
the program. Some companies are resistant to change, and others are limited by the
computing power of their systems. For example, thousands, if not millions, of local
government employees are happily using early versions of Word.

Thank goodness then for Word's built-in text converters that enable you to open documents created in earlier versions of Word and in other applications. All you have to
do is open the file and let Word's text converters do all the work.

When you save a converted document, Word asks whether you want to save the file in Word format. If you want to keep this document in Word format from now on, choose **Yes**. Choose **No** if you are returning the document to someone who isn't using Word. Then open the Save As dialog box to select the originating format in the **Save as Type** drop-down list.

If you get an `Invalid format` error message when you try to open a file in a different format, you have a couple of options:

■ Try saving the file in another format before you open it in Word. Get the file in a Rich Text Format (`*.rtf`) or Plain Text (`*.txt`) format if you can.

■ You may need to install additional conversion files. Have your CD ready just in case you are prompted to insert it. Click **Start**, **Control Panel**, **Add/Remove Programs**. Locate the entry for Office or Word 2003. Choose **Change** and then choose **Add or Remove Features**. In the next screen, enable the **Choose advanced customization of applications** radio button. In the next screen, open the **Office shared features** list. Open the **Converters and filters** list. Choose **Text Converters**. A picture of a hard drive appears next to the converters that are currently installed. For those that aren't, open the list and choose **Run from My Computer**. Choose **Update** to install the additional text converters.

THE ABSOLUTE MINIMUM

After reading this chapter, you now know how to

■ Use the Open dialog box so you're comfortable working in the file management dialog boxes in Word.

■ Navigate through the drives and folders on your system so you can work with files in another folder.

■ Search for a file, even if you don't remember the name or where it was located.

■ Move, copy, rename, and delete files from within the file management dialog boxes.

■ Convert documents from a different format. The built-in text converters do all the work for you.

In the next chapter, you'll learn how to move and copy text, adjust the way you view a document onscreen, and preview and print documents.

IN THIS CHAPTER

- Selecting text to perform numerous operations.

- Using the Undo feature as the ultimate "oops" fixer.

- Adjusting the zoom setting so that you can read tiny print or check a detailed graphic.

- Opening multiple documents at once so that you can easily create a new document from pieces of existing documents.

- Using Word's collection of view modes to review, edit, and format documents.

- Previewing a document in Print Preview before you send it to the printer.

- Faxing and emailing documents.

3

EDITING DOCUMENTS

When you're learning a new program, there is a certain amount of information that you *have* to learn before you can move on to the more advanced features. One of the most critical skills you can develop is selecting with the mouse or the keyboard. You'll soon see that many actions that you take in a document involve selecting text.

Another important concept is learning how to send out your documents. Back in the "old days" you had to print a document and either mail it or hand carry it to the recipient. In Word 2003, you can fax or email documents just as easily as you would print them. Add the Print Preview feature, which helps you proof your documents onscreen, and you are well on your way to saving trees.

Selecting Text

The Select feature is a powerful tool. Whenever you want to work with a specific section of text, you can select just that portion and work on it separately from the rest of the document. Selecting text gives you maximum flexibility because you can isolate the text or other items that you want to work with. Whatever action you take on the selection won't affect the rest of the document. When you edit documents, you'll do a lot of selecting, so take a few minutes to learn some shortcuts.

Selecting Text with the Keyboard

You can use either the mouse or the keyboard to select text. Each method has its own advantages, so it's a good idea to learn both techniques. Let's look at selecting text using the keyboard first.

To select a portion of text, follow these steps:

1. Position the insertion point at the beginning of the area you want to select.

2. Hold down the **Shift** key.

3. Use the arrow keys, or any of the navigation shortcuts that you prefer, to move to the end of the selection. For example, to select text a word at a time, hold down the **Shift** key while pressing **Ctrl+right arrow**. To select everything from the cursor to the end of the line, hold down the **Shift** key and press **End**.

Word shows the selection with a background color (see Figure 3.1). You can now work with this area of the document as a single unit.

Selecting Text with the Mouse

Selecting text with the mouse is also easy, although you might need a bit of practice before you become really good at it. Table 3.1 shows several methods of using the mouse to select text.

TABLE 3.1   Selecting Text with the Mouse

Mouse Action	What It Selects
Drag across text	One whole word at a time
Double-click	Entire word
Ctrl+click	Entire sentence
Triple-click	Entire paragraph
Single-click in left margin	Entire line
Double-click in left margin	Entire paragraph

FIGURE 3.1

Selected text is shown with a different background color to differentiate it from the rest of the text.

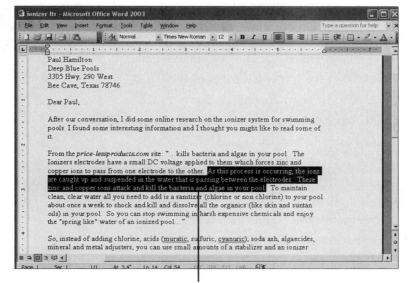

Selected text

Moving and Copying Text

Now that you have selected text, you might be thinking, "Okay, now what?" As you read through this book, you'll learn dozens of things that you can do with selected text. One of the most basic functions you will probably use is to move or copy text. If you move the text, deleting it from the original location and placing it somewhere else, you are *cutting and pasting* text. When you make a copy of the text, leaving a copy in the original location and placing the new copy in a different place, you are *copying and pasting* text.

tip

When you move the mouse pointer into the left margin, the pointer reverses direction and points to the right (instead of the regular left-facing pointer). When you see this special pointer, you can click to select a line or double-click to select a paragraph.

When you cut or copy a section of text, it is moved to the Windows Clipboard, which holds the cut or copied sections until you are ready to paste them. Because the Clipboard is Windows-based, you can use it in all Windows applications, not just Word. You'll learn how to use the Clipboard to cut and copy information between programs in Chapter 12, "Using Data from Other Sources."

One thing that makes Word so popular is that you can choose from a number of different methods to accomplish the same result. There are several different ways to cut or copy and paste selected text. The different alternatives are listed here. Generally, the basic steps to copy and move are as follows:

1. Select the text you want to copy or move.
2. Copy (or cut) the selected text.
3. Reposition the insertion point at the target location.
4. Paste the text you copied (or cut).

Some methods for copying, cutting, and pasting text work better in certain situations. For example, if your hands are already on the keyboard, the keyboard methods might be more convenient. Others prefer to use the mouse. Experiment with the different methods and find your favorites.

To copy selected text, perform one of the following actions:

- Click the **Copy** button.
- Choose **Edit**, **Copy**.
- Right-click the selected text and choose **Copy**.
- Press **Ctrl+C**.
- Press **Ctrl+Insert**.

To cut selected text, perform one of the following actions:

- Click the **Cut** button.
- Choose **Edit, Cut**.
- Right-click the selection and choose **Cut**.
- Press **Ctrl+X**.
- Press **Shift+Delete**.

To paste selected text, perform one of the following actions:

- Click the **Paste** button.
- Choose **Edit, Paste**.
- Right-click in the document and choose **Paste**.
- Press **Ctrl+V**.
- Press **Shift+Insert**.

note

If you cut or copy more than one section of text during a Word session, a special Clipboard task pane appears when you paste text. The last several sections of text that you cut or copied to the Clipboard are shown in a list. Click an item to paste that section of text at the insertion point. To view the Clipboard task pane at any time, choose **Edit**, **Office Clipboard**, or press **Ctrl+C** twice.

If you prefer, you can also use the mouse to drag selected text from one location and drop it in another. The drag-and-drop method works best if you are moving or copying text within the document window. When you have to scroll up or down, the process becomes a little tricky.

To drag and drop text, do the following:

1. Select the text you want to move or copy.

2. Position the mouse pointer on the highlighted text. The pointer changes to an arrow.

3. If you want to move the text, click and hold down the mouse button; if you want to copy the text, hold down the **Ctrl** key before you click and hold down the mouse button.

4. Drag the mouse to the target location. The mouse pointer changes to an arrow along with a small rectangular box (see Figure 3.2). An insertion point also appears showing you exactly where the text will be inserted when you release the mouse button.

5. Release the mouse button.

6. The text is still selected, so if you didn't get the text right where you wanted it, click and drag it again.

7. When you have the selection where you want it, click in the document window to deselect the text.

caution

If you don't see the Cut, Copy, or Paste buttons on the toolbar, you can select them from a palette of additional toolbar buttons. On the Standard toolbar, click the down arrow on the right side of the toolbar to open the palette of additional buttons. Click the button that you need. That button is added to the toolbar so you will have quick access to it next time. If you don't see the button you're looking for, choose **Add or Remove Buttons** and then select **Standard** or **Formatting**.

tip

If you are copying a selection, you'll see a box with a plus sign in it attached to the move/copy pointer. This is a nice touch because if you don't see the plus sign, you'll know that you are moving the selection, not copying it.

Insertion point shows where the pasted text will appear.

FIGURE 3.2
You can use the
mouse to move
selected text
with drag and
drop.

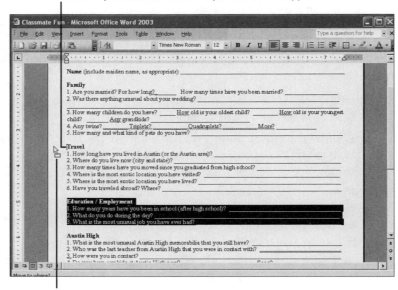

Move/copy mouse pointer

Using Undo to Fix Your Mistakes

Thank goodness for the Undo feature. How many times have you been a little hasty in a dialog box and done something you really didn't want to do? Simply put, Undo reverses the last action taken on a document. For example, if you delete selected text, Undo brings it back. If you change the margins, Undo puts them back the way they were. The text will look as if you never took the action.

Undo has a twin feature called Redo. Redo reverses the last Undo action. If you accidentally undo too many things, Redo puts them back.

To use the Undo feature, perform one of the following actions:

- Click the **Undo** button on the toolbar.
- Choose **Edit, Undo**.
- Press **Ctrl+Z**.

To use the Redo feature, perform one of the following actions:

- Click the **Redo** icon on the toolbar.
- Choose **Edit, Redo**.

The Undo and Redo buttons have drop-down arrows next to them. Click the arrow to display a list of the most recent actions (see Figure 3.3). Instead of repeatedly clicking the Undo or Redo buttons, you can choose an action from one of the lists. Stay with me now because this procedure gets a little tricky. If you choose an action from this list, all the actions up to and including that selected action will be reversed, not just the selected action.

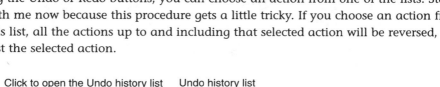

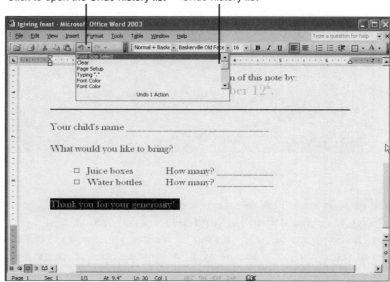

FIGURE 3.3

Use the Undo and Redo history lists to select which action to undo or redo.

Working with More Than One Document

Stop for a minute and think about how you use your computer. On any given day, you probably have two or three applications running at once—Word, your email application, several Web browser windows, a scanner or digital camera program, and so on. Your Windows taskbar contains buttons for each of the programs that you are running so that you can quickly switch back and forth between programs.

Likewise, Word enables you to work on more than one document at a time. Each document has a button on the Windows taskbar (at the bottom of the screen), so you can quickly switch back and forth between documents. When the taskbar is full, the application button shows a number next to the application name, indicating how many windows for that application are currently open (see Figure 3.4).

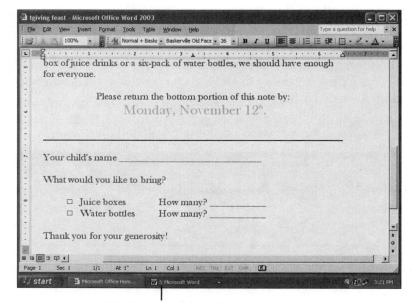

Number of open windows in Word

You already know how to open a document, but what you might not realize is that when you open a document, Word automatically places it in a new document window. So if you are already working on a letter, you can open other documents without affecting the letter document. Also, you can open more than one file at a time while you're in the Open File dialog box. Simply click the first file and then hold down the **Ctrl** key to click the other files.

You can switch from one document to another by using any of the following methods:

- Click the application button on the taskbar to open a pop-up list of open documents. Select an item from this list.
- Choose **Window** and then select the document you want.
- Press **Ctrl+F6** (Previous Window) repeatedly until Word displays the document you want to work on.

Multiple document windows make it a snap to cut, copy, and paste between documents. Simply cut or copy while viewing one document, and then switch to another document and paste.

Changing the Way You View a Document Onscreen

Everyone who picks up this book has a unique set of documents to work on and a unique style of working on them. If you are designing presentation materials with vivid graphics and informational charts, you can benefit from the ability to view details up close. Someone else might be generating a report where consistency in appearance is critical, and he or she can benefit from the ability to view more than one page at a time. And regardless of your industry, you probably spend lots of time simply just reading documents onscreen.

Word has built-in tools that enable you to customize the way you view documents onscreen. The idea is to give your eyes a break while you edit or read documents, and to make document review less of a chore.

The first options I'll discuss are part of the Zoom feature. Zoom allows you to adjust the magnification of a document. You can blow it up or scale it down. This is the tool you will use when you want to "zero in" on details such as figure captions, graphics, or small print in footnotes.

The second options I'll discuss are called *view modes*. These options allow you to view your documents in a variety of different layouts. You can choose from a special view mode just for reading documents onscreen and another for reviewing a document as it will look when printed.

Zooming In and Out

No matter what type of document you're working on, whether you're working with finely detailed graphics, charts with tiny legends, or very small print, Word has a way for you to view that document to make your job easier. Zoom controls the magnification of the document as it appears onscreen. Because the magnification doesn't affect the printed copy, you can use whatever Zoom setting you need for the task at hand.

By default, Word displays documents at a zoom ratio of 100%, which displays the text and graphics in the same size that they will be when printed. A zoom setting of 50% displays the document at half the printed size. A zoom setting of 200% displays the document twice as large as the printed copy.

tip

If you have a Microsoft IntelliMouse or other type of mouse with a scroll wheel, you can adjust the zoom ratio by holding down the **Ctrl** key and rotating the wheel. Notice that the wheel has small notches. Word zooms in or out at intervals of 10% for each notch on the wheel.

To adjust the zoom setting, follow these steps:

1. Click the drop-down arrow next to the **Zoom** button on the toolbar. A pop-up menu of zoom settings appears (see Figure 3.5).

2. Select a zoom setting.

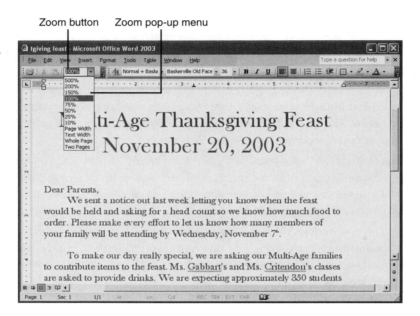

Zoom button   Zoom pop-up menu

FIGURE 3.5
Changing the
zoom setting
improves the
readability of a
document with-
out affecting the
printed copy.

You may decide that you don't like any of the preset zoom settings. You can type the zoom ratio that you want in the Zoom box, or you can choose **View**, **Zoom** to open the Zoom dialog box where you can type the preferred zoom ratio.

Switching to a Different Document View

There are no written rules for choosing a particular layout to view your documents. It really just depends on your work habits. Most people prefer to work in Print Layout view, which displays the document as it will appear when printed. Others prefer to work in the simpler Normal view, so they can focus on content and then switch to another view when they want to polish the appearance. My favorite is the new Reading Layout view because it's so much easier to read documents onscreen.

There are eight different options, all on the View menu. Some of the different options have buttons (next to the horizontal scrollbar) that you can click to quickly switch back and forth between view modes.

■ **Normal**—This view is designed for general editing and formatting tasks. No discernable page borders are visible onscreen, and page breaks are shown as a dotted line (see Figure 3.6).

Page break

FIGURE 3.6

Normal view is the most frequently used view mode in Word.

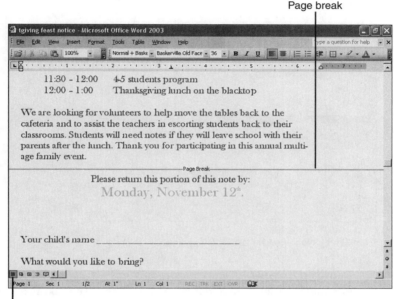

Normal View button

■ **Web Layout**—In this view, the document is shown as it will appear when viewed in a browser. Text wraps within the window, backgrounds are shown, and graphics are positioned as they will appear in a browser window.

■ **Print Layout**—This view displays the document as it will look when printed. Text, graphics, headers, footers, footnotes, columns, and other screen elements are shown in their correct positions and can be easily edited. A vertical ruler is added on the left side of the screen (see Figure 3.7). Pages are shown with a gray border around them, so you can easily see the dimensions of the paper. Page breaks are easily identified by the gray border between the pages.

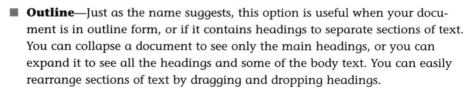

■ **Outline**—Just as the name suggests, this option is useful when your document is in outline form, or if it contains headings to separate sections of text. You can collapse a document to see only the main headings, or you can expand it to see all the headings and some of the body text. You can easily rearrange sections of text by dragging and dropping headings.

Vertical ruler   Page break

FIGURE 3.7
Print Layout
view gives you a
good representa-
tion of how your
document will
look when you
print it.

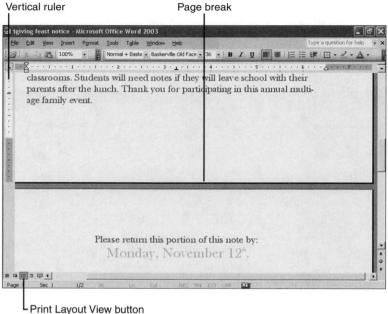

classrooms. Students will need notes if they will leave school with their
parents after the lunch. Thank you for participating in this annual multi-
age family event.

Please return this portion of this note by:
Monday, November 12th.

Print Layout View button

■ **Reading Layout**—A new feature in Word 2003, Reading Layout is designed
to make it easier to read documents onscreen. The text is reformatted to fit
the screen, and the font size is increased so you can read it without reaching
for your glasses (see Figure 3.8). This view does not reflect the true pagination
and formatting of the document. You can find a Reading Layout button on
the Standard toolbar, although it might not be visible until you use it for the
first time.

■ **Document Map**—In this view mode, the screen is split into two panes. The
left pane contains a list of headings in the document; the right pane contains
the document text. You can click a heading in the left pane to quickly jump
to that place in the document.

■ **Thumbnails**—Another new feature in Word 2003, the Thumbnails option
displays a thumbnail image, which is a smaller version, of each page of the
document. The left pane contains the thumbnails; the right pane contains
the actual text (see Figure 3.9). Advantages include the ability to jump
quickly to a specific page by clicking it in the left pane and the ease of
reviewing multiple pages for a consistent appearance. The Thumbnails
option is not available in Web Layout view or in conjunction with
Document Map.

FIGURE 3.8

The new
Reading Layout
view is well
suited for read-
ing documents
onscreen.

Display two screens at once

Pages are divided into screens   Click here to close Reading Layout

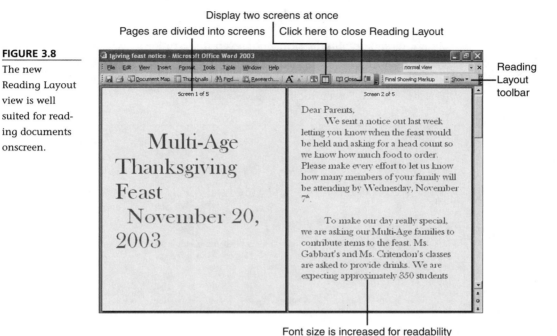

Reading
Layout
toolbar

Font size is increased for readability

Click a page to jump to it

FIGURE 3.9

The Thumbnails
option is helpful
when you need
to navigate
through a long
document.

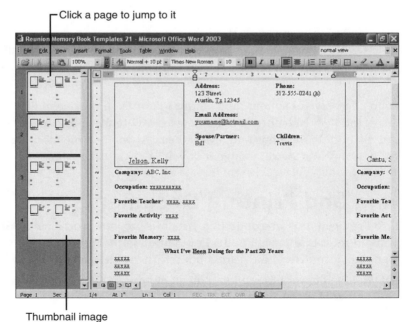

Thumbnail image

- **Full Screen**—This option has been around for a long time, but it is easily overlooked. Full Screen removes every single screen element—title bar, menu bar, toolbars, scrollbars, status bar, even the Windows taskbar. Why? To give you the most screen real estate possible. The trick is remembering how to switch back to the previous view mode, by clicking the Close Full Screen button on the Full Screen toolbar (see Figure 3.10).

FIGURE 3.10

In Full Screen mode, the screen elements are cleared off, giving you more room to review the document text.

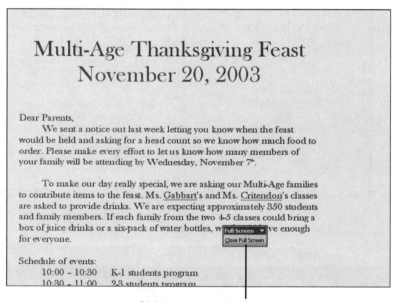

Click here to return to the previous view mode

Word offers several options, and all this information may seem like a lot to digest at this point. Just remember that the view modes are there, and when you're ready, you can flip back to this page and review them. As you become more familiar with Word, your favorites will jump out at you.

Previewing and Printing Documents

If you've spent any time at all in a Windows program, you already know how to print. In most cases, you'll find a Print button in the menu bar that automatically sends the document to the default printer. The same is true in Word.

But what if you want to print to a different printer? Or maybe you need to increase the number of copies from one to five. I'll cover the most frequently used print options for Word in this section.

Switching to Print Preview

The Print Preview feature shows you how your document will look when you print it. Print Preview offers the advantage of seeing multiple pages of your document in a smaller size. The Print Preview image isn't static. You can make editing and formatting changes to create just the right look before you print the document.

Using buttons on the Print Preview toolbar, you can switch to a multiple page view, or you can use the Zoom feature to adjust the size of the page. Other buttons give you access to the Magnifier, the ruler, the Shrink to Fit feature, and Full Screen view.

To use the Print Preview feature, do the following:

1. Choose **File, Print Preview** from the menu. The current page is displayed (see Figure 3.11).

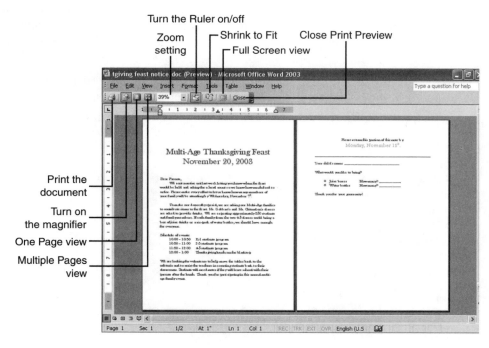

FIGURE 3.11

Print Preview displays a fully editable representation of how the document will look when printed.

2. Make any necessary adjustments.

3. When you are finished, click the **Close** button to switch back to the document window.

Most of the buttons in Print Preview are self-explanatory. The others, like the Magnifier button, are not, so I'll try to clarify them here:

- **Magnifier**—Click this button to turn on Magnifier. Then click the section of text that you want to magnify. Click the text again to go back to "normal."

- **Multiple Pages view**—Click this button to open a palette of pages. Click and drag across the palette to select the number of pages you want to view at once. The maximum number of pages is six.

- **Shrink to Fit**—Click this button to activate the Shrink to Fit feature, which makes small adjustments that allow the text to fit on one page.

Changing the Number of Copies

The cost of printing multiple copies on a laser printer is virtually identical to the cost of running copies on a copier. However, it's much faster just to print three copies of a document than it is to print a copy, walk to the copier, punch in your account number, figure out which buttons to press to get three copies, and wait for them to be finished.

Follow these steps to change the number of copies you want to print:

1. Choose **File**, **Print** (**Ctrl+P**) to display the Print dialog box (see Figure 3.12).

Type the number of copies here

FIGURE 3.12

If you need more than one original, change the number of copies to print as many as you need.

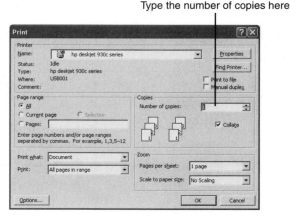

2. Change the number in the **Number of copies** text box.

If you choose to print more than one copy, Word groups the copies as illustrated in the Copies area of the dialog box. The **Collate** option is enabled by default. To see how the pages will print without collating, disable the **Collate** check box and notice the difference in the sample pages.

Printing Specific Pages

When you're revising a multipage document, printing the whole thing again doesn't make sense when you need to check only a few pages. Save some trees and print just the pages that you need. The following options are found in the Print dialog box (**File**, **Print**).

- To print the current page, choose **Current Page**.

- To print multiple pages, type the page numbers that you want to print in the **Pages** text box. For example, if you need to print pages 3 through 9, type **3-9**. If you also want to print page 15, type **3-9, 15** in the text box. Finally, if you type a page number followed by a dash, Word prints from that page number to the end of the document. For example, **13-** prints page 13 and everything that follows it.

- To print selected text, select the text before you open the Print dialog box. Then choose **Selection**.

- To print on both sides of the paper, print the odd pages, reinsert the paper, and then print the even pages. Open the **Print** drop-down list and choose **Odd pages** or **Even pages**.

tip

It almost goes without saying, but the default paper orientation in Word is portrait, which means the paper is taller than it is wide. With landscape orientation, the paper is wider than it is tall. Think of a typical spreadsheet with lots of columns. Landscape orientation is well suited for that type of document because there is more room from left to right. To switch to landscape orientation, choose **File**, **Print**, **Properties**. In the Orientation section, choose **Landscape**. Bear in mind that this setting will stick, so if you want to print in portrait orientation again, you'll have to go back and change it here.

Faxing Documents from Word

How many times have you printed out a document, fed it into a fax machine, and then put the printout in the recycle bin? You can save some time, paper, and printing resources by faxing directly from within Word.

There are essentially two ways to send a fax from Word: using a fax service or using a fax modem. To send through a fax service, you must be signed up with a fax service provider. Fax services offer several advantages, one of which is the ability to use the fax service to fax from Excel, PowerPoint, or Microsoft Office Document Imaging in addition to Word.

Whether you use a fax modem or an Internet fax service, you'll need software. Most modems ship with fax software, so check your documentation and install the necessary software.

Both Windows 2000 and Windows XP have a built-in fax service that is easy to use and integrates well with Office 2003 applications. It is not installed by default, however, so you'll need to update your Office 2003 installation.

To install the Fax component, follow these steps:

1. Choose **Start**, **Control Panel**, **Add or Remove Programs**.
2. Click the **Add/Remove Windows Components** button on the My Places bar.
3. Enable the **Fax Services** check box and then follow the instructions to update your installation.
4. After the Fax component is installed, you can start it by clicking **Start**, **All Programs**, **Accessories**, **Communications**, **Fax**, **Fax Console**. The Fax Console dialog box appears (see Figure 3.13). For more information on the Fax Console, choose **Help**, **Help Topics** in the Fax Console dialog box.

FIGURE 3.13

Use the Fax Console to send and receive faxes through an Internet fax service provider.

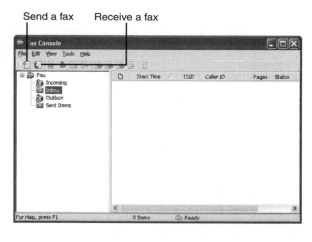

To send a fax from Word using a fax modem, do the following:

1. With the document that you want to fax in the active window, choose **File**, **Send To**, **Recipient Using a Fax Modem**.
2. Follow the instructions in the Fax Wizard to send the fax.

If your fax modem appears in the Print dialog box, you can also send a fax by choosing the fax modem as the printer. You can use this method in other Microsoft Office applications as well.

To send a fax from Word using Internet Fax Service, do the following:

1. With the document that you want to fax in the active window, choose **File**, **Send To**, **Recipient using Internet Fax Service**. An email message window opens in Outlook with the document attached as a .tif file. If you have other files that you want to send, you can attach them as well.

2. Fill in the fields to address the fax. You'll be able to send your fax to a fax number or an email address.

3. In the Fax Service pane, select the necessary options.

4. Complete the cover sheet (in the body of the email) message.

5. Click **Send**.

The first time you use the Internet Fax Service option, you are prompted to sign up with an Internet provider. Click **OK** to open your Web browser so you can locate a provider. By default, Microsoft takes you to the information page for the Venali Internet Fax Service. You can use Venali to send and receive faxes (as attachments to email messages) through Microsoft Outlook 2003 from your desktop, laptop, or wireless device. After you choose a service, close the Web browser and switch back to Word.

After the document is scheduled for sending, you can use the fax modem's software to monitor the fax status, check the fax logs, or even cancel the fax if it hasn't been sent yet. The Fax Console serves the same purpose for Internet Fax Services.

Sending Documents via Email

If you know how to send an email message, you can send Word documents via email. There are two ways to send a document: You can attach the file to the message, or you can send the document as the body of an email message.

If you want to send the entire file as an email attachment, you must be using Microsoft Outlook 2003, Microsoft Outlook Express, Microsoft Exchange, or other MAPI-compatible email programs, such as Juno, Yahoo, or HotMail. (MAPI stands for Messaging Application Programming Interface, which Microsoft developed to allow different email programs to work together.)

To send the active document as an attachment, do the following:

1. Choose **File**, **Send To**, **Mail Recipient (as Attachment)**.

2. In the To: and Cc: boxes, enter the recipient names, separated by semicolons. Alternatively, click the **To:** and **Cc:** buttons to select the names from a list.

3. If necessary, replace the document name as the subject with something more descriptive.

4. Choose **Send**.

note

To use the Internet Fax Service, you must have both Word and Outlook installed on your computer. If you want to send the fax right away, open Outlook. If Outlook isn't open when you send a fax, it is placed in the Outbox and sent the next time you open Outlook.

You can also send the document as the body of the email message. One method is to copy and paste the contents of the Word document into the body of an email message. Another method is to use the **File**, **Send To** menu option.

To send the active document as the body of a message, follow these steps:

1. Click the **E-Mail** button or choose **File**, **Send To**, **Mail Recipient**.

2. In the To: and Cc: boxes, enter the recipient names, separated by semicolons. Alternatively, click the **To:** and **Cc:** buttons to select the names from a list.

3. If necessary, replace the document name as the subject with something more descriptive.

4. If you like, type an introduction in the Introduction text box. For example, you might enter instructions for the recipients to follow (see Figure 3.14).

5. Choose **Send a Copy**.

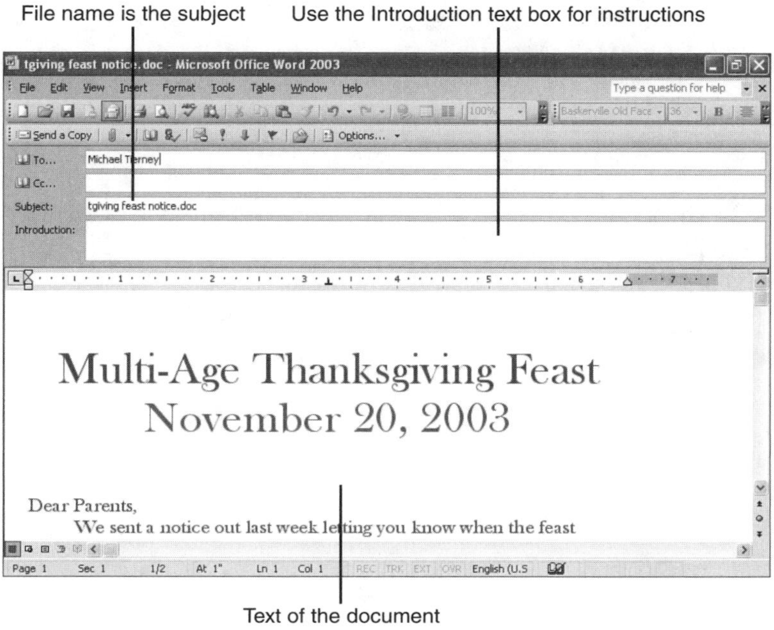

File name is the subject   Use the Introduction text box for instructions

FIGURE 3.14

If the recipient doesn't need to edit the document, send the document in the body of an email message.

Text of the document

THE ABSOLUTE MINIMUM

After reading this chapter, you now know how to

- Select text with the mouse or the keyboard so you can work with that section of text independently from the rest of the document.

- Move and copy selected text so you can rearrange text as you edit your documents.

- Correct your mistakes with the Undo feature, which reverses the last action you took on a document.

- Open multiple documents at the same time and switch back and forth between the open documents.

- Adjust the zoom setting to make it easier to inspect small details in a document.

- Switch to a different document view to make it easier to review your documents.

- Preview a document before printing so you can catch last-minute corrections.

- Adjust the number of copies and specify which pages you want to print.
- Use your fax modem to fax a document directly from Word, without printing it first.
- Use your email program to attach a document to an email message or to include the text in the body of the message.

In the next chapter, you'll learn the basics of formatting documents, including changing fonts, adjusting margins, creating envelopes and labels, inserting symbols, and learning how to use Reveal Formatting.

IN THIS CHAPTER

- Learning how to use bold, italics, and underline to emphasize important text.

- Selecting different fonts and font sizes to improve the appearance of your documents.

- Changing the margin settings to fit more text on a page.

- Creating an envelope with the mailing address automatically inserted for you.

- Inserting symbols and special characters into documents.

- Displaying the new Reveal Formatting task pane and learning how to make changes to the formatting.

4

LEARNING BASIC FORMATTING TECHNIQUES

You've learned a lot in the first three chapters, and now it's time to put those skills into practice. This chapter covers a collection of features that fall into the "basic formatting" category. These are things you will likely want to do right away, such as applying bold, changing to a different font, adjusting margins, printing envelopes, and inserting symbols.

One of the most exciting new features in Word 2003 is the Reveal Formatting feature. You will learn how easy it is to use the Reveal Formatting pane to adjust formatting and correct conflicts. You can even compare the formatting of two sections of text to see the differences.

Getting an Overview of Formatting in Word

The rules of formatting in Word follow a strict hierarchy of characters, paragraphs, and sections. Let's start with paragraph formatting because it is used most often. Strictly speaking, a paragraph is anything that ends with a hard return. (You may recall that a hard return is inserted when you press Enter.) The date at the top of a letter is considered a paragraph because it ends with a hard return. The same goes for a five-line paragraph—both end with a hard return, both are considered paragraphs, the length is irrelevant.

So, if you want to format anything from a single line up to a multi-line paragraph, you apply the formatting to a paragraph. In contrast, you apply character formatting when you don't want the formatting to affect the entire paragraph. For example, you might want to apply bold to several words on a line, but not to the entire line.

All the formatting that you apply to a paragraph is stored in the paragraph mark at the end of the paragraph. This is a *very* important point, and one that took me a while to grasp. First of all, if you don't know what a paragraph mark looks like, take a look at that now.

To show or hide paragraph marks, follow these steps:

> **caution**
>
> When you edit your documents, you have to be very careful not to accidentally delete a paragraph mark because if you do, you'll lose all the formatting that was applied to that paragraph. This is one situation in which you'll be very thankful for the Undo feature.

1. Open a document.
2. Click the **Show/Hide ¶** button on the Standard toolbar. You should see a paragraph symbol where there is a hard return and dots where there are spaces (see Figure 4.1).

At the top of the hierarchy is the section. Word documents can be divided into sections, and each section can be formatted independently. Say you print your letters on preprinted letterhead and second sheets. Your letterhead may appear at the top of the page or along the left side. In either case, you need to adjust the margins on the first page to accommodate the letterhead. On the second page, however, you need to revert back to "normal" margin settings for the second and subsequent pages. To do this, you have to set up two sections: one for the letterhead page and one for the other pages. Section formatting is stored in the section break (that you insert) just as paragraph formatting is stored in the paragraph mark.

Paragraph mark   Space

FIGURE 4.1

While you're editing, it's a good idea to display the paragraph marks so you don't accidentally delete them.

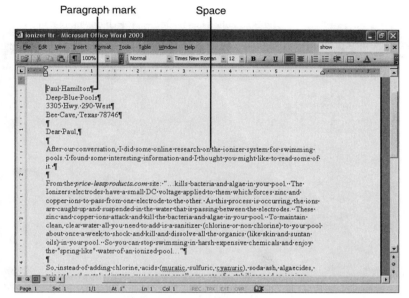

Applying Bold, Italics, and Underline

The most common forms of character formatting are bold, italics, and underline. These effects can help emphasize important passages and draw attention to key points.

To apply bold, italics, or underline, do the following:

1. Select the text.

2. Click the **Bold**, **Italic**, or **Underline** button on the Formatting toolbar (or any combination of the three).

When bold, italics, or underline has been applied to a section of text, the buttons on the toolbar appear "pushed in" (see Figure 4.2).

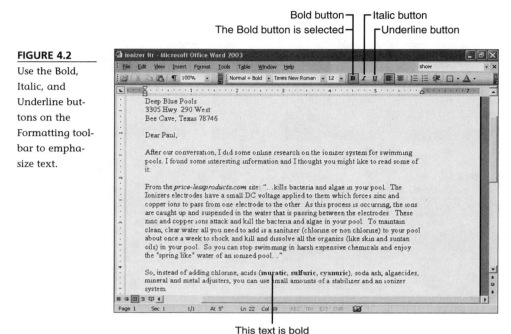

FIGURE 4.2

Use the Bold, Italic, and Underline buttons on the Formatting toolbar to emphasize text.

Choosing the Right Font

Choosing a font can be intimidating, especially when you have so many different fonts to choose from (and thousands more are available online). It's worth the time and effort, though, because the right font can improve the appearance of a document and make the text easier to read. Attractive fonts generate interest in your subject.

You can also make adjustments to the font size where appropriate. As a general rule, titles and headings should be larger than the body text so that they stand out a bit. Headers, footers, and page numbers should be slightly smaller so they don't detract from the body text.

In Word, the default font is Times New Roman, 12 point. The default differs a bit from previous versions, where the default point size was 10 point.

Selecting Fonts and Font Sizes with the Toolbar Buttons

The quickest way to choose a different font is to click the **Font** drop-down arrow on the Formatting toolbar. A drop-down list of fonts appears (see Figure 4.3). Notice that each font name is shown in that font so you get an idea of what a particular font looks like.

Font drop-down list arrow

FIGURE 4.3
The Font drop-down list has a small sample of each font.

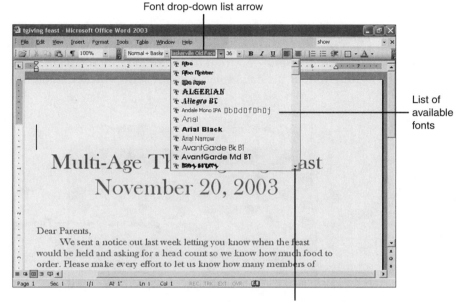

List of available fonts

Scroll down to see more fonts

Choosing a different font size works essentially the same way as choosing a different font. Click the **Font size** drop-down list arrow on the Formatting toolbar to open a drop-down list of sizes. If you click the scroll arrows, you'll see that the list has sizes ranging from 8 point to 72 point.

Selecting Fonts and Font Sizes in the Font Dialog Box

If you prefer, you can select a new font and/or font size in the Font dialog box. You can still see a small sample of the font, and you can easily select a font and font size.

caution

As you apply fonts in your document, remember to always position the insertion point (or select the text) first. As a general rule, your changes take effect at the insertion point, which may or may not be where you want them. You can always use **Undo** if you make a mistake.

To select fonts and font sizes in the Font dialog box, do the following:

1. Choose **Format**, **Font**. The Font dialog box appears (see Figure 4.4). As you can see, the default font, Times New Roman 12 point, is selected.

2. Make your selections.

3. Click **OK**.

If you locate a font that you want to use for most, if not all, of your documents, you can set that font as the default for the current document and all new documents.

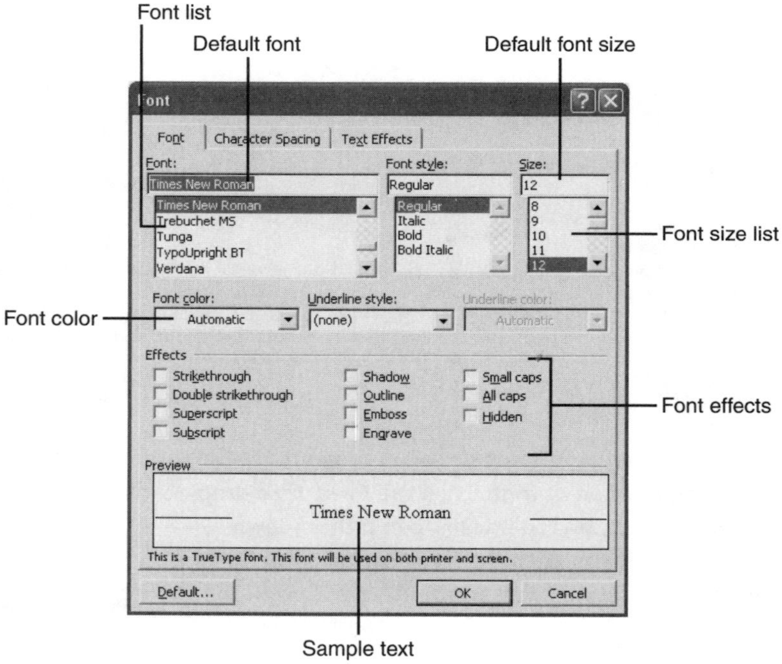

FIGURE 4.4

In the Font dialog box, you can select a font and font size at the same time.

To set a font as the default for all new documents, do the following:

1. Choose **Format**, **Font** to open the Font dialog box.

2. Make your selections.

3. Click **Default**.

4. Click **OK**.

Applying Other Font Effects

Bold, italics, and underline are used most often, so you can find buttons for them located on the Formatting toolbar. The other font effects are located in the Font dialog box. One of the most popular is strikethrough, which is used to show deleted text in a revised document. There is also an option to hide text, which is great for tests because a teacher can hide the answers from the students. Decorative effects such as shadow, outline, emboss, and engrave add a creative touch to headings, titles, and announcements.

To use the other font effects, follow these steps:

1. Position the insertion point where you want the effects to start (or select some existing text).

2. Choose **Format**, **Font** to open the Font dialog box (refer to Figure 4.4).

3. Make your selections by placing check marks next to the effect(s) that you want to use. The sample text in the Preview window shows what the text will look like with the selected effect(s).

4. Click **OK** when you're finished.

tip

The Font color drop-down arrow opens a palette of colors that you can apply to the text. For documents that will be reviewed onscreen, you can use font colors to help guide the reader. I use different colors for key terms, financial data, cautionary information, and so on.

Changing Margins

Margins may not be something you think about every day, but you can improve the readability of a document by making adjustments to the margins. A wider margin creates more whitespace around the text and keeps down the number of words on a line. And remember, the shorter the line, the less likely the reader is to lose his or her place.

On the other hand, if you're trying to keep down the number of pages, you might want to make the margins smaller so that you can fit more on a page. When you use headers and footers, for example, you might want to cut down the top and bottom margins to 1/2". The default margins in Word are 1" on the top and bottom, and 1.25" on the left and right. These settings differ from WordPerfect, which has margins of 1" on all four sides as the default.

You can adjust the margins in two different ways. Using the mouse, you can click and drag the margin indicators on the ruler. Or you can open the Page Setup dialog box and change the settings there.

Adjusting the Margins with the Ruler

The ruler is a nice feature for people who use tabs a lot in their documents. With the ruler displayed, you can easily add, move, or delete tabs. For more information on setting tabs with the ruler, see Chapter 6, "Working with Paragraphs."

Margin indicators on the ruler show what the current margins are. The indicators divide the margin space from the text space. You can click and drag the indicators on the horizontal ruler to adjust the left and right margins, and click and drag the indicators on the vertical ruler to adjust the top and bottom margins.

> **tip**
>
> The default unit of measure that Word uses for measurements in dialog boxes and rulers is inches, but you can change that to centimeters, millimeters, picas, or points. Choose **Tools**, **Options** and then click the **General** tab. Click the **Measurement units** drop-down arrow and choose your preferred unit of measure.

To adjust the left and right margins with the horizontal ruler, do the following:

1. If necessary, display the ruler by choosing **View**, **Ruler**. The ruler appears under the toolbars. Also, switch to Print or Web Layout by choosing **View**, **Print Layout** or **Web Layout**.

2. Position the pointer over the margin indicator and wait for the double arrow to appear.

3. Click and drag the margin indicator to the left or right to adjust the margin (see Figure 4.5). A guideline appears to show you where the new margin will be when you release the mouse button.

To adjust the top and bottom margins with the vertical ruler, follow these steps:

1. If necessary, switch to Print Layout view by choosing **View**, **Print Layout**.

2. If necessary, choose **View**, **Ruler** to display the rulers. The vertical ruler appears on the left side of the screen (see Figure 4.5).

3. Position the pointer over the top or bottom margin indicator and wait for the double arrow.

4. Click and drag the margin indicator up or down to adjust the margins.

Changing Margins in the Page Setup Dialog Box

If you're not comfortable with clicking and dragging, or if you just want to be more precise, you can make your changes in the Page Setup dialog box.

Follow these steps to set the margins in the Page Setup dialog box:

1. Choose **File, Page Setup** to open the Page Setup dialog box (see Figure 4.6).

2. If necessary, click the **Margins** tab.

3. Either type the measurements in the **Top**, **Bottom**, **Left**, or **Right** text boxes or click the spinner arrows to bump the value up or down—in this case, 0.1" at a time.

4. Click **OK** when you're done.

caution

Finding the left margin indicator can be a little tricky when the Hanging Indent and First Line Indent markers are sitting on top of it. Believe me—it's there. You have to point at the indent markers and wait for the double arrow to appear.

Vertical ruler   Margin indicator   Text space   Double arrow

FIGURE 4.5

Click and drag the margin indicators on the horizontal ruler to adjust the left and right margins.

Margin space

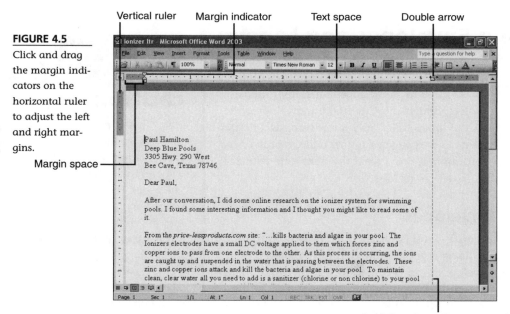

Guideline shows the new margin

Type a new value here

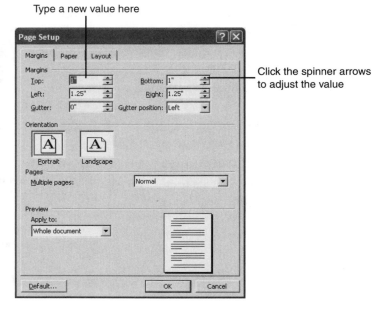

FIGURE 4.6
Use the options on the Margins tab of the Page Setup dialog box to adjust the margin settings.

Click the spinner arrows to adjust the value

Creating Envelopes and Labels

I send a lot of my documents out via fax and email, but I still need to print envelopes and labels for letters, announcements, invitations, invoices, and so on. Creating an envelope or a sheet of labels takes only a few seconds. Plus, you need to type your return address only once. Word saves it and uses it the next time you create envelopes or labels.

Creating Envelopes

Because email is such a popular way to communicate, you're probably addressing fewer envelopes than you used to. Still, creating them is fast and easy, so why not let Word do all the work? Word figures out where the mailing address is in the document and pulls it into the envelope dialog box, so you don't even have to retype it.

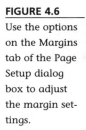

caution

Certain types of printers (such as inkjet and laser printers) are not capable of printing to the edge of the paper. This area is called the *unprintable zone*. The size of this zone varies from printer to printer, so the information is stored in the printer driver that Windows uses. If you try to set a margin within the unprintable zone, Word automatically adjusts it to the printer's minimum margin setting.

To create an envelope, do the following:

1. Choose **Tools, Letters and Mailings, Envelopes and Labels** to display the Envelopes and Labels dialog box (see Figure 4.7). In most cases, the mailing address will be inserted for you.

2. If you want to enter or revise either of the two addresses, you have a couple of options:

   ▪ Click in the **Delivery address** or **Return address** text box and enter (or edit) the information.

    ▪ Click the **Insert Address** icon if you want to select an address from one of the available address books. (The type and number of address books that you have available will vary depending on your system setup.)

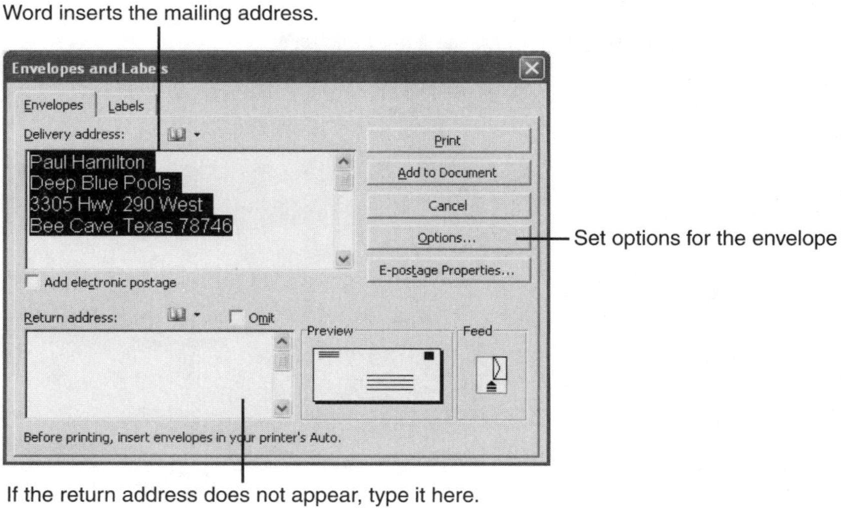

Word inserts the mailing address.

FIGURE 4.7

Word locates the mailing address and inserts it in the Envelopes and Labels dialog box so you don't have to type it again.

Envelopes and Labels

Envelopes | Labels

Delivery address:

Paul Hamilton
Deep Blue Pools
3305 Hwy. 290 West
Bee Cave, Texas 78746

□ Add electronic postage

Return address: □ Omit

Before printing, insert envelopes in your printer's Auto.

Print

Add to Document

Cancel

Options...

E-postage Properties...

— Set options for the envelope

Preview

Feed

If the return address does not appear, type it here.

3. If necessary, click the **Options** button to open the Envelope Options dialog box (see Figure 4.8). You may also need to click the **Envelope Options** tab to display the following options:

   ▪ Open the **Envelope size** list to select another envelope size.

   ▪ Enable the **Delivery point bar code** check box if you want Word to add a bar code to the envelope. (This option may not be available in international editions of Microsoft Office or Word 2003.)

   ▪ Click the **Font** button to change the font and/or font size for the delivery address.

- Click the **Font** button to change the font and/or font size for the return address.
- Set specific locations for the mailing address and return address in the **From left** and **From top** boxes.

4. When you're finished, click **OK** to close the Envelope Options dialog box.

5. Click the **Print** button to send the envelope directly to the printer or click the **Add to Document** button if you want to place the envelope at the top of the current document.

Include a bar code

FIGURE 4.8

Switch to a different envelope size or set the address fonts in the Envelope Options dialog box.

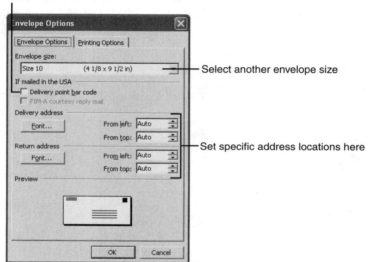

Select another envelope size

Set specific address locations here

Creating Labels

Creating labels works essentially the same way as creating envelopes. If you've already typed a return address, Word will use that in the label form. You can also create a sheet of identical labels so you can keep frequently used labels on hand.

To create labels, do the following:

1. Choose **Tools**, **Letters and Mailings**, **Envelopes and Labels** to display the Envelopes and Labels dialog box (refer to Figure 4.7).

caution

Some printers have a large unprintable zone on the left side, which interferes with printing the return address on the envelope. If this is a problem on your printer, you may have to set a specific location for the return address in the Envelope Options dialog box.

2. Click the **Labels** tab to display the label options.

3. Choose **Options** to open the Label Options dialog box (see Figure 4.9).

FIGURE 4.9

Select a label
definition in the
Label Options
dialog box.

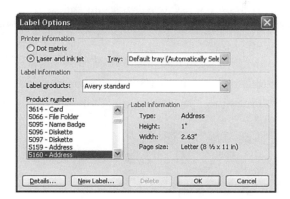

4. Select a product in the **Label products** drop-down list.

5. Select a label in the **Product number** list.

6. Click **OK** to close the Label Options dialog box.

7. Click in the **Address** text box and type the address information, or click the **Insert Address** button and select an address from one of the available address books. (The type and number of address books that you have available will vary depending on your system setup.)

8. Insert the label page into the printer and then click the **Print** button or click the **New Document** button to place the labels in a new document.

Inserting Symbols

You can insert symbols (such as the asterisk, dollar sign, pound sign, percent sign) with your keyboard by holding down the Shift key and pressing the key. Word also gives you access to a tremendous collection of symbols, special characters, and language characters that you can insert in your documents. The variety and types of symbols available depend on the font that you want to use. The same goes for the language characters; they are available only in the "expanded" fonts, such as Times New Roman or Arial.

Using the Symbol Dialog Box

The Symbol dialog box provides a complete list of the available symbols for the fonts that you have installed on your system. After you choose a font, you can select a symbol from the list. The special characters are accessible through the Special Characters tab of the Symbol dialog box.

To insert symbols using the Symbol dialog box, follow these steps:

1. Click in the document where you want to insert the symbol.
2. Choose **Insert**, **Symbol** to open the Symbol dialog box (see Figure 4.10).

FIGURE 4.10

Through the Symbol dialog box, you can insert symbols, language characters, and special characters.

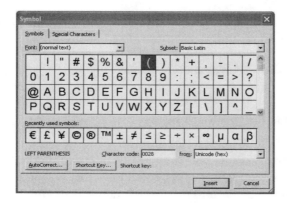

3. Click the **Font** drop-down list arrow and select a font from the list.
4. Click the **Subset** drop-down list arrow and select a subset from the list.
5. When you find the symbol you want (you may have to scroll down), click it and then choose **Insert**. The dialog box stays open to make it easier for you to insert other symbols.
6. Click **Close** when you're finished.

To insert a special character using the Symbol dialog box, follow these steps:

1. Click in the document where you want to insert the special character.
2. Choose **Insert**, **Symbol** to open the Symbol dialog box.
3. Click the **Special Characters** tab.
4. Select the special character and then choose **Insert**.
5. Click **Close** when you're finished.

Using AutoCorrect to Insert Symbols

The AutoCorrect feature is designed to automatically correct common spelling errors and typos while you type. You'll learn more about AutoCorrect in the section titled "Customizing the AutoCorrect Feature" in Chapter 5, "Using the Writing Tools." For now, I want to show you how to use AutoCorrect to insert more than a dozen common symbols (see Table 4.1). This is the absolute fastest method to insert these symbols, so if you use any of the symbols in the list, take a minute to memorize the AutoCorrect combination.

TABLE 4.1   Inserting Symbols with AutoCorrect

To Insert This Symbol	Type This
Right-facing arrow	-->
Copyright symbol	(c)
Registered symbol	(r)
Trademark symbol	(tm)
Ellipsis	...
Frown face	:(or :-(
Happy face	:) or :-)
Straight face	:| or :-|
Left-facing arrow	<--
Thick left-facing arrow	<==
Two-way arrow	<=>
Thick right-facing arrow	==>

AutoCorrect makes these replacements automatically to save you time. However, if you don't want AutoCorrect to make these automatic replacements, you can take these symbols out of the list. To remove a symbol from the AutoCorrect list, do the following:

1. Choose **Tools**, **AutoCorrect Options** to open the AutoCorrect dialog box (see Figure 4.11).
2. Select the symbol you want to remove.
3. Choose **Delete**.
4. Click **OK** to close the AutoCorrect dialog box.

FIGURE 4.11
AutoCorrect automatically substitutes symbols for the right keystrokes.

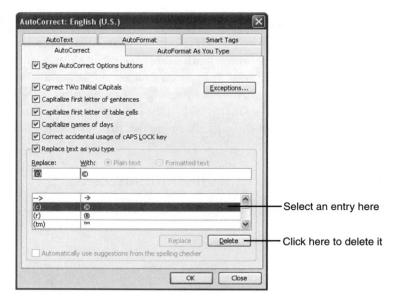

Select an entry here

Click here to delete it

Using Reveal Formatting

In response to thousands of requests for a feature like the "Reveal Codes" feature in WordPerfect, Microsoft has added the Reveal Formatting feature to Word 2003. The idea behind Reveal Formatting is to give you a peek under the hood of your document and show you how the text is formatted. This feature can be especially useful when you're troubleshooting a problem.

But wait, there's more! When the Reveal Formatting pane is displayed, you get one-click access to dialog boxes where you can make adjustments to the formatting. Using this feature is harder to explain than it is to "do," so let's display the Reveal Formatting pane and talk some more about what you can do with it.

Choose **Format**, **Reveal Formatting (Shift+F1)** to display the Reveal Formatting task pane (see Figure 4.12).

To focus on another part of the text, select it in the document window. The Reveal Formatting task pane automatically updates to reflect the formatting for the newly selected text.

Making changes to the formatting is easy; all you have to do is click one of the blue labels in the task pane (see Figure 4.12).

Reveal Formatting task pane

FIGURE 4.12

The Reveal Formatting task pane shows you how the selected text is formatted.

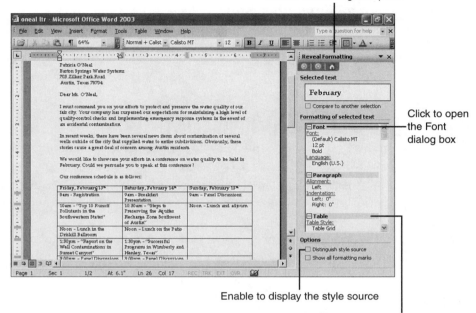

Click to open the Font dialog box

Enable to display the style source

Click to open the Table AutoFormat dialog box

You might have two sections of text in a document that look different. If you can't figure out why, compare the two selections. Enable the **Compare to another selection** check box. Select the second section of text. You should now have two boxes of text in the **Selected text** section. If the two sections of text are formatted exactly the same, you'll see **No formatting differences**. Otherwise, you'll see a list of formatting differences. If you want to format the second section of text so that it matches the first section of text, point to the second box. When the arrow appears, click it and choose **Apply Formatting of Original Selection**.

If you want to be able to distinguish between formatting that was set manually from formatting that was set through a style, enable the **Distinguish style source** check box.

tip

If you're concerned about someone making formatting changes to one of your painstakingly formatted presentations, you should protect the document. For more information, see "Protecting Documents" in Chapter 15, "Collaborating on Documents."

To display the formatting marks, such as paragraph marks and spaces, enable the **Show all formatting marks** check box.

As you work through these chapters, turn on Reveal Formatting now and then so you can see how the selections you make in dialog boxes result in changes to the formatting of a document.

THE ABSOLUTE MINIMUM

In this chapter, you learned how to perform basic formatting tasks. You now know how to

- Follow Word's strict set of rules for formatting. Understand how the formatting is applied and where it is saved can help you prevent a formatting disaster.
- Use good judgment when selecting fonts and font attributes to emphasize important sections of text and to improve the appearance and readability of your document.
- Use several methods to change the margins.
- Create and print an envelope.
- Insert characters from foreign alphabets and a huge variety of symbols and other special characters.
- Display the formatting for selected text and make changes to the formatting.

In the next chapter, you'll learn how to use Word's writing tools to improve accuracy and ensure consistency in your documents.

IN THIS CHAPTER

- Checking your documents for spelling errors and using an electronic thesaurus.

- Working with different languages by using the tools in the Microsoft Office 2003 Multilingual User Interface Pack.

- Translating short passages of text to and from different languages.

- Searching and replacing text and/or formatting to save you from long hours of repetitive editing.

- Taking advantage of all the tools in the "Auto" collection, including AutoCorrect, AutoComplete, AutoText, and AutoSummarize.

5

USING THE WRITING TOOLS

Word processors have evolved from typing tools to document production machines. During this time, the people using word processors have also evolved. Not many people have the luxury of an assistant, so most of us produce our own materials. People who rarely type their own documents are learning how to use spelling and grammar checkers to improve the readability and credibility of their work.

Word includes a powerful collection of productivity tools to help automate the daily tasks that we all perform. In this chapter, you'll learn how to use the writing tools to improve your efficiency and accuracy. From automatically correcting common typos, to flagging misspelled words, to locating key passages of text, Word's writing tools can help you work faster.

Using Word's Automatic Proofreading Features

You may notice that as you type a document, red underlines appear under some words. The underlines indicate that the Check Spelling as You Type feature is working for you. These words are marked as possible misspellings.

Check Spelling as You Type is one of the two automatic proofreading features in Word; the other is Check Grammar as You Type, which checks for grammatical errors. The theory behind these two features is that it's faster to correct errors while you are typing than to go back and fix them later. If Check Grammar as You Type is activated, you may see green underlines in the text as well.

To correct a word with Check Spelling as You Type, do the following:

1. Right-click a red underlined word to open a list of suggested replacement words that you can choose from (see Figure 5.1).

Choose a replacement word from this list.

FIGURE 5.1

When you right-click a red underlined word, a list of suggested replacements appears.

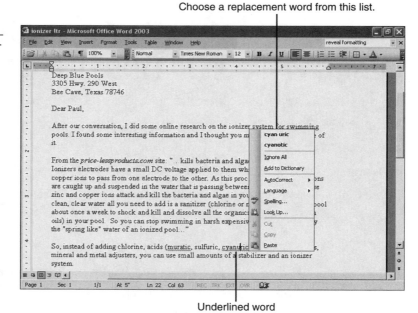

Underlined word

2. Click the correctly spelled word in the list.

That's it! You just corrected the misspelled word. Selecting a word from this list automatically replaces the underlined word with the word you chose.

If you find these proofing marks distracting, you can disable the Check Spelling as You Type and Check Grammar as You Type features.

To disable the automatic proofing features, follow these steps:

1. Choose **Tools, Options** to open the Options dialog box.

2. Click the **Spelling & Grammar** tab to display the options for these writing tools (see Figure 5.2).

Check spelling as you type is turned on.

FIGURE 5.2

The Spelling & Grammar tab of the Options dialog box controls the automatic proofing tools.

Check grammar as you type is turned on.

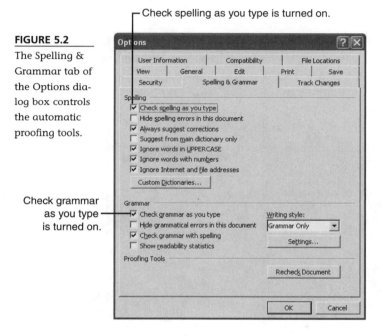

3. Remove the check mark next to **Check Spelling as You Type** and/or remove the check mark next to **Check Grammar as You Type** to disable these features.

4. Click **OK** to close the dialog box.

Checking a Document for Spelling and Grammatical Errors

Who would think that something as simple as a few mistakes could undermine hours and hours of hard work? Well, they can and they will. Like it or not, readers will question a writer's credibility if they find typos and grammatical errors in the text. The solution? Run Word's spelling and grammar checker on every document, no matter how short it is, before you send it out. Read over the suggestions and decide whether you want to make the edits. You can always skip over something if you decide not to make the change.

Follow these steps to start the spelling and grammar checker and correct mistakes in your document:

1. Choose **Tools, Spelling and Grammar** or click the **Spelling and Grammar** button on the Standard toolbar. If Word finds a spelling or grammatical error in the document, the Spelling and Grammar dialog box appears. (Otherwise, you see a message box telling you that the spelling and grammar check is finished.) Word immediately begins checking the document. If a potential error is found, it is highlighted, and a suggested replacement word or words appear in the **Suggestions** list box (see Figure 5.3).

FIGURE 5.3

Word uses red text to point out potential spelling errors and green text to point out potential grammatical errors.

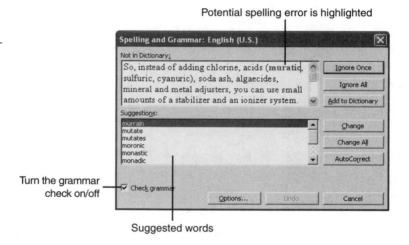

2. Choose from the following options to correct the potential error:

   ■ To correct an error manually, click in the document window, correct the problem, and then choose **Resume** to continue checking.

   ■ To fix a spelling or grammatical error, select an entry in the **Suggestions** list box and then click **Change**.

   ■ To replace a misspelled word now and for the rest of the document, without any further intervention from you, select the correctly spelled word in the **Suggestions** list box and then choose **Change All**.

- To correct a frequently misspelled word, select the correct spelling in the **Suggestions** list box and then click **AutoCorrect** to add the combination to the AutoCorrect list. (See "Customizing the AutoCorrect Feature" later in this chapter for more information.)

- To skip a potential spelling or grammatical error here but have the spelling and grammar checker stop if it finds that error again, click **Ignore Once**.

- To skip a potential spelling problem here and for the rest of the document, click **Ignore All**.

- To stop checking the document for a particular grammatical rule, choose **Ignore Rule**. You'll see the Ignore Rule option when the spelling and grammar checker stops on a grammatical error.

- To skip past potential grammatical errors in the current sentence and move on to the next, choose **Next Sentence**. You see the **Next Sentence** option only when the spelling and grammar checker stops on a grammatical error.

- To add a word to the dictionary, click **Add to Dictionary**.

- To locate more information on a grammatical problem, choose **Explain**. You see the **Explain** option only when the spelling and grammar checker stops on a grammatical error.

- To correct a mistake you make while running the spelling and grammar checker, choose **Undo** to reverse your action.

note

Choosing **Ignore All** prevents the spelling and grammar feature from stopping on the error again. This change doesn't affect other documents. The strength of this feature becomes clear when you work with documents that are full of complex or technical terms. Building the list takes only a few mouse clicks, so after you've built it, the spelling and grammar checker runs faster because it doesn't stop on those terms anymore.

In the first section of this chapter, you learned how to turn off the automatic proofreading features in the Options dialog box. You can access the same options from the Spelling and Grammar dialog box. There, you can click the **Options** button to review the options for the spelling and grammar checkers (refer to Figure 5.2).

Choose from the following options in the Spelling section:

- **Check spelling as you type**—Turns the automatic spelling checker on/off.

- **Hide spelling errors in this document**—Turns off the automatic spelling checker for this document only.

- **Always suggest corrections**—Activates and deactivates the list of suggestions that Word builds when a potential error is found.

- **Suggest from main dictionary only**—Deselect this option if you want suggestions from alternate dictionaries in addition to the main dictionary.

- **Ignore words in UPPERCASE**—Excludes words in all uppercase letters from the spell check.

- **Ignore words with numbers**—Excludes words with numbers, such as *fy2004* or *800-micrsft*, from the spell check.

- **Ignore Internet and file addresses**—Skips Internet and file addresses during a spell check.

- **Custom dictionaries**—Enables you to create, edit, remove, and activate custom dictionaries (see Figure 5.4). You might want to add dictionaries that are specific to your industry (that is, legal, medical, scientific, engineering).

FIGURE 5.4

The Custom Dictionaries dialog box enables you to activate additional dictionaries to supplement Word's main dictionary.

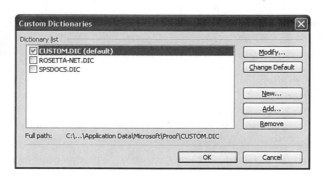

Choose from the following options in the Grammar section:

- **Check grammar as you type**—Turns the automatic grammar checker on/off.

- **Hide grammatical errors in this document**—Turns off the automatic grammar checker for this document only.

- **Check grammar with spelling**—Enables you to deactivate the grammar checker so that when you start the spelling and grammar feature, you run only a spell check.

- **Show readability statistics**—Turns the readability statistics on/off. These statistics are based on word choice and sentence structure and are displayed after you run the spelling and grammar checker.

No spelling checker or grammar checker is foolproof, so don't count on it to correct all your writing mistakes. In some situations, these checkers flag something that is perfectly acceptable, and in some cases, accepting a change can alter your meaning. There is no replacement for a careful read-through before you hand off your documents.

Looking Up Words in the Thesaurus

A thesaurus helps you find just the right word to describe something. Some concepts are more complex than others, and ideas can be expressed in a number of ways. Using the right words enables you to convey exactly the message you want to the reader. Word's thesaurus looks up synonyms (that is, words with similar meanings), antonyms, and related words.

To look up a word in the thesaurus, follow these steps:

1. Select the word (or just click in it) that you want to look up.

2. Choose **Tools**, **Language**, **Thesaurus (Shift+F7)**. The thesaurus looks up the word and, by default, displays a list of synonyms and, if available, a list of antonyms and related words in the Research task pane (see Figure 5.5).

3. Choose from the following options to look up words in the thesaurus:

   - If you selected a word in step 1, the thesaurus looks up the word and displays the results in the window. Otherwise, you need to type the word you want to look up in the Search for text box and then click the green arrow (see Figure 5.5). You can also select the word and press **Shift+F7**.

   - To see a list of related words under a suggested synonym or antonym, click the suggested word or click the plus sign in the box.

   - To look up one of the words in the list, click the word.

   - To replace a selected word in the document with a word from the thesaurus, point to the word, click the drop-down list arrow, and choose **Insert**.

   - To copy a word so you can insert it somewhere other than the current document, point to the word in the list, click the drop-down list arrow, and choose **Copy**.

   - If you change your mind about replacing a word, click the **Undo** button or choose **Edit**, **Undo** (in the document window) to reverse the change.

   - The thesaurus has a history list so you can jump back to a word that you noticed earlier. Click the drop-down list arrow next to the **Back** button to select from the previous search history list. By the same token, click the drop-down list arrow next to the right-facing arrow button to open a list of next searches. This feature enables you to basically move forward and backward through the words you've searched for in this thesaurus session.

FIGURE 5.5

The thesaurus helps you improve your writing by showing you alternate words to use.

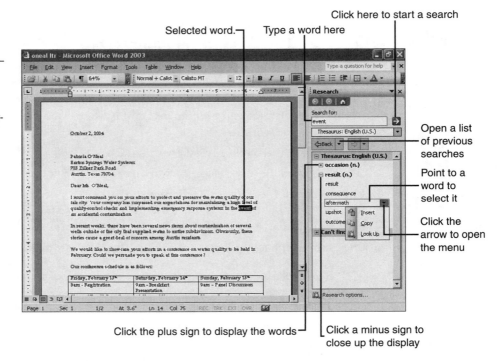

Selected word.

Type a word here

Click here to start a search

Open a list of previous searches

Point to a word to select it

Click the arrow to open the menu

Click the plus sign to display the words

Click a minus sign to close up the display

Switching to a Different Language

We are truly working in a global marketplace. It's not unusual to work with individuals and companies from all over the world. So, when you write in a different language, you need to be able to do more than just enter, display, and print the non-English characters. You also need to be able to correct spelling, check grammar, use proper punctuation, and implement the correct sorting conventions. Two add-in products are available to provide support for other languages:

- You can purchase the Microsoft Office 2003 Multilingual User Interface (MUI) Pack and change the user interface and help files so that the menus, prompts, wizards, templates, and help topics are all in that language.

- The Microsoft Office 2003 MUI Pack also includes Microsoft 2003 Proofing Tools, which enables you to get proofing tools for more than 30 different

languages. You can use fonts, spelling and grammar checkers, AutoCorrect lists, AutoSummarize rules,
translation dictionaries, and other tools
that help you create and edit Word documents in the language of your choice.

To switch to a different language, do the following:

1. If you want to mark a section of text,
   select it first. Otherwise, click in the text
   where you want to switch to a different
   language.

2. Choose **Tools**, **Language**, **Set
   Language**. The Language dialog box
   appears, with a list of available languages
   (see Figure 5.6).

3. Scroll through the list and double-click the
   language you want.

> **caution**
>
> Some fonts do not sup-
> port languages other
> than English. If you type
> text with a language
> enabled in a font that
> does not support that language, the
> font automatically switches to a
> comparable font that does support
> the language. If this problem per-
> sists, consider purchasing the
> Proofing Tools package from
> Microsoft.

FIGURE 5.6

Select another
language for
selected text, or
the entire docu-
ment, in the
Language dia-
log box.

└─ Set the selected language as the default

If you frequently switch back and forth between languages, you'll love this shortcut.
You can add a Language button to the Formatting toolbar so you can always see
the current language.

To display the current language on the Formatting toolbar, follow these steps:

1. Click the down arrow on either toolbar to open the button palette.

2. Choose **Add or Remove Buttons**, **Formatting**.

3. Slide over and click **Language** in the list of buttons.

4. Click in the document window to clear the toolbar button list. A new Language button appears on the far-right side of the toolbar.

5. Click this button to open a list of available language modules (identical to the one in the Language dialog box).

Translating Text

My daughter has a pen pal who lives in Mexico. Her pen pal doesn't speak English and my daughter doesn't speak Spanish, but the girls are able to write letters to each other. How? They use Microsoft Word to translate the text into the other's native language.

You can use the bilingual dictionaries that come with Word 2003 to look up words and short phrases in a dictionary for other languages. With Internet access, you can get a basic translation for words, phrases, or an entire document, using online dictionaries and machine translation over the Web.

> **note**
>
> The first time you try to use the translation services, you need to confirm the installation of the bilingual dictionaries so the Research pane translation services can be activated. If you receive an error message during the installation of the dictionaries, you may need to install system support for multiple languages. The Microsoft Office 2003 Multilingual User Interface Pack includes translation dictionaries, among other things. Contact Microsoft to purchase the MUI Pack.

You can choose from several methods for translating text:

- Hold down the **Alt** key and then click a word in the text. When the Research task pane appears, open the **Search for** drop-down list and choose **Translation**. Choose the original language in the **From** drop-down list and then choose the destination language in the **To** drop-down list.

- Select a short phrase. Then hold down the **Alt** key and click in the selected text. When the Research task pane appears, open the **Search for** drop-down list and choose **Translation**. Choose the original language in the **From** drop-down list and then choose the destination language in the **To** drop-down list. The translation results are shown in Figure 5.7.

- Choose **Tools**, **Research**. In the **Search for** text box, type the word or phrase you want to translate. Open the **Search for** drop-down list and choose **Translation**. Choose the original language in the **From** drop-down list and then choose the destination language in the **To** drop-down list.

■ If you have an active Internet connection, you can translate the entire document. Open the Research task pane. Choose the original language in the **From** drop-down list and then choose the destination language in the **To** drop-down list. Click the green arrow under **Translate whole document**. A translation of your document appears in the Web browser window.

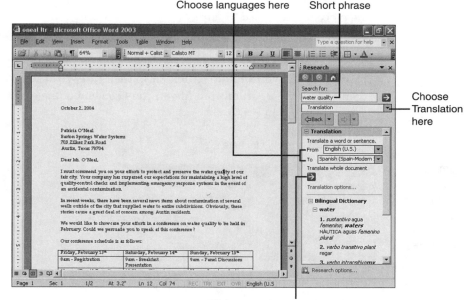

FIGURE 5.7

Using bilingual dictionaries, you can translate words and phrases in the Research task pane.

Finding and Replacing Text

Say you accidentally misspelled someone's name in a long document. You could look through the document manually correcting each occurrence, hoping that you don't miss one. Or you could search for all occurrences of that person's name and replace them with the correct spelling.

The Find feature in Word can locate a snippet of text or a specific type of formatting in your document in just a few seconds. The Replace feature takes the process a step further by allowing you to substitute something else for the search item.

The same concept can be applied for formatting. If you decide you want to search for a particular font and replace it with another one, you can use the Find and Replace feature. You can really unlock the power of the Find and Replace feature and combine these two methods to perform a search for only the text that has specific formatting assigned to it. Let's start with a basic text search and progress onto a search for formatting.

Searching for Text

Searching for text is fairly straightforward. You can do broad searches by searching for the first several characters in a word, or you can be very specific by searching for a particular sentence or phrase.

On long and complex documents, I use Find to quickly jump to the text that I need to work on. Using this feature is much faster than scrolling through a document to find the place where I need to start.

To search for text, follow these steps:

1. Choose **Edit**, **Find (Ctrl+F)** to open the Find and Replace dialog box.

2. Type the text you want to search for in the **Find what** text box. You can enter a word, a partial word (if you can't remember the exact spelling), or a phrase (see Figure 5.8).

Type the text to search for here

FIGURE 5.8
The Find feature can help you to jump quickly to the section of a document that you need to work on.

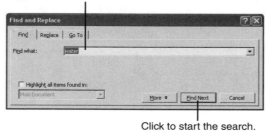

Click to start the search.

3. Choose **Find Next** to start the search.

When Word locates the search text, you have the following options:

■ Click **Find Next** to continue the search.

■ Click **Cancel** to discontinue the search and to close the Find and Replace dialog box so you can start working.

Searching and Replacing Text

Don't make the mistake of underestimating the Replace side of the Find and Replace feature. When you need to make a change throughout a

tip

If you want to delete selected instances of the search text, leave the **Replace with** text box empty. As you go through the search, you can selectively replace the search text with nothing, deleting it from the document.

long document, nothing beats this feature for speed and accuracy. Consider a difficult-to-spell technical term that you painstakingly typed throughout a long document, only to discover that you've misspelled it. You can read through the entire document, correcting each misspelled term, hoping that you don't make any mistakes. Or you can spend 30 seconds doing a Find and Replace that fixes every misspelled term in one pass.

To search and replace text, follow these steps:

1. Choose **Edit, Replace (Ctrl+H)** to open the Find and Replace dialog box.

2. Type the text you want to search for in the **Find what** text box.

3. Type the replacement text in the **Replace with** text box (see Figure 5.9). The replacement text must be exact because it will be inserted in the document exactly as it appears in the text box.

Type the text to search for here

FIGURE 5.9

With Find and Replace, you can quickly locate a section of text and replace it with something else.

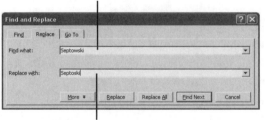

Type the replacement text here

4. Choose **Find Next** to locate the first entry.

When Word locates the search text, you have the following options:

- Click **Replace** to replace the search text with the replacement text.

- Click **Replace All** to replace all the rest of the occurrences without further confirmation from you.

- Click **Find Next** to skip this entry and move to the next one, without making a change.

- Click **Cancel** if you're just using Find to locate your place in a document and you want to get to work.

Extending the Search for Text

When you search for text, you can extend and refine the search using Search options. These options allow you to locate all forms of a word and other words that sound like the search word. You can also perform wildcard searches, which give you an added measure of flexibility. You can narrow down a search by matching the case exactly and by searching for whole words only (so you don't locate words that have the search word embedded in them).

Click the **More** button to expand the Find and Replace dialog box (see Figure 5.10).

FIGURE 5.10

The Search options give you more flexibility to conduct a more or less precise search.

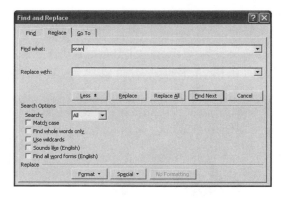

Here's a quick rundown of the additional options:

- **Match case**—Locates only those words that match the case used in the words you type in the **Find what** text box.

- **Find whole words only**—Locates only those words that exactly match the word you typed in the **Find what** text box. This option prevents Word from stopping on words that contain the search word. For example, the word scan appears in *scanning* and *scanner*.

- **Use wildcards**—Allows you to use wildcards in place of text. The two commonly used wildcards are * and ?. An asterisk (*) stands for any number of characters; a question mark (?) stands for a single character. For example, a search for lymph* locates *lymphoma, lymphatic, lymphangial*, and so on.

- **Sounds like**—Locates words that *sound* like the search word. For example, searching for here locates *here* and *hear*.

- **Find all word forms**—Searches for variations of the search word. For example, searching for wire locates *wire, wired*, and *wiring*.

Searching for Formatting

In addition to searching for text, you can also search for a specific type of formatting. This tool can be a powerful ally when you're making global changes to a document. For example, you might need to change the text color in a document from indigo to teal. Instead of locating every instance, selecting the text, and applying teal, you can use the Find and Replace feature to search for the indigo text color and replace it with teal.

Follow these steps to search for a format setting:

1. Choose **Edit**, **Find (Ctrl+N)** to open the Find and Replace dialog box.

2. If necessary, click the **More** button to expand the dialog box.

3. If you want to perform a find and replace operation, click the **Replace** tab to expose the **Replace with** text box.

4. With the insertion point in the **Find what** text box, click the **Format** button to open a list of format categories (see Figure 5.11).

FIGURE 5.11

Using Find and Replace, you can search for quite a few formatting options.

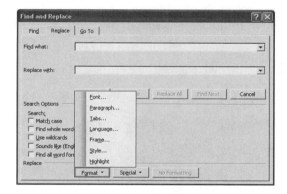

5. Choose a category from the list. The dialog box you see next depends on which category you select. To continue with the scenario mentioned earlier, Figure 5.12 shows the Find Font dialog box where you can make selections to search for font formatting.

6. Make your selections and then click **OK** to insert the information into the Find and Replace dialog box.

7. If necessary, click in the **Replace with** text box, click the **Format** button, select a category, and make the necessary selections. Figure 5.13 illustrates a search for indigo text and a replacement of teal text.

8. Choose **Find Next** to start the search or **Replace All** to make the replacements without any further confirmation.

To remove the formatting options from the Find what or Replace with text boxes, click in either of the two text boxes and click the **No Formatting** button.

FIGURE 5.12
In the Find Font dialog box, you can specify a font, font size, font color, or font effect to search for.

FIGURE 5.13
The formatting options that you are searching for appear below the Find what and Replace with text boxes.

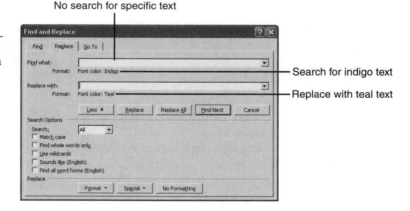

Searching for Special Formatting Characters

A handful of formatting characters and document elements, such as page breaks and tabs, can also be included in a search. I use this aspect of Find and Replace frequently to search for em dashes and replace them with en dashes because I often confuse the two.

To search for a format character, follow these steps:

1. Choose **Edit**, **Find (Ctrl+F)** to open the Find and Replace dialog box.

2. If necessary, click the **More** button to expand the dialog box.

3. If you want to perform a find and replace, click the **Replace** tab to expose the **Replace with** text box.

4. With the insertion point in the **Find what** text box, click the **Special** button to open a list of format characters and document elements (see Figure 5.14).

5. Choose an item from the list to insert it in the **Find what** text box. You'll notice that a code is inserted in the text box, not the actual format character. This is how Word searches for these elements.

6. If necessary, click in the **Replace with** text box and specify a format character or document element as the replacement. Figure 5.15 shows a search to replace an em dash code with an en dash code.

> **tip**
>
> You also can create a combination search for text and formatting. This type of specific search is simple to put together and an incredible timesaver when you compare it to the manual editing that you would have to do to accomplish the same result.

FIGURE 5.14

Find and Replace can search for a variety of format characters and document elements.

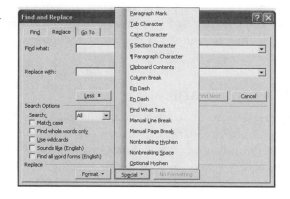

Em dash code   En dash code

FIGURE 5.15

It's a simple process to search for a particular format character and replace it with another.

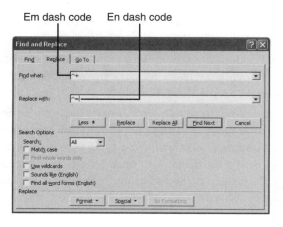

7. Choose **Find Next** to start the search or **Replace All** to make the replacements without any further confirmation.

Discovering the Power of the "Auto" Features

Word provides four great productivity tools: AutoCorrect, AutoComplete, AutoText, and AutoSummarize. They all have different functions, but the general idea behind them is that they fix things for you automatically.

AutoCorrect recognizes commonly misspelled (or mistyped) words and replaces them with the correct spelling. AutoComplete identifies words as you type them, and if you let it, AutoComplete will finish typing the word for you. AutoText gives you the opportunity to store frequently used blocks of text, such as your company name and address or a signature block, so you can quickly insert them in your documents. AutoSummarize identifies the key points in a document and produces a concise summary of a complex document.

Customizing the AutoCorrect Feature

The AutoCorrect feature is designed to correct common mistakes while you type, without any intervention from you. AutoCorrect fixes capitalization errors and corrects common spelling mistakes and typos. AutoCorrect has a predefined list of entries that it uses to make corrections in your documents. You can customize the way AutoCorrect works by enabling or disabling the options and by adding and removing entries in the AutoCorrect list.

To customize AutoCorrect, choose **Tools**, **AutoCorrect Options**. The AutoCorrect dialog box then opens (see Figure 5.16).

Most of the AutoCorrect options are self-explanatory. You can turn off any of the individual options by removing the check mark in the check box. Likewise, you can activate an option by enabling the check box.

AutoCorrect comes with a long list of frequently misspelled words and typos. You can add your own common typing mistakes to the AutoCorrect list and have Word make the replacements automatically, while you type. The result is that you'll spend a lot less time proofing your documents. Also included in the list are shortcuts to inserting common symbols, such as the copyright, registered mark, and trademark.

FIGURE 5.16

In the AutoCorrect dialog box, you can add, delete, and edit the AutoCorrect entries, or you can disable AutoCorrect so that it won't correct words while you type.

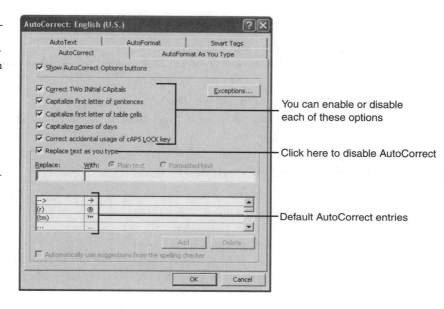

You can enable or disable each of these options

Click here to disable AutoCorrect

Default AutoCorrect entries

To add words or phrases to AutoCorrect, do the following:

1. Choose **Tools, AutoCorrect Options** to open the AutoCorrect dialog box.
2. Type the word or phrase in the **Replace** text box.
3. Type the replacement word or phrase in the **With** text box (see Figure 5.17).

FIGURE 5.17

You can add your frequent misspellings and typos to the AutoCorrect list and let Word fix your mistakes automatically.

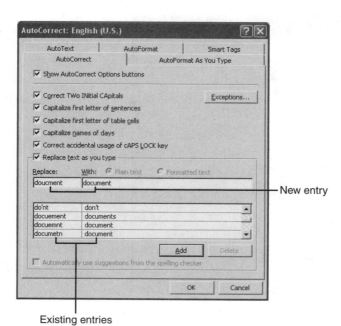

New entry

Existing entries

4. Click **Add** to include the new entry in the list.

If you prefer not to use the AutoCorrect feature, you can turn it off completely. To do so, choose **Tools, AutoCorrect Options** and deselect the **Replace text as you type** check box (that is, remove the check mark).

A better solution might be to remove the entries that you don't like so that you can continue to take advantage of those that are helpful. To remove an entry, select it in the list and then click **Delete.**

Understanding How AutoComplete Works

You may have already seen the prompts popping up as you type today's date, days of the week, or the name of a month. The prompts are called ScreenTips; the feature is called AutoComplete. AutoComplete monitors your typing, and if it recognizes an entry, a ScreenTip appears. You can press **Enter** to accept the entry in the ScreenTip, or you can continue typing without accepting it. AutoComplete is designed to recognize the months, days of the week, today's date, your name, and other AutoText entries.

If you don't want to use the AutoComplete feature, you can turn it off as follows:

1. Choose **Insert**, **AutoText**, **AutoText** to display the AutoText tab of the AutoCorrect dialog box (see Figure 5.18).

┌ Disable AutoComplete

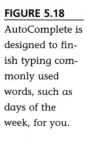

FIGURE 5.18

AutoComplete is designed to fin-ish typing com-monly used words, such as days of the week, for you.

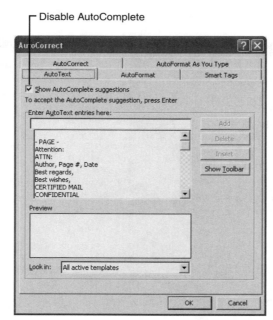

2. Disable the **Show AutoComplete suggestions** check box.

3. Click **OK** to close the dialog box.

Creating and Editing AutoText Entries

AutoText entries are blocks of text or graphics that you use over and over in your daily routine. You can assign an abbreviation to a word, phrase, or graphic image. As you create a document, you type in the abbreviation. When you type the first four characters, AutoComplete recognizes the entry and displays a ScreenTip. At this point, you can insert the entry or ignore the ScreenTip.

AutoText entries aren't limited to words or phrases. You can create AutoText entries with formatting codes, such as font attributes, or graphics that you would use for logos.

To create an AutoText entry, do the following:

> **caution**
>
> Make sure that you use names that won't normally come up in your documents for AutoText abbreviations. For example, you could use *compadd* to expand your company address, *clogo* for the company logo, or *sigblock* for your signature block. If you use a word or phrase that comes up naturally, AutoText displays a ScreenTip with the information. Pressing Enter inserts the information into your document. If you don't see the ScreenTip or if you press Enter by mistake, you can end up with information in the wrong places.

1. Select the text or graphic you want to assign to AutoText. If you want to store the formatting with the entry, make sure you include the paragraph mark in the selection. To display the paragraph marks, click the down arrow at the end of the Standard toolbar and then click the **Show/Hide ¶** button on the button palette.

2. Choose **Insert**, **AutoText**, **New (Alt+F3)** to display the Create AutoText dialog box (see Figure 5.19).

3. If necessary, replace the suggested AutoText name with one of your own.

4. Click **OK.**

Use one of the following methods to insert AutoText in a document:

- Type the first four letters of the AutoText name. When a ScreenTip appears, press **Enter** to insert the AutoText entry.

- Choose **Insert**, **AutoText**, **AutoText** to display the AutoText tab of the AutoCorrect dialog box (see Figure 5.20). Select an entry from the list and then choose **Insert**.

FIGURE 5.19
With AutoText, you can assign an abbreviation to text or graphics, and then simply type the abbreviation to insert them into a document.

Suggested name

Selected entry

FIGURE 5.20
Select an item in the list of AutoText entries to add the information in the document.

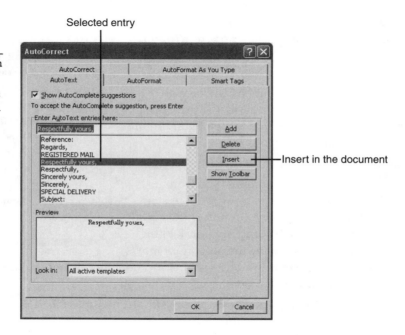

Insert in the document

- Right-click a toolbar to open the toolbar list. Choose **AutoText**. Click the **AutoText** button to open the AutoText dialog box where you can choose an entry.

- Right-click a toolbar to open the toolbar list. Choose **AutoText**. Click the **All Entries** button to open a pop-up list of AutoText categories. Point to a category to display a list of entries (see Figure 5.21). Select an entry to insert it in the text.

It's a simple matter to update an AutoText entry if the text changes or if you want to insert a different graphic image with a certain AutoText entry. To replace an AutoText entry, follow these steps:

AutoText button

FIGURE 5.21
The AutoText
toolbar gives
you quick access
to your AutoText
entries.

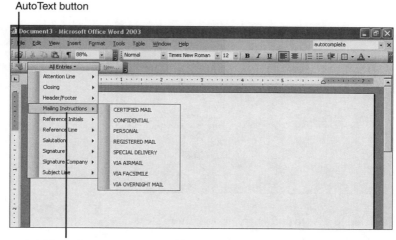

AutoText category

1. Insert the original AutoText entry.
2. Make the necessary changes.
3. Select the revised text or graphic.
4. Choose **Tools**, **AutoText**, **New**.
5. Type the original name of the AutoText entry.

Say your company has merged with another company, and you've been revising your AutoText entries. As you change the content of AutoText entries, you might want to assign a new name at the same time. You may also want to delete those entries that you won't be using anymore.

To rename an AutoText entry, follow these steps:

1. Choose **Tools**, **Templates and Add-Ins**.
2. Click the **Organizer** button to open the Organizer dialog box.
3. Click the **AutoText** tab to display the list of AutoText entries (see Figure 5.22).
4. In the **In Normal** box on the left, click the entry you want to rename.
5. Click **Rename** to open the Rename dialog box.
6. Type a new name for the entry.
7. Click **OK** and then click **Close**.

Select an entry here

FIGURE 5.22

Revisions to the
AutoText entries
are made
through the
Organizer dia-
log box.

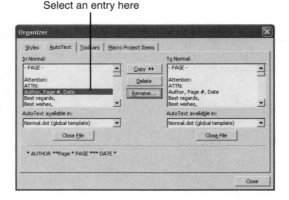

To delete an AutoText entry, follow these steps:

1. Choose **Tools**, **Templates and Add-Ins**.
2. Click the **Organizer** button to open the Organizer dialog box.
3. Click the **AutoText** tab to display the list of AutoText entries.
4. In the **In Normal** box on the left, click the entry you want to rename.
5. Click **Delete**.
6. Choose **Yes** to delete the entry.
7. Click the **Close** button.

Using the AutoSummarize Feature

Another new feature in Word 2003, AutoSummarize identifies key points in a document and produces a summary from these points. This feature works best in a well-
structured document such as reports, proposals, legal briefs, and research papers that
contain headings and subheadings.

So, how does AutoSummarize identify the key points? By analyzing the document
and assigning a score to each sentence. Sentences that contain words used often in
the document are given a higher score. You get to choose a percentage of the
highest-ranking sentences, and they are displayed in the summary.

Follow these steps to summarize a document with AutoSummarize:

1. Choose **Tools**, **AutoSummarize** to display the AutoSummarize dialog box
   (see Figure 5.23).

Click a summary type

FIGURE 5.23
Identify the type
and length of
summary that
you want
AutoSummarize
to build.

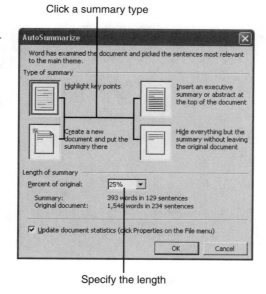

Specify the length

2. Click one of the sample pages to choose
   which type of summary you want to produce.

3. Open the **Percent of original** drop-
   down list and choose a length for the
   summary. The longer the summary, the
   more detail you'll see.

4. Click **OK** to create the summary.

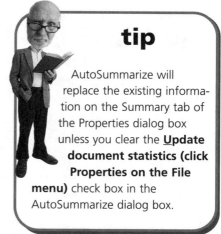

tip

AutoSummarize will
replace the existing information on the Summary tab of
the Properties dialog box
unless you clear the **Update
document statistics (click
Properties on the File
menu)** check box in the
AutoSummarize dialog box.

If you choose the option to highlight key points,
or to hide everything but the summary, you can
switch back and forth between the two options.
In other words, you can view only the key points
(where the rest of the document is hidden) and
then switch to a view where the key points are high-
lighted. Furthermore, as you read through the summary, you can change the level of
detail. All of this is done through the AutoSummarize toolbar that appears with a
completed summary (see Figure 5.24).

Highlighted summary information   Highlight/Show Only Summary button

FIGURE 5.24

The buttons on the AutoSummarize toolbar allow you to switch back and forth between views and to increase the level of detail.

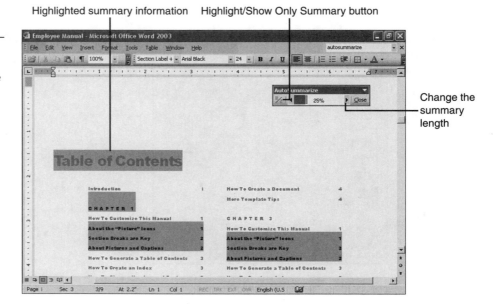

Change the summary length

The Absolute Minimum

After reading this chapter, you now know how to

- Identify Word's automatic proofreading features that correct your work as you type.
- Run a spelling and grammar check on a document.
- Look up words in a thesaurus so you can avoid using the same words over and over.
- Switch to a different language for the user interface, help files, and writing tools.
- Translate words and phrases using the bilingual dictionaries.
- Search and replace text, formatting, or a combination of both.
- Use AutoCorrect to correct common typing mistakes while you type.
- Understand how the AutoComplete feature can save you keystrokes.
- Set up AutoText to create abbreviations for frequently used passages of text.
- Use the AutoSummarize feature to create a summary of a document.

In the next part of the book, you'll learn how to make your document look polished and professional through a variety of formatting techniques.

PART

MAKING IT LOOK NICE

IN THIS CHAPTER

- Using the Justification features to align paragraphs between the left and right margins.

- Setting specific tabs so you can type information in columns.

- Increasing the spacing between lines and paragraphs to make long passages of text easier to read.

- Using Word features that keep important text from being split apart by a page break.

- Using the AutoFormat feature to automatically apply formatting while you type or when you're finished.

6

WORKING WITH PARAGRAPHS

Because this chapter discusses ways to format paragraphs, I want to stop for a minute and clarify the definition of a *paragraph*. Generally, you might think of a paragraph as several lines of text all together in one chunk. You would be right; that is a paragraph, but so is a single line. In fact, anything that ends with a hard return is considered to be a paragraph. You may recall that a hard return is inserted into the document each time you press the Enter key. The hard return ends the current line and moves the insertion point down to the next line.

Now that you know what you're working with, you're ready to learn about the features that help the text flow more smoothly on the page and across page breaks. This chapter focuses on working with paragraphs; Chapter 7, "Working with Pages," covers formatting pages.

Aligning Text with Justification

Justification controls how text flows between the left and right margins. Word offers four justification options that you might be interested in, especially if you work with columns, newsletters, and formal documents (see Figure 6.1). For example, one of the most common formatting tasks is centering a line. When you use justification to center text on a line, Word does the math and makes sure that an equal amount of space appears on both sides of the text. If you add or remove text, Word automatically adjusts the position of the text so it is always at the exact center of the page.

Flush right text is a little less common, but it still has an important place, especially in legal documents. Text that is flush right is aligned against the right margin, so it stretches out to the left.

FIGURE 6.1

This sample document illustrates the different justification settings.

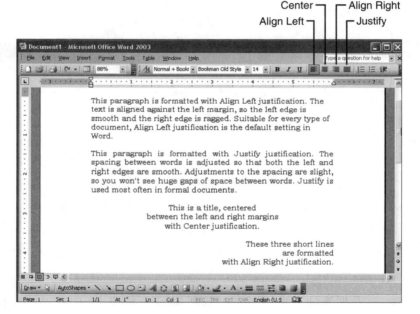

Word offers the following justification options:

- **Align Left**—Text is aligned against the left margin so that the left margin is smooth and the right is ragged. This type of justification is suitable for almost every type of document, especially those with long passages of text. To align text on the left side, click the **Align Left** button or press **Ctrl+L**.

- **Center**—Text is centered between the left and right margins. To center text, click the **Center** button or press **Ctrl+E**.

- **Align Right**—Text is aligned against the right margin so that the right side is smooth and the left is ragged. The placement draws attention, but because it's difficult to read, you might not want to use it on more than three or four lines. To align text on the right, click the **Align Right** button or press **Ctrl+R**.

- **Justify**—Text is aligned against the left and right margins, so both edges are smooth. Documents with this type of justification have a more formal and organized appearance. To justify text, click the **Justify** button or press **Ctrl+J**.

Before you choose which type of justification you want to use in your document, decide where you want the justification to take effect and then move the insertion point there. This may be at the top of the document, the top of a column, or the beginning of a paragraph. If you want to apply justification to a section of text, such as a multiline title, select the text first.

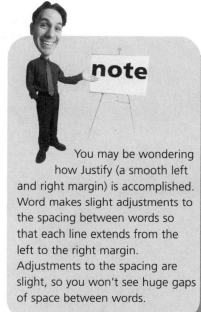

You may be wondering how Justify (a smooth left and right margin) is accomplished. Word makes slight adjustments to the spacing between words so that each line extends from the left to the right margin. Adjustments to the spacing are slight, so you won't see huge gaps of space between words.

Setting Tabs

Tabs may be one of the most misunderstood features in a word processor. Most of us press the Tab key without really thinking about it. We want to move over a bit, and Tab does that for us. What most people don't realize is that there is a lot more to the Tab feature than just moving over a bit.

To start with, Word offers five different types of tabs:

- **Left tab**—Text flows from the right side of the tab stop. This is the "normal" tab.
- **Center tab**—Text is centered over the tab stop.
- **Right tab**—Text flows from the left side of the tab stop.
- **Decimal tab**—The numbers are aligned on their decimal points, which rest on the tab stop. You can change the alignment character to something other than a period (decimal point).
- **Bar tab**—This tab doesn't actually align text. It just inserts a vertical bar at the tab stop.

If you don't see the ruler at the top of the screen, turn it on by choosing **View**, **Ruler**. The default tab settings (every one-half inch) are shown with lines in the tab area of the ruler (see Figure 6.2). The blue area identifies the margin area; the white area is the text area.

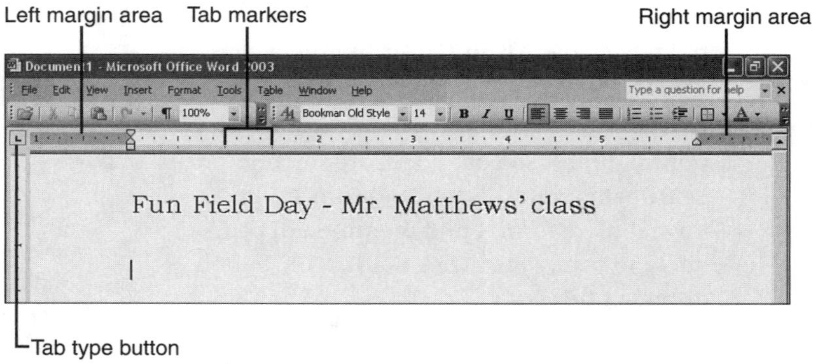

FIGURE 6.2

Using the ruler, you can set all types of tabs with just a few mouse clicks.

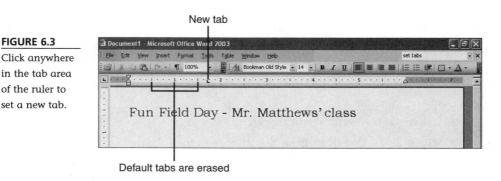

Creating New Tabs

Setting new tabs is fast and easy. All you have to do is click on the ruler where you want a tab to be and voilà! You'll notice that when you set a specific tab, the default tabs in front of it are erased. Word erases them so you don't have to tab past the defaults. Pressing Tab once moves you directly to the specific tab that you set.

To set a new tab, follow these steps:

1. Click in the tab area of the ruler, in the place where you want to create a tab. By doing so, you insert the default tab, which is left-aligned (see Figure 6.3).

New tab

FIGURE 6.3

Click anywhere in the tab area of the ruler to set a new tab.

Fun Field Day - Mr. Matthews' class

Default tabs are erased

2. If you change your mind and need to remove a tab, simply click and drag it off the ruler.

Changing to a Different Tab Type

By default, clicking in the ruler sets a left tab. If you want to use the other tab types, you should choose the tab type before you set the tab. When you change the tab type, it stays selected until you select another tab type. So, if you change the tab type to Decimal, every time you click on the ruler, you set a decimal tab.

To change the tab type, do the following:

1. Click the **tab type** button to scroll through all the different types of tabs. Stop when you locate the desired tab type.

2. Click on the ruler where you want to set the tab.

> **tip**
>
> If you're unsure which tab type is displayed on the tab type button, hold the cursor arrow over it and wait for the ScreenTip to appear and identify the tab type.
>
> You can change the type of tab after it's been set. Double-click the tab to open the Tabs dialog box; then select a different tab type in the **Alignment** section.

Moving Tabs

After you've typed your text, you may decide to move things around a bit. Good news! You don't have to delete a tab and create a new one. You can just move it instead.

When you're working with tabs, be sure to select the text first. If you don't, and the insertion point is in the middle of the tabbed text, some of the text will be formatted with the original tab settings, and the rest of the text will be formatted with the new tab settings. Believe me, it isn't pretty. This is where Undo comes in handy.

Follow these steps to move a tab:

1. Select the tabbed text.

2. Click and drag the **tab** marker. When you do, a guideline appears in the text so you can see where the text will be placed when you release the tab marker (see Figure 6.4).

3. When you're satisfied with the tab position, release the mouse button to drop the tab.

Tab guideline   Selected text

Even if you've
already typed
the text, you
can freely move
the tabs around.

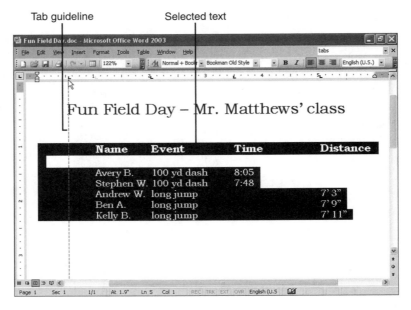

Clearing Tabs

When you're ready to return to default tab settings (so you can use regular tabs and indent later in the document), you need to clear your tab settings. As explained in the preceding section, you can clear a tab by clicking and dragging it off the ruler. However, there is a faster way: Clear all the tabs at once by using the Tabs dialog box. Everything you can do from the ruler (and some things that you can't), you can do in this dialog box.

To clear all the tab settings, follow these steps:

1. Choose **Format**, **Tabs** (or double-click a tab on the ruler) to open the Tabs dialog box (see Figure 6.5).

2. Choose **Clear All**.

3. Click **OK**.

When you clear the tabs that you created, the default tabs are automatically put back in place. You can adjust the interval between the default tabs by changing the value in the **Default Tab Stops** box.

Type the tab location

FIGURE 6.5
The Tabs dialog
box offers
options that
aren't available
when you use
the ruler.

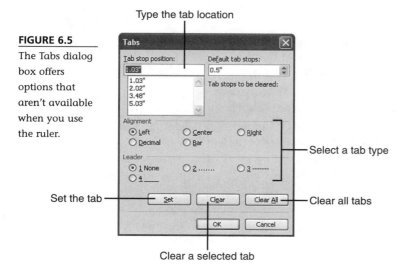

Set the tab

Select a tab type

Clear all tabs

Clear a selected tab

If you aren't comfortable using the mouse to set tabs, you can set the tabs in the Tabs dialog box. You can type in an exact location and select a tab type from a list, rather than click on the ruler. If you have already set your tabs with the mouse, you can use the Tabs dialog box to fine-tune the locations instead of clicking and dragging the tabs on the ruler.

Adding Leaders to Tabs

A *leader* is a series of dots, dashes, or a single line before a tab setting. You can add leaders to all the tab types except the Bar tab. Leaders are useful when the space between columns is wide because they help the reader's eye travel across the gap. Dot leaders are standard formatting for a table of contents.

To add dot leaders to a tab setting, follow these steps:

1. Choose **Format**, **Tabs** (or double-click a tab on the ruler) to open the Tabs dialog box (refer to Figure 6.5).

2. Select the tab you want to add leaders to.

3. Select one of the three leader styles in the **Leader** section.

4. Choose **Set**.

5. Click **OK** when you're finished.

If you change your mind, you can easily remove dot leaders from a tab. To do so, simply select the tab in the Tabs dialog box and then choose **1 None** in the Leader section.

Indenting Text

Indentation is often used to set quotations apart from the rest of the text. It is also used to emphasize text or to place a paragraph in a subordinate position beneath another paragraph. When you create a bulleted or numbered list, Word inserts an Indent command after the bullet or number so that the text you type isn't aligned under the bullet or number, but rather under the first word of the text. For more information on creating bulleted or numbered lists, see Chapter 10, "Creating Lists and Outlines."

You can set up indentation in two ways: using the indent markers on the ruler (see Figure 6.6) or using the options in the Paragraph dialog box. The quickest method is clicking and dragging the indent markers on the ruler, but it also requires a steady hand.

> **caution**
>
> The Indent feature uses the tab settings to indent your text. Changing the default tab settings affects the way text is indented. If you plan on indenting text and setting specific tabs in the same document, don't change the tabs at the top of the document. Change them just before you want to type the tabbed text. Then, after you've typed the text, restore the default tab settings.

FIGURE 6.6

Click and drag the indent markers on the ruler to set indents.

Creating a First-Line Indent

If you want the first line of every paragraph to be indented automatically (rather than your having to press Tab each time), use the First Line Indent option. Because Word carries the current paragraph formatting forward to the next paragraph, all your paragraphs will have the same first line indent setting, all without your pressing Tab once.

To set a first-line indent on the ruler, do the following:

1. Select the paragraph(s) that you want to indent.
2. If necessary, turn on the ruler by choosing **View**, **Ruler**.

3. Click and drag the **First Line Indent** marker to the position where you want the first line of text to start (see Figure 6.7).

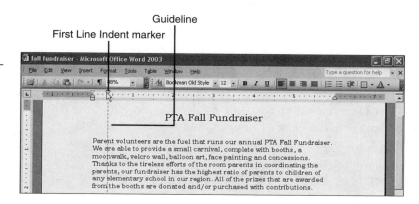

FIGURE 6.7

The guideline helps you visualize where the text will be placed with the indent setting.

Follow these steps to set a first-line indent using the Paragraph dialog box:

1. Select the paragraph(s) that you want to indent.

2. Choose **Format**, **Paragraph** or double-click one of the indent markers to open the Paragraph dialog box (see Figure 6.8).

FIGURE 6.8

Type the value for the first-line indent in increments of inches. For example, one-quarter inch would be .25".

3. If necessary, click the **Indents and Spacing** tab.

4. Open the **Special** drop-down list and choose **First Line**.

5. Type the amount (or use the spinner arrows) that you want the first line indented in the **By** text box. (The default is for one tab setting, or one-half inch.)

6. Click **OK**.

When you're ready to turn off the first-line indent, you can either click and drag the **First Line Indent** marker on the ruler back on top of the **Hanging Indent/Left Indent** markers, or you can open the Paragraph dialog box, open the **Special** drop-down list, and choose **(None)**.

Indenting on the Left and Right Sides

A left indent moves every line within a paragraph to the next tab setting (to the right). By default, this indent moves the text over one-half inch. The quickest way to set a left indent is to use the Increase Indent and Decrease Indent buttons on the Formatting toolbar.

A right indent moves every line in a paragraph over to the left, so the right side of the paragraph is indented. To create this indent, you can click and drag the **Left Indent** and **Right Indent** markers on the ruler. Or, if you prefer to use the Paragraph dialog box, you can specify the indent settings there.

To use the Increase Indent and Decrease Indent buttons to indent text on the left, follow these steps:

1. Select the paragraph(s) that you want to indent.

2. Click the **Increase Indent** button to indent the paragraph to the right by one tab setting. Click the button again to indent to the next tab setting.

3. To move the text back to the left by one tab (reducing the indent), click the **Decrease Indent** button on the toolbar. Click the button again to move the text to the next tab setting to the left.

To set a left or right indent on the ruler, follow these steps:

1. Select the paragraph(s) that you want to indent.

2. If necessary, turn on the ruler by choosing **View**, **Ruler**.

3. Click and drag the **Left Indent** marker to the position where you want the left side of the paragraph indented (see Figure 6.9). Alternatively, click and drag the **Right Indent** marker to the position where you want the right side of the paragraph indented.

Follow these steps to set indents in the Paragraph dialog box:

1. Select the paragraph(s) that you want to indent.

2. Choose **Format**, **Paragraph** (or double-click an indent marker) to open the Paragraph dialog box (refer to Figure 6.8).

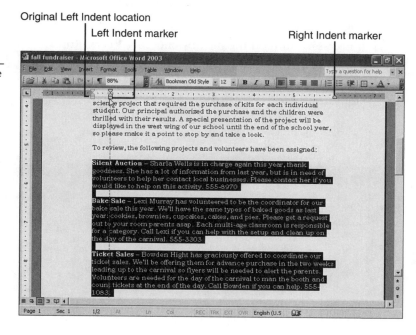

Original Left Indent location

Left Indent marker

Right Indent marker

FIGURE 6.9

Every line in the selected paragraphs will be indented to the left when you release the Left Indent marker.

3. If necessary, click the **Indents and Spacing** tab.

4. Type the amount (or use the spinner arrows) that you want the paragraph indented on the left and right in the **Left** and **Right** text boxes. Watch the text in the Preview window to see how it will look.

5. Click **OK**.

When you're ready to turn off the left or right indents, click and drag the **Left Indent** or **Right Indent** markers on the ruler back to the original locations (at the left and right margins). Alternatively, open the Paragraph dialog box and reset the values in the **Left** and **Right** text boxes to 0.

Creating a Hanging Indent

A hanging indent leaves the first line at the left margin, and all the other lines are indented (on the left side) by one-half inch. Bulleted and numbered lists frequently use this type of indent to align the text underneath the first line of text, rather than under the bullet or number.

As you've already seen, you can set up this type of indent either on the ruler or in the Paragraph dialog box. There is also a nifty keyboard shortcut that you can use.

To create a hanging indent on the ruler, do the following:

1. Select the paragraph(s) that you want to indent.

2. If necessary, turn on the ruler by choosing **View**, **Ruler**.

3. Click and drag the **Hanging Indent** marker to the location where you want the second line of text to be placed. Figure 6.10 is shown in Print Layout so you can see the left margin.

First line is against the left margin
Hanging Indent marker

FIGURE 6.10

A hanging indent leaves the first line at the left margin and indents the rest of the lines in the paragraph.

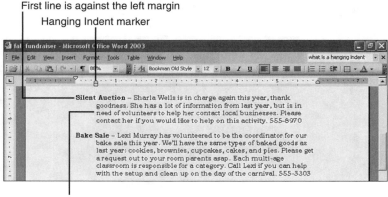

Other lines are indented

To set a hanging indent in the Paragraph dialog box, follow these steps:

1. Select the paragraph(s) that you want to indent.

2. Choose **Format**, **Paragraph** to open the Paragraph dialog box (refer to Figure 6.8).

3. If necessary, click the **Indents and Spacing** tab.

4. Open the **Special** drop-down list and choose **Hanging**.

5. Type the amount that you want the second and subsequent lines indented in the **By** text box.

6. Click **OK**.

When you're ready to turn off the hanging indent, either click and drag the **Hanging Indent** marker on the ruler back to the original location (at the left margin) or, in the Paragraph dialog box, open the **Special** drop-down list and choose **(None)**.

Creating a Negative Indent

A negative indent releases the left margin so that the first line of a paragraph starts at the tab setting inside the left margin; all the other lines are aligned at the left margin.

To create a negative indent on the ruler, follow these steps:

1. Select the paragraph(s) that you want to indent.

2. If necessary, turn on the ruler on by choosing **View**, **Ruler**.

3. Click and drag the **First Line Indent** marker to the location where you want the first line of text to be placed. Figure 6.11 is shown in Print Layout so you can see the left margin and, therefore, the negative indent.

When you're ready to turn off the negative indent, click and drag the **First Line Indent** marker on the ruler back to the original location (at the left margin). You can also reset the indent on the Indents and Spacing tab of the Paragraph dialog box.

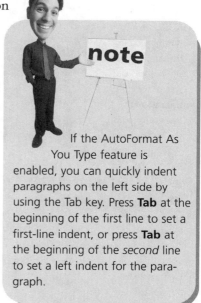

note

If the AutoFormat As You Type feature is enabled, you can quickly indent paragraphs on the left side by using the Tab key. Press **Tab** at the beginning of the first line to set a first-line indent, or press **Tab** at the beginning of the *second* line to set a left indent for the paragraph.

tip

I really like keyboard shortcuts, and I use them whenever I can. I save a lot of time by leaving my hands on the keyboard instead of reaching for the mouse, making selections, and then finding the home keys again. To create a hanging indent, press **Ctrl+T**. To reduce a hanging indent, press **Ctrl+Shift+T**. Cool, huh?

First line is in the left margin space

FIGURE 6.11

A negative indent pushes the first line into the left margin space, leaving the rest of the lines aligned on the left margin.

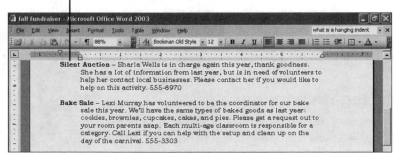

Adjusting the Spacing Between Lines and Paragraphs

As you may recall, the default line spacing in Word is set to single-spacing. Some types of documents, such as manuscripts, grants, and formal reports, require a certain line-spacing setting for submission.

The accepted standard is to leave a blank line between paragraphs, so you just press Enter twice after you type a paragraph, right? That's not a problem—until you decide to change the line spacing to double. Now you have the space of two lines between each paragraph. Furthermore, these extra lines leave space at the top of a page.

Making adjustments to the spacing between lines and paragraphs is another way to tailor your document to certain specifications and accepted standards.

Adjusting the Line Spacing

Line spacing can be a predefined amount, such as single, 1.5, or double, or you can set a specific amount, such as 3.3 lines. Say that you want to print out a document for someone else to review. You might consider changing to double- or triple-spacing, so that person has room for writing comments. After you incorporate that person's changes, you can just switch back to single-spacing.

To change line spacing, follow these steps:

1. Click in the paragraph where you want the change to take effect (or select the paragraphs that you want to change).

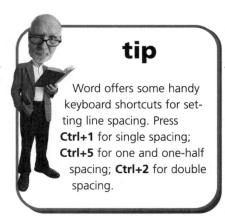

tip

Word offers some handy keyboard shortcuts for setting line spacing. Press **Ctrl+1** for single spacing; **Ctrl+5** for one and one-half spacing; **Ctrl+2** for double spacing.

2. Choose **Format**, **Paragraph** to open the Paragraph dialog box (refer to Figure 6.8).

3. Open the **Line spacing** drop-down list and choose an option (see Figure 6.12).

4. If you select **Exactly** or **At Least**, enter the amount of space you want in the **At** text box.

5. If you select **Multiple**, enter the number of lines in the **At** text box.

6. Click **OK** when you're finished.

FIGURE 6.12

You can specify exactly the amount of blank space you want between each line of text in the Paragraph dialog box.

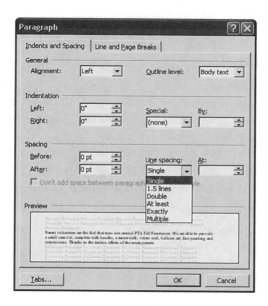

The new line-spacing setting takes effect at the beginning of the paragraph where the insertion point is resting, and it remains in effect throughout the rest of the document, or until you change the line spacing again. You might change the line spacing, for example, in a double-spaced document, where you switch to single-spacing for lists or quotations.

Adjusting the Spacing Between Paragraphs

Rather than insert extra blank lines, you can adjust the spacing between paragraphs. This way, you always have the same amount of space between each paragraph (no matter what you do to the line spacing), and you don't have extra blank lines floating around.

Follow these steps to change the spacing between paragraphs:

1. Click in the paragraph where you want to start the spacing.

2. Choose **Format**, **Paragraph** to open the Paragraph dialog box (refer to Figure 6.8).

3. In the **Spacing** section, select the number of points that you want between each paragraph in the **Before** and **After** drop-down lists.

The options in the Before and After drop-down lists depend on the current font size. If you're working in a 12-point font, you can adjust the spacing by 6-point increments, or half a line at a time.

Keeping Text Together

As you create or revise a document, you never have to worry about running out of room. Word creates a new page for you as soon as you reach the bottom of the current page. This feature is so transparent that you probably don't even stop to think about it. That is, until you preview the document and realize that you have headings and paragraphs separated by a page break. You can prevent this situation by identifying the text that should stay together when a page break is encountered.

To keep text from being separated by a page break, do the following:

1. Choose **Format**, **Paragraph**.

2. Click the **Line and Page Breaks** tab to display that section of the Paragraph dialog box (see Figure 6.13).

FIGURE 6.13

The options in the Line and Page Breaks tab of the Paragraph dialog box prevent important information from being separated by a page break.

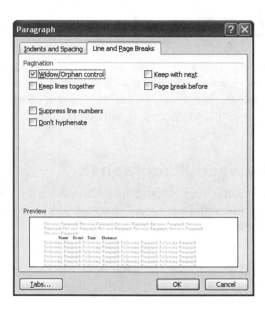

3. Choose from one of the following options:

- **<u>W</u>idow/Orphan control**—Prevents a single line of a paragraph from being left behind at the bottom of a page or being pushed to the top of the next page. The first line of a paragraph that is left behind at the bottom of a page is called an *orphan*. A *widow* is the last line of a paragraph that is pushed to the top of the next page. Select the paragraphs in which you want to control widows or orphans and then enable the **<u>W</u>idow/Orphan control** check box.

caution

If you keep large sections of text together, you may end up with extra whitespace in the middle of a page.

- **Keep with ne<u>x</u>t**—Prevents a page break between the selected paragraph and the next paragraph. Keep with Next works well for keeping figures or tables and explanatory text together. You can also use it to protect numbered paragraphs, lists, and outlines. Select the paragraphs that you want to keep together on a page and then enable the **Keep with ne<u>x</u>t** check box.

- **<u>K</u>eep lines together**—Prevents a page break within a paragraph. Select the paragraphs that contain the lines you want to keep together and then enable the **<u>K</u>eep lines together** check box.

- **Page <u>b</u>reak before**—Always places the selected paragraph at the top of a new page. Select the paragraph that you want to follow a page break and then enable the **Page <u>b</u>reak before** check box.

Using AutoFormat

AutoFormat does exactly what the name says: It automatically applies formatting to paragraphs. AutoFormat can be used to create headings, bulleted and numbered lists, symbols, fractions, hyperlinks, em dashes, bold, and italics. You can use AutoFormat to format a document as you type, and/or you can run it through after you finish.

Word analyzes each paragraph and based on how it is used in the document, Word applies a style to that paragraph. For example, if Word detects a number, followed by a period, followed by a tab, it assumes a numbered list and so applies a numbered list style. Some people like this feature, others don't. The important point is that you can customize AutoFormat to suit your preferences.

AutoFormatting as You Type

AutoFormat can work with you, as you type a document. When a style is applied, Word displays an icon that enables you to open a short menu from which you can choose to undo the action or change the AutoFormat settings. You'll find AutoFormat to be a friendly partner and one that can save you lots of repetitious formatting.

Before you turn on AutoFormat, you should look at the different AutoFormat options and make sure you want to leave them all enabled.

To review or edit the AutoFormat As You Type settings, do the following:

1. Choose **Tools**, **AutoCorrect Options**.

2. Click the **AutoFormat As You Type** tab to display that section of the AutoCorrect dialog box (see Figure 6.14).

FIGURE 6.14

Word can apply the most common types of formatting to your document, as you type.

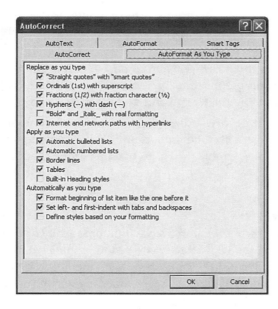

3. Enable or disable each option by adding or removing the check mark in its box. For more information on the different options, search help for "automatic formatting results."

4. Click **OK** when you're finished.

If you want to disable AutoFormat As You Type so Word doesn't attempt any formatting changes, clear the check boxes in the AutoFormat As You Type tab.

As you type a document, you may notice Word making changes automatically. When this happens, an AutoCorrect Options button appears in the text (see Figure 6.15).

FIGURE 6.15

When AutoFormat applies a style, the AutoCorrect Options button appears so you can undo the action.

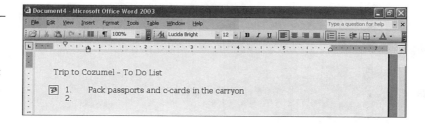

To accept or reject the AutoFormat changes, follow these steps:

1. Click the **AutoCorrect Options** button to open a drop-down list of options (see Figure 6.16).

FIGURE 6.16

Choose from the drop-down list of options, or clear the list and leave the formatting as it is.

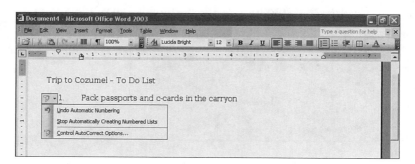

2. Either undo the action, turn off the AutoFormat As You Type option, or open the AutoFormat As You Type tab so you can make changes. Alternatively, ignore the options and leave things the way they are; just click in the document window to clear the drop-down list.

Running AutoFormat After You Finish Typing

Instead of stopping and accepting or rejecting AutoFormat changes while you type, you can wait until you're finished and then run the entire document through AutoFormat. This way, you can accept or reject the changes all at once. When you do the formatting all at once, Word doesn't display the AutoCorrect Options button, but you can still review the changes before they are implemented.

Follow these steps to run AutoFormat after you have typed a document:

1. Choose **Format**, **AutoFormat** to open the AutoFormat dialog box (see Figure 6.17). The **AutoFormat now** option is enabled by default.

FIGURE 6.17
Use the AutoFormat dialog box to switch between an AutoFormat As You Type and an AutoFormat pass.

2. Choose **AutoFormat and review each change.**

3. If necessary, open the drop-down list and choose a document type.

4. Click **OK**. Word formats the document and displays the AutoFormat message box (see Figure 6.18).

FIGURE 6.18
Either accept or reject all the changes at once, or review each change individually.

5. Choose one of the following options:

   ■ **Accept All**—Allows you to accept all the formatting changes without reviewing them first.

   ■ **Reject All**—Allows you to reject all the formatting changes in one step.

   ■ **Review Changes**—Displays the Review AutoFormat Changes dialog box. Click the **Find** button to move forward through the document and

tip

If you're having problems with the AutoFormat or the AutoFormat As You Type option and can't figure out what is going on, search Help for "troubleshooting automatic formatting" for a list of potential problems and their solutions.

start reviewing changes. When a change is made, Word highlights it and displays an explanation (see Figure 6.19). Either reject the change or click a **Find** button to continue moving forward or backward through the document.

FIGURE 6.19

You have an opportunity to accept or reject each AutoFormat change as you run AutoFormat on the document.

Selected change

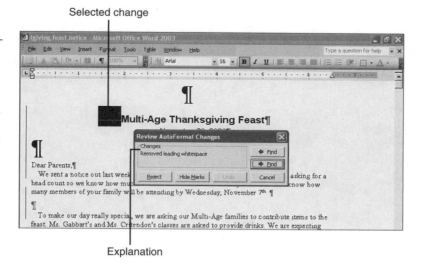

Explanation

THE ABSOLUTE MINIMUM

After reading this chapter, you now know how to

- Use the Justification feature to center and flush right text, as well as justify the text so that both margins are smooth.

- Define tabs stops to format information in columns.

- Correctly indent text for quotations and numbered lists.

- Adjust the spacing between lines and paragraphs to make it easier to read long passages of text.

- Keep sections of text together and prevent headings from being separated from the text, a single line left at the top or the bottom of a page, or key pieces of information split between two pages.

- Use the AutoFormat feature and save time by allowing Word to apply formatting automatically.

In the next chapter, you'll learn how to apply formatting to pages.

IN THIS CHAPTER

- Changing to a different paper source when you need to print envelopes or on a different size of paper.

- Including page numbers, headers, footers, and watermarks in your documents.

- Setting up columns so you can format text into smaller, easy-to-read chunks.

- Adding some punch with a plain or fancy border around a page.

- Using Shrink to Fit to shrink or expand a document into a certain number of pages.

7

WORKING WITH PAGES

In Chapter 6, "Working with Paragraphs," you learned how to format lines and paragraphs, which are pieces of a single page. This chapter deals with formatting that you apply to the entire page. I'll introduce features such as headers and footers, page numbers, and borders that are applied to a whole page, not just a section of a page.

Most simple documents may require a few changes to the format, but for the most part, those changes are generally applied to the entire document. However, more complex documents may have more than one header or page number style. When you need to change the formatting within this type of document, you need to divide the document into sections. This chapter begins with a short explanation of these sections and how they are created.

Formatting Sections of a Document

Before starting on the features that let you format pages, I want to stop for a minute and explain section formatting. In Word, page formatting can be applied to the whole document, or from the insertion point forward. Sections allow you to divide a document into separate parts that can be formatted independently of each other. Say you want to create a header for a document, but you need to be able to change the text of that header several times throughout the document. To do so, you simply create a new section each time you need to modify the text of the header. Section breaks don't affect page layout; they merely divide the document for formatting purposes.

To clarify, if you want the formatting to be the same throughout the document, you do not need to create any sections. However, if you want to change any of the following formatting from page to page or within a page, you need to create a new section:

- Top/bottom margins, paper size, paper orientation
- Page numbers (format, position, or numbering)
- Headers and footers (content or placement)
- Footnotes and endnotes (numbering and placement)
- Number of columns

To break a document into sections, insert a section break where you want the new section to start:

1. Choose **Insert**, **Break** to open the Break dialog box (see Figure 7.1).

FIGURE 7.1
Choose the type of section break you want to insert in the Break dialog box.

2. Choose one of the following options under **Section Break Types**:

   - **Next page**—A page break is inserted after the section break so the text after the break starts on a new page.

- **Continuous**—The text after the section break continues on the same page.
- **Even page**—A page break is inserted after the section break, forcing the text after the break to appear on an even-numbered page.
- **Odd page**—A page break is inserted after the section break, forcing the text after the break to appear on an odd-numbered page.

3. Click **OK**. In the Normal view, a section break appears onscreen (see Figure 7.2).

FIGURE 7.2

Depending on the view mode you're using, you may or may not see a section break onscreen.

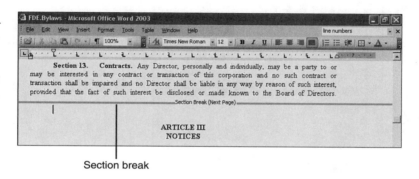

Section break

Defining Paper Size, Source, and Orientation

When you are ready to print a document, you have to stop and ask yourself, "What type of paper do I want to print this on?" In my office, I do most of my printing on plain white 8.5-by-11-inch paper. Your situation may be different; you may use several different types of paper depending on the project you're working on. You may print on letterhead, second sheets, legal size paper, and envelopes. The key is telling Word exactly how you want the document printed, what size paper you're using, and where that paper is coming from.

Changing to a Different Paper Size

By default, the paper size in the U.S. version of Word is 8.5 inches by 11 inches (other countries have different standards for paper size, such as A4). If you create only standard business documents, you might not ever need to switch to a different paper size. However, when you need to create an envelope or print on legal size paper, you need to know how to switch to a different paper size.

To select a different paper size, do the following:

1. Choose **File, Page Setup.** The Page Setup dialog box appears.

2. Click the **Paper** tab to display the Paper section of the dialog box (see Figure 7.3).

Select a page size here

FIGURE 7.3

You can choose a different paper size in the Page Setup dialog box.

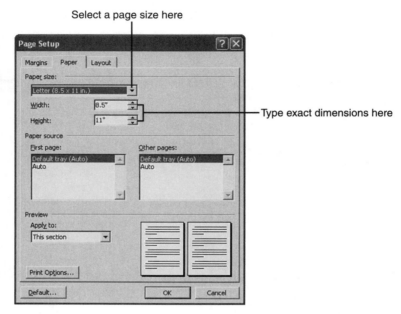

Type exact dimensions here

3. Open the **Paper size** drop-down list and select an item from the list. The measurements for the selected paper size are shown in the **Width** and **Height** text boxes.

4. If you don't find the right paper size in the list, choose **Custom size** (at the bottom of the list) and then type the page dimensions, or use the spinner arrows to set the value, in the **Width** and **Height** text boxes.

5. Open the **Apply to** drop-down list and choose **Whole Document** if you want to change the paper size for the entire document. Alternatively, select **This Point Forward** to apply the change to the current page and the rest of the document.

6. Click **OK** when you're finished.

Selecting the Paper Source

My printer has only one paper tray, so if I want to print a letter with more than one page, I have to manually feed in first the letterhead and then the second sheets. Offices that generate more paper than I do typically have a multitray printer that pulls letterhead from one tray and second sheets from another. To take advantage of the convenience of multiple trays, you need to identify a paper source.

Follow these steps to select a different paper source:

1. Choose **File, Page Setup** and then click the **Paper** tab to display the Paper section of the Page Setup dialog box.

2. Select the printer tray from which you want to print the first page of the section from the **First page** list box.

3. If necessary, select the printer tray from which you want to print the second and subsequent pages of a section from the **Other pages** list box.

4. Click **OK** when you're done.

> **note**
>
> The Eirst page and Other pages list boxes contain the paper feed options available on the current printer. If you don't see the paper source that you need, make sure that you have the correct printer selected. To switch to a different printer, choose **File, Print (Ctrl+P)**. Open the **Name** drop-down list and then choose another printer.

If you need to pull paper from more than two sources, you must insert a section break and then choose the paper source(s) for that section. A good example of this might be a letter with letterhead, second sheets, and an envelope.

Switching to Another Orientation

By default, text is formatted in *portrait orientation*, which means the paper is taller than it is wide. Think of a portrait photograph. If necessary, you can switch to *landscape orientation*, which means the paper is wider than it is tall. Spreadsheets are often printed in landscape orientation because more columns will fit on a page.

If you're having trouble visualizing the way the pages print, take a piece of paper and hold it up as if you were about to review a form letter. This is portrait orientation. Rotate the paper 90 degrees (turn the piece of paper over on its side). This is landscape orientation.

To switch between portrait and landscape orientation, follow these steps:

1. Choose **File**, **Page Setup**. If necessary, click the **Margins** tab of the Page Setup dialog box to display those options (see Figure 7.4).

FIGURE 7.4

You can switch between portrait and landscape orientation on the Margins tab of the Page Setup dialog box.

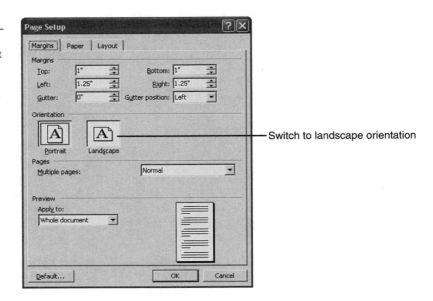

Switch to landscape orientation

2. Click the **Landscape** box in the Orientation section.
3. Click **OK** to close the Page Setup dialog box.

When you're ready to switch back to portrait orientation, open the Page Setup dialog box and click the **Portrait** box.

Adding Page Numbers

Word keeps track of your page numbers and displays a counter at the bottom of the document showing you the current page number and the total number of pages in the document. As you add or remove text, the page numbers are automatically updated, so the numbers are always current. If you want page numbers to show up in the actual document, however, you need to insert a page number.

I highly recommend adding page numbers if your document is longer than five or six pages. Think about what might happen if you accidentally drop the printout when you grab it off the printer. Without page numbers, you'll have to sort through the text to put the pages back in order. The same goes for someone who is reading your document. Often, readers spread out a document to review it, and the same problem crops up: If the document doesn't have page numbers, they have to reread parts of it to reorder the pages.

There are two ways to add pages numbers to your documents. You can add them to the header or footer region, which I'll show in the next section, or you can insert them directly into the text.

Inserting Page Numbers into a Header or Footer

When you insert a page number at the top of the page, you are actually inserting it in the header region of the page, which is inside the top margin area. Likewise, when you insert a page number at the bottom of the page, you are inserting it in the footer region of the page, which is inside the bottom margin. Therefore, adding page numbers to a document does not affect the page layout at all.

To insert page numbers at the top or bottom of the page, follow these steps:

1. Choose **Insert**, **Page Numbers** to open the Page Numbers dialog box (see Figure 7.5).

Top or bottom

FIGURE 7.5

Select where you want the page number placed in the Page Numbers dialog box.

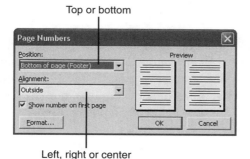

Left, right or center

2. Select the location on the page from the **Position** drop-down list.
3. Select the location on the line from the **Alignment** drop-down list.
4. Click **OK** (see Figure 7.6).

Page numbers are visible in the Print Layout view, so if you aren't currently in that view, you need to switch to it so you can preview the page numbers. Also, you won't be able to insert page numbers in Web Layout.

Page number

FIGURE 7.6

When you place
a page number
in a footer, it
appears at the
bottom of the
page.

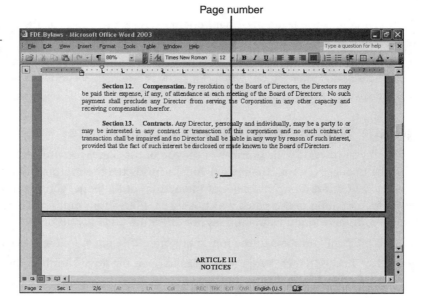

Customizing Page Numbers

Don't be misled by the simplicity in the steps for inserting a page number. Sure, this
procedure is quick and easy, but there is more to this feature than meets the eye.
Long documents often utilize different types of page numbers. For example, a table
of contents typically uses Roman numeral page numbers, and the body text uses
Arabic page numbers. And an index might have a different style, such as page
numbers surrounded by dashes.

By default, Word continues the page numbering from section to section. If necessary,
you can restart page numbering at any point in the document by creating a new
section and inserting a new page number. Finally, if you're working on a document
with multiple sections, or chapters, you can include a chapter number with the page
number. To customize the page number, do the following:

1. In the Page Numbers dialog box, choose **Format** to display the Page
Number Format dialog box (see Figure 7.7).

Choose a page number format

FIGURE 7.7
Choose a page
number format
and a new page
number in the
Page Number
Format dialog
box.

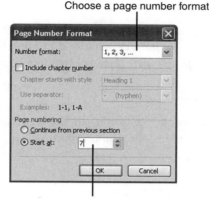

Set a new page number

2. Choose from one of the following options:

- Open the **Number format** drop-down list and choose a style for the page number.

- Enable the **Include chapter number** check box and then make your selections in the **Chapter starts with style** and **Use separator** drop-down lists.

- Enable the **Start at** radio button and then type a new page number in the text box.

3. Click **OK** when you're finished.

Inserting a Page Number in the Text

In some situations you want to include a page number in the body of the document, not in the header or footer regions. You can insert a basic page number with just a simple keystroke combination. However, this page number cannot be customized in the Page Number Format dialog box. To insert a page number in the text, press **Alt+Shift+P**.

Inserting Headers and Footers

A *header* is the area between the top of the page and the top margin; a *footer* is the area between the bottom margin and the bottom of the page. When you add page numbers to the top or bottom of the page, you do so in a header or footer. This section explains how to create a header/footer that can contain the page number and any other type of information that you want to include. You might want to include the title or author of the document and the date it was modified, for example.

Creating Headers and Footers

In Word, you can create a simple header/footer that appears on every page, or you can get fancy and create a header/footer for odd pages and another header/footer for even pages. I'll start with the steps to create a simple header or footer and then progress to the more advanced options.

To insert a header or footer, do the following:

1. Choose **View**, **Header and Footer** to display the header region at the top of the page (see Figure 7.8). The header region is outlined so you can see how much room you have to work with.

Header region

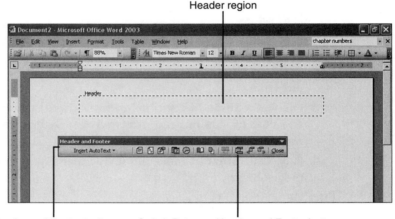

FIGURE 7.8
Word automatically switches to Print Layout view when you work with headers and footers.

Header and Footer toolbar   Switch Between Header and Footer button

2. Type the header text. To create a footer, click the **Switch Between Header and Footer** button to switch to the footer region and then type the footer text.

3. Use the following buttons on the Header and Footer toolbar to add information and change the page setup:

   - **Insert Page Number**—Inserts a simple page number at the insertion point.

   - **Insert Number of Pages**—Inserts a page number that represents the total number of pages in the document.

- **Format Page Number**—Opens the Page Number Format dialog box (refer to Figure 7.7) where you can change to a different page number style, add a chapter number, or reset the page number.

- **Insert Date**—Inserts the current date.

- **Insert Time**—Inserts the current time.

- **Page Setup**—Opens the Page Setup dialog box. You might want to decrease the top or bottom margins to allow for the header or footer text.

4. Using the menus, change to a different or smaller font, add graphics, or set up other formatting. (Features that can't be used in a header or footer are grayed out on the menus.)

5. Click the **Close** button on the Header and Footer toolbar when you're finished.

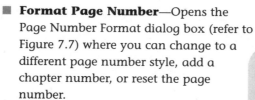

The header and footer regions have two preset tabs: a center tab and a right tab. This means that you can press **Tab** once to move to the center of the line and twice to move to the right margin. You may recall that with a right tab, the text that you type extends to the left, so the last character is always positioned at the right margin.

Editing Headers and Footers

Okay, you've created a simple header or footer. Now you need to know how to edit it—especially if you spend more time revising existing documents to create new documents rather than creating them from scratch. If you don't remember to edit the header or footer, you could get caught in an embarrassing mistake. And yes, I'm speaking from personal experience.

Follow these steps to edit a header or footer:

1. Choose **View**, **Header and Footer**.

2. If necessary, click the **Switch Between Header and Footer** button to switch to the footer region.

3. Make your changes.

4. Click the **Close** button when you're finished.

Creating Different Headers and Footers for Specific Pages

Up to this point, you've created a header or footer that will appear on every page of the document. But what if you need to use several different headers and footers in a document?

In Word, you can create one header or footer for odd pages and another header or footer for even pages. Having a different header/footer for odd and even pages is useful when you're printing on both sides of the paper and binding the document.

You can also divide your document into sections and have a different header/footer in each section. For the first chapter, you create a header with the chapter name and number. For the second and subsequent chapters, you edit the header/footer to change the name and number. Because each chapter is in a different section, you can work with each header/footer independently.

To create headers and footers for specific pages, do the following:

1. Choose **View**, **Headers and Footers**.
2. Click the **Page Setup** button on the Headers and Footers toolbar to open the Page Setup dialog box.
3. Click the **Layout** tab to display those options (see Figure 7.9).
4. Select one of the following options from the Headers and Footers section:
   - **Different Odd and Even**—Creates a different header and footer for the odd and even pages. You'll see that the headers are now identified as Odd Page Header or Even Page Header.
   - **Different First Page**—Creates one header or footer for the first page and another header or footer for the second and subsequent pages.
5. Open the **Apply to** drop-down list and choose **This section** if you are using sections, **Whole document**, or **This point forward**.
6. Click **OK** when you're finished.

 A couple of buttons on the Header and Footer toolbar come in handy when you're working with more than one header or footer. Click the Show Previous and Show Next buttons to move to the previous section or the next section, respectively, so you can work on the headers or footers in that section.

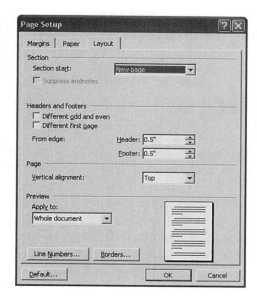

Creating Watermarks

A *watermark* is a design that is printed on fine paper and can only be seen by hold-ing the paper up to a light. Watermarks were traditionally used to identify the type and maker of a certain type of paper. Your business may be using paper with a watermark design for letterhead and second sheets.

Today watermarks are printed behind the document text and are usually done in a light gray so they don't detract from the rest of the document. They are used to iden-tify the type of document and, in some cases, impose restrictions on a document. For example, you could create a watermark that states the document cannot be copied or that the document is confidential. A printed watermark will certainly transfer over if the document is copied, even if the watermark is very light.

To create a watermark, follow these steps:

1. Choose **Format**, **Background**, **Printed Watermark** to open the Printed Watermark dialog box (see Figure 7.10).

2. Choose one of the following two options:

   ■ **Insert a picture as a watermark**—Choose **Picture Watermark** and then choose **Select Picture**. Select the picture you want to use and then choose **Insert**.

■ **Insert a text watermark**—Choose **Te_x_t Watermark**, and then either select the text from the drop-down list or enter the text that you want. Select any additional options that you want, such as changing the font or color.

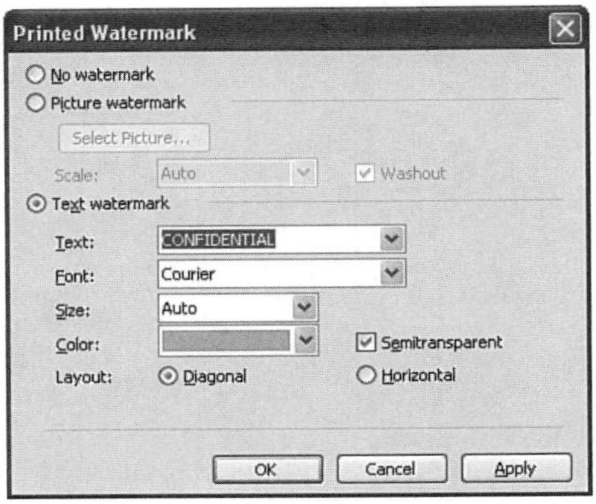

FIGURE 7.10

Create a text or picture water-mark in the Printed Watermark dia-log box.

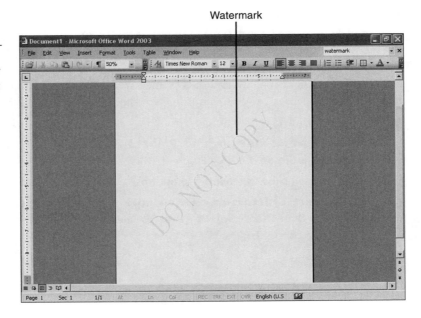

3. Click **OK**.

If you can't see the watermark, switch to Print Layout view to see the watermark onscreen. Choose **View**, **Print Layout**. Figure 7.11 shows the watermark at a 50% zoom so you can see the whole mark.

Watermark

FIGURE 7.11

The default watermark color is light gray, but it will transfer if the document is copied.

Setting Up Columns

You may have glanced at the newspaper this morning or read an article in a magazine over the weekend. These publications present information in narrow columns, rather than extending the text from the left to the right side of the paper. Why is that? Because the news printers from a long time ago realized that narrow columns are easier to read than longer blocks of text. It's harder to lose your place if you're reading across a short line than if your eye is traveling from one side of the page to the next.

The columns used in newspapers and magazines are called *newspaper columns*. Text flows down the column until the bottom margin is reached; then it is carried over to the next column. The text flows up and down, from left to right, following the natural movement of a reader's eye.

It makes no difference whether you define your columns before or after you type the text. Just make sure you click in the paragraph where you want the columns to start, or select the text that you want to format into columns, before you open the dialog box.

To divide a page into columns, do the following:

1. Click the **Columns** button on the toolbar to open a palette where you can specify how many columns you want to define (see Figure 7.12).

Columns button   Columns palette

FIGURE 7.12

You can easily choose the number of columns by using the Columns button.

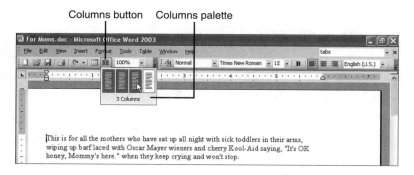

2. Click in the palette and drag across the columns to select the number of columns you want to define.

3. Release the mouse button to reformat the text into columns (see Figure 7.13).

That's the "quick and easy" method for defining columns. You can also use the Columns dialog box, which gives you more flexibility to set more than four columns and to define specific column widths.

FIGURE 7.13

Text in columns flows down until the bottom of the page is reached and then crosses over to the next column.

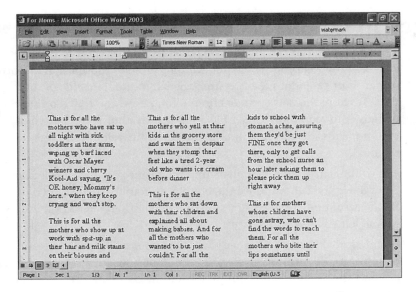

Follow these steps to define columns with the Columns dialog box:

1. Choose **Format**, **Columns** to display the Columns dialog box (see Figure 7.14).

2. In the **Presets** section, click one of the boxes to quickly set a frequently used column format or type the number of columns you want to define in the **Number of columns** text box. The Preview window shows you how the text will look with that column definition.

3. If you want, adjust the column widths and spacing between columns in the **Width and spacing** section. The **Equal column width** option needs to be disabled for this to work.

4. Open the **Apply to** drop-down list and choose **This section**, **Whole document**, or **This point forward**.

5. Click **OK** when you're finished.

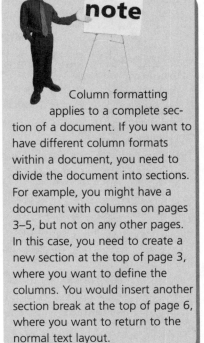

note

Column formatting applies to a complete section of a document. If you want to have different column formats within a document, you need to divide the document into sections. For example, you might have a document with columns on pages 3–5, but not on any other pages. In this case, you need to create a new section at the top of page 3, where you want to define the columns. You would insert another section break at the top of page 6, where you want to return to the normal text layout.

FIGURE 7.14

You can create a set of columns with specific widths in the Columns dialog box.

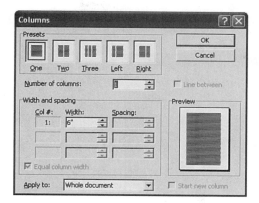

Creating Page Borders

Word comes with a collection of borders that you can place around a page. These ready-to-use designs are perfect for announcements, invitations, and a variety of presentation materials. Some of the designs can even be used to create your own decorative paper.

Selecting a Line Border

Word offers several different line styles and a selection of clip art to choose from. The line borders are more formal, but they are also more versatile. You can choose from 24 predefined line borders, and because you can edit these predefined borders to change the color and the line style, there are endless possibilities.

To add a line border around a page, follow these steps:

1. Either click on the page where you want the page border to start, or click in the section in which you want to place the page border.

2. Choose **Format**, **Borders and Shading**. The Borders and Shading dialog box appears.

3. Click the **Page Border** tab to display those options (see Figure 7.15).

4. Click one of the boxes in the **Setting** section to select a border style. You'll have to change the selection from None or you won't be able to create a border.

5. Scroll through the **Style** list box to see all the available borders and then click the one you want to use.

Select an effect

Choose a style

FIGURE 7.15
In the Borders and Shading dialog box, you can choose the border that you want to place around the page.

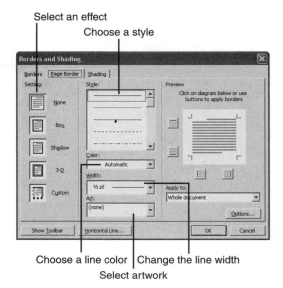

Choose a line color | Change the line width

Select artwork

6. (Optional) Click the **Color** drop-down arrow and then select a color for the border lines from the palette (see Figure 7.16). The Preview window shows you how the color will be applied to the border.

7. (Optional) Open the **Width** drop-down list and choose a line width from the list.

8. (Optional) Click one of the buttons in the Preview window to enable or disable the line border on the top, bottom, left, or right side of the page. You can also click the border sides in the Preview window to add or remove sides of a border.

9. Open the **Apply to** drop-down list and choose one of the options to apply the page border to every page in the document, pages in the current section, the first page in the current section, or all pages but the first page in the current section.

10. Click **OK** when you're finished.

To remove a line style page border, follow these steps:

1. Click in the page.

2. Choose **Format**, **Borders and Shading** to open the Borders and Shading dialog box.

3. Click the Page Borders tab.

4. Click the **None** button in the Settings section.

5. Click **OK**.

Enable/disable border sides

FIGURE 7.16

You can choose any color from this palette to add color to the border lines.

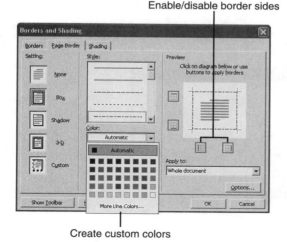

Create custom colors

Selecting a Clip Art Border

The line borders are the "serious" borders. The fun borders are called "art" borders. There are 166 (no kidding) borders to choose from. You can choose from a huge selection of clip art and other types of decorative borders.

Follow these steps to select a clip art page border:

1. Either click on the page where you want the page border to start, or click in the section in which you want to place the page border.

2. Choose **Format**, **Borders and Shading**.

3. Click the **Page Border** tab to display the options for creating a page border.

4. Open the **Art** drop-down list and choose one of the clip art borders (see Figure 7.17). If this is the first time you've tried to use the clip art borders, you may be prompted to install these borders. It only takes a second.

5. (Optional) Open the **Width** drop-down list and choose a width for the border.

6. (Optional) Click one of the buttons in the Preview window to enable or disable the line border on the top, bottom, left, or right side of the page. You

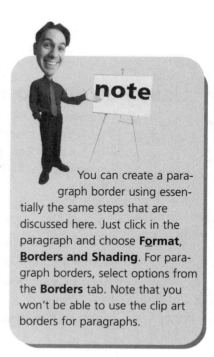

note

You can create a paragraph border using essentially the same steps that are discussed here. Just click in the paragraph and choose **Format**, **Borders and Shading**. For paragraph borders, select options from the **Borders** tab. Note that you won't be able to use the clip art borders for paragraphs.

can also click the border sides in the Preview window to add or remove sides of a border.

7. Click **OK** when you're finished.

FIGURE 7.17
Word offers a nice collection of clip art borders that you can apply to create decorative paper, invitations, certificates, and banners.

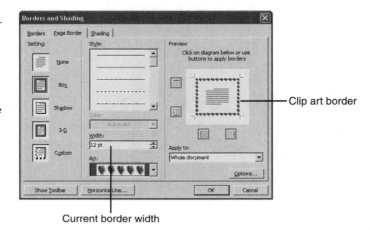

Clip art border

Current border width

To remove a clip art style page border, use the steps to remove a line style page border in the previous section.

Using Shrink to Fit

It happens to the best of us. You've just finished a carefully thought-out memo, and you're ready to send it off. However, when you print it, you notice that the last two lines of the memo have spilled over to the second page. Ack! You really need to make it fit on one page, so you sit down to play around with the margins and font size.

Stop! A Word feature can handle this job for you, in just seconds. Shrink to Fit decreases the size of each font used in the document in an effort to make the text fit on one page. If you don't like the result, you can always undo it.

To use Shrink to Fit on your document, follow these steps:

1. Choose **File**, **Print Preview** to display the document in the Print Preview window.

2. Click the **Shrink to Fit** button.

If you aren't happy with the results of a Shrink to Fit operation, press **Ctrl+Z**, or choose **Edit**, **Undo** to reverse the action. If you accidentally save the document before you undo the Shrink to Fit, you have to manually restore the original font sizes.

THE ABSOLUTE MINIMUM

After reading this chapter, you now know how to

- Break up a document into sections to allow you to format each section independently.
- Switch to a different paper size and orientation.
- Add page numbers, headers, footers, and watermarks to your documents.
- Break up text into smaller chunks to make it easier to read.
- Set up columns and adjust column widths and the gutter space between them.
- Work with borders to give simple documents a polished appearance.
- Force a document into a certain number of pages by using the Shrink to Fit feature.

In the next chapter, you'll learn how to create styles to automate repetitive formatting tasks and to ensure formatting consistency across documents.

8

Using Styles for Consistency

In Chapter 6, "Working with Paragraphs," and Chapter 7, "Working with Pages," you learned how to use most of the formatting commands that control lines, paragraphs, and pages. This chapter teaches you how to use those same formatting commands to create *styles*.

Styles speed up the formatting process and enable you to make editing changes on the fly. They also ensure a consistent appearance among documents. You might, for example, use styles for book manuscripts, presentation materials, financial reports, legal briefs, medical records, and more.

Understanding Styles

A *style* is basically a collection of formatting commands, such as font type, size, typestyle, and so on, that you put together and save with a name. The next time you want to apply those commands to some text, you can use the style instead of having to repeat all the commands. Obviously, applying a style is much faster than repeating a series of steps to generate the proper format.

But that isn't the only reason you want to use styles. The real benefit occurs when you start fine-tuning the format. Say you decide not to italicize your headings. If you had italicized the headings by selecting the text and applying italics, you would have to go back to each heading and remove the italics code. Instead, you can create a heading style so that all you have to do is remove the italics from the style and voilà! Every heading is automatically updated to reflect the new formatting in the style.

Think about the benefits for a minute. You can format an entire project, such as a newsletter, and then go back and play around with the styles and have the changes reflected automatically, throughout the whole document. Furthermore, if you're trying to achieve some sort of consistency among the documents that you and your co-workers create, a set of standard styles is the way to go.

Word employs four types of styles:

- **Paragraph**—Controls the formatting for a paragraph (that is, tabs, line spacing, justification, indentation).
- **Character**—Controls the formatting of text within a paragraph (that is, font, font size, bold, italics).
- **Table**—Controls the formatting of tables (such as borders, shading, justification, fonts).
- **List**—Controls the placement, bullet or number characters, and fonts used in lists.

As you work in a document, Word keeps track of the formatting that has been applied to the text and stores it in the Styles and Formatting task pane (see Figure 8.1). To display the Styles and Formatting task pane, choose **Format**, **Styles and Formatting**, or click the **Styles and Formatting** button on the toolbar.

By default, the list shows you the formatting that has been applied to the document. You can switch to a view of formatting in use, available styles, and all styles. You can also create your own customized view.

As you'll see in the following sections, you use the Styles and Formatting task pane to create, apply, and edit styles. I'll start with creating styles from formatted text; then I'll show you how to use Word's built-in styles. From there, I'll show you how to create your own styles from scratch and how to modify styles.

FIGURE 8.1

Word saves the formatting in the document to the Styles and Formatting task pane.

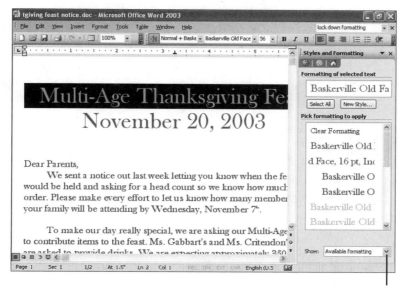

Select which styles you want displayed

Creating a New Style from Formatted Text

What if I told you that all you need to create your own collection of styles is a document that you've already formatted? Seriously. You've already spent the time to set everything up; here's your chance to take advantage of it! All you have to do is click in the formatted text and type a name for the style. That's it!

Follow these steps to create a style from formatted text:

1. Move the insertion point to the formatted text. For example, in Figure 8.2, the heading is 36-point Baskerville Old Face with a font color of navy.

Position the insertion point in the formatted text.   Type the style name here

FIGURE 8.2

You can format text first and then create a style based on the format you used.

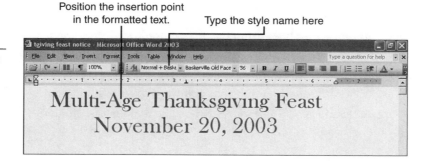

2. Click in the **Style** box on the toolbar and type a name for the style. For example, enter `notitle` for *notice title*. That's it; you just created a style from the formatted text!

3. If the Styles and Formatting task pane isn't already displayed, click the **Styles and Formatting** button to turn it on. Your new style is displayed in the list (see Figure 8.3).

FIGURE 8.3

The newly created style appears in the Styles and Formatting task pane.

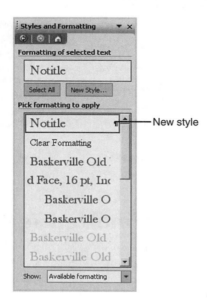

New style

Applying Styles

Word offers a few predefined styles that you can use right away in your documents. If you're in a hurry, or you don't care to learn how to create your own styles, you can use Word's heading styles to format your headings and titles. If you've created your own styles, or if you are using a template of styles that someone else created, you can apply the styles using the Style drop-down list on the toolbar or the Styles and Formatting task pane.

To apply a style, follow these steps:

1. Click in the paragraph that you want to format.

2. Click the **Style** drop-down list on the toolbar (see Figure 8.4).

Style name shows formatting
Style drop-down list

FIGURE 8.4

The fastest way to select a style is to choose one from the Style list on the tool-bar.

3. Click the style you want to use. Word applies the style to the text. Notice that the style name shows the formatting that is in the style.

Alternatively, you can use the Styles and Formatting task pane to apply a style as follows:

1. Click in the paragraph you want to format.

2. Click the **Styles and Formatting** button (or choose **Format**, **Styles and Formatting**). Word displays the Styles and Formatting task pane.

3. In the **Show** list, choose **Available Styles**. Word displays a list of the styles in the current document. Here again, notice that the style name is shown with the formatting of the style applied. When you position the mouse pointer over a style, a ScreenTip appears with detailed information on what is in the style (see Figure 8.5).

tip

If you frequently work with styles, you might find it helpful to display the name of the style alongside the text. Choose **Tools**, **Options** and then click the **View** tab. Click the spinner arrows or type a measurement in the **Style area width** text box. I have mine set to .3'', but my styles have only three letters in them. For longer style names, you might want to go to .5'' or higher.

Current style

FIGURE 8.5

FIGURE 8.5

The style name in the Styles and Formatting task pane is also shown with the formatting applied.

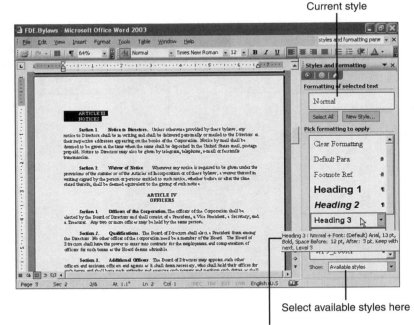

Select available styles here

Formatting in Heading 3 style

4. Click a style in the list to apply the style to the selected text.

Creating Your Own Styles

The heading styles are convenient, but they have limited use, so you'll probably want to start creating your own styles right away. You've already seen how to create styles from text that you have already formatted. When you're ready, you can create your own styles—either from scratch or based on another style. The next time you start a new project, take a few minutes and create the styles that you will need. Then you can apply the styles as you generate the content.

To create your own style, follow these steps:

tip

Word keeps track of both the available styles and the formatting that you've used in the document and saves this information in the Styles and Formatting task pane. You can reapply this formatting to selected text without creating a style. To do so, simply select the text, display the task pane, and select the formatting description in the list. If you don't see any format descriptions, make sure **Available Formatting** or **Formatting in Use** is selected in the Show list at the bottom of the task pane.

1. If the Styles and Formatting task pane isn't displayed, click the **Styles and Formatting** button (or choose **Format**, **Styles and Formatting**) to turn it on.

2. If you have text in the document that you want to use as a basis for the new style, select it now.

3. Click the **New Style** button in the task pane to open the New Style dialog box (see Figure 8.6).

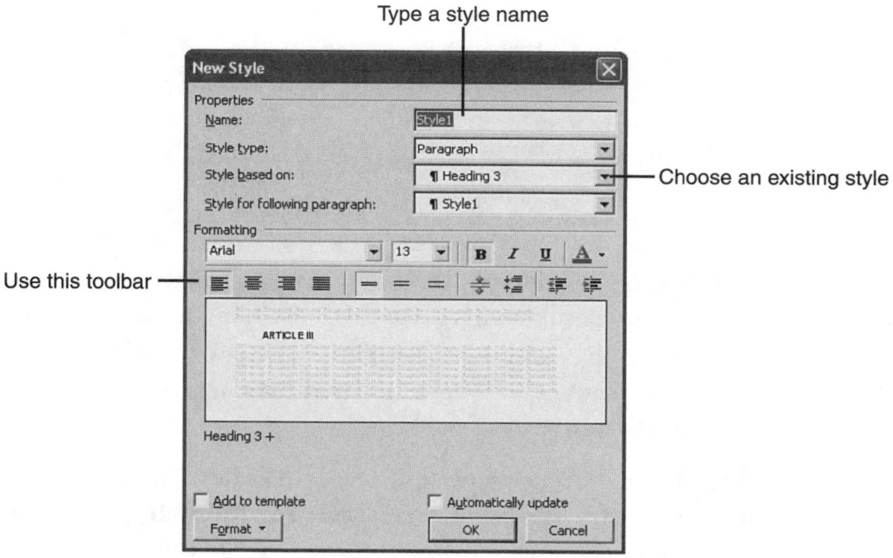

Type a style name

FIGURE 8.6

When you create a style in the New Style dialog box, you can base it on an existing style.

Choose an existing style

Use this toolbar

4. Type a name for the style in the **Name** text box.

5. If necessary, open the **Style type** drop-down list and choose a different style type.

6. If possible, open the **Style based on** drop-down list and choose a style to base your new style on. You can save yourself oodles of time this way. When you choose a style to base your style on, that formatting is copied over to your new style, so all you have to do is make minor adjustments or add to it.

7. Use the toolbar in the New Style dialog box and the options under the **Format** button (see Figure 8.7) to adjust formatting just as you would in a document.

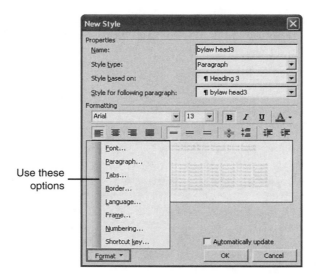

Use these
options

8. If you want this new style to be available to all new documents (not just the current document), place a check mark in the **Add to template** check box.

9. When you're finished, click **OK** to save your style. Word saves the new style to the current document (and to the default template if you enabled the **Add to template** check box).

When you create a new style in the New Style dialog box, you may have noticed that the new style is selected as the **Style for following paragraph**. This means that if you are creating a new document, and you stop and apply a style to a paragraph, when you continue typing, that new paragraph will be formatted with the style that you just selected. This is the way Word works: The formatting for one paragraph is automatically carried over to the next.

You can get a little fancy with this feature and *pick* a style to apply to the following paragraph. An example might be a heading, followed by text that should have a different style applied to it. In the example shown in Figure 8.6, the Heading 3 style is followed by Style1. For this manuscript, I used a style to identify the type of heading and used a body text style for the following paragraph.

To select a style for the following paragraph, open the **Style for following paragraph** drop-down list and choose a style from the list.

If you've painstakingly formatted a presentation and need to send it out for review, you might consider restricting the formatting that can be done to the document so that a review doesn't inadvertently reformat portions of the text. You can do this by limiting the styles available in the document. When the formatting is restricted, the commands and keyboard shortcuts to apply formatting directly are unavailable. See "Limiting the Available Styles" in Chapter 15, "Collaborating on Documents."

Editing Styles

Using the same techniques you learned in the preceding section on creating your own styles, you can edit your styles and make adjustments to them. You can also edit the default template, which contains the formatting codes for all new documents. The default template is the key to setting up Word just the way you like it.

Revising Your Styles

As mentioned previously, after you create a style and apply it to some text, you can make changes to that style, and those changes are automatically reflected in any text to which the style has been applied. This is the real strength of the Styles feature—the ability to tweak the formatting and have the changes reflected immediately in the document.

Follow these steps to edit a style:

1. If necessary, click the **Styles and Formatting** button to display the Styles and Formatting task pane.
2. Click the down arrow next to the style that you want to edit.
3. Click **Modify** to open the Modify Style dialog box (see Figure 8.8). A description of the style is shown under the preview area.
4. Use the toolbar and/or the options under the **Format** button to make your additions and/or changes.
5. If you want this style to be available to other documents, choose **Add to Template**.
6. Click **OK** when you're finished.

The description in Figure 8.8 is for the newly created style that was based on Heading 3, hence the "Heading 3+" at the beginning. This description shows that this style will apply all the formatting in Heading 3 plus the additional formatting that you added.

Some styles have "Normal+" next to them because those styles are based on the formatting in the Normal style, which contains the settings in the default template. Therefore, whatever is in the Normal style plus the formatting you've added to the style will be applied to the text.

FIGURE 8.8

The Modify Style dialog box is virtually identical to the New Style dialog box.

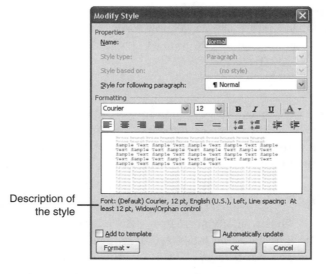

Description of the style

Customizing the Default Settings

As mentioned in Chapter 4, "Learning Basic Formatting Techniques," Word has a set of default format settings. The margins are 1 inch on the top and bottom and 1.25 inches on the left and right, documents are single-spaced, tabs appear every .5 inch, and so on. These settings are stored in the default template. Because of these defaults, you can start creating documents as soon as the software is installed.

After you've worked in Word for a while, you may develop a set of formatting standards that you use in your documents. Instead of making these selections every time you create a document, you can edit the default settings to meet your needs.

You can edit the default style, the Normal style, to change these default settings. Before you do, make a backup copy of the default template, which contains the default style. And yes, they are both called Normal. Search your system for the Normal.dot file. When you find it, make a copy of it and save it in another folder. Give it a name like normal-bak.dot. Now you have a safety net if your changes to the default style should go awry.

> **tip**
>
> If, after you create a style, you make some adjustments to the text that you want to add to that style, you can do so without going through the same steps again. How is this done? Select the paragraph, open the Styles and Formatting task pane, click the drop-down arrow next to the style that you want to update, and choose **Update to match selection**. Word then updates the selected style to match the formatting in the paragraph.

To edit the default style, do the following:

1. Display the Styles and Formatting task pane.

2. Click the drop-down arrow next to **Normal** and choose **Modify**. Word displays the Modify Style dialog box with the default settings shown in the description (see Figure 8.9).

3. Make the necessary changes.

4. Select **Add to template**. This saves the updated styles to the Normal.dot template so they are available to other documents.

FIGURE 8.9
Edit the Normal style to customize the default settings for all new documents.

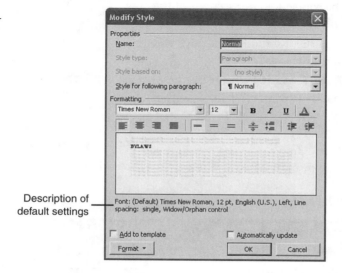

Description of default settings

The changes you make to the default style do *not* affect the documents that you have already created. Such changes apply only to new documents that you create after updating the default style

For more information on the normal.dot template, see "Customizing the Default Template" in Chapter 14, "Using Templates and Wizards to Build Documents."

Using Format Painter

Word's Format Painter feature enables you to copy formatting that you can then apply to other parts of the document. It's perfect for those situations in which you need to do some repetitive formatting, but you don't really need to create a style.

Say you have a document with a series of headings. You decide not to create a style because this isn't something you will use again. All you have to do is format the first heading and then use the Format Painter to copy the formatting to the other headings.

You use the Format Painter as follows:

1. Begin by applying the formatting you want to a section of text. This formatting will be copied to other sections of the document.

2. Position the insertion point anywhere in the formatted text.

3. Click the **Format Painter** button on the toolbar. A new mouse pointer appears; this one is shaped like a paint brush (see Figure 8.10).

4. Click and drag across the text that you want to format. When you release the mouse button, Word formats the text.

tip

After you adjust your styles so they are just perfect, you can copy them to other documents and templates. This is a great way to distribute a model that people can use to create documents. Que Publishing makes extensive use of styles to create and format these books. See "Transferring Items to Templates and Documents" in Chapter 14 for more information on copying styles to other documents or templates.

The Format Painter pointer

FIGURE 8.10

The mouse pointer changes to indicate that you will copy formatting when you click and drag the mouse.

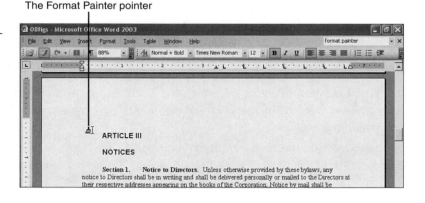

THE ABSOLUTE MINIMUM

After reading this chapter, you now know how to

- Create styles that are based on text that you had already formatted.

- Apply styles, including Word's heading styles.

- Create your own styles in the Modify Style dialog box.

- Create new default settings for all your documents so you don't have to make the same formatting adjustments for every new document.

- Duplicate formatting using the Format Painter feature when you don't necessarily want to create a style.

In the next chapter, you'll learn how to use one of the most versatile features in Word: the Table feature. From a simple list with several columns, to forms, to a mini-spreadsheet, you'll use the Table feature often.

PART III

Organizing Information

9

CREATING AND FORMATTING TABLES

At this point, you may not be sure what a table is, let alone why you might want to use one. I promise—after you learn how easy and useful Word tables can be, you'll wonder how you ever got along without them!

Whenever you need to organize information in rows and columns, as you would for a team roster or an inventory list, you should use a table. In fact, with very little effort you can use tables to create lists, forms, invoices, schedules, calendars, dialogue scripts, and more. And even if you're not quite ready to venture off into the world of spreadsheets, you can still use Word to perform spreadsheet-like calculations.

Creating a Table

Before you create a table, take a few minutes and consider how your information needs to be organized (see Figure 9.1). Grab a sheet of notebook paper and sketch out a rough draft so you can get an idea of how many columns of information you need (for example, name, address, phone number, and email). If you can, estimate roughly the number of rows you need. Don't worry if you have trouble coming up with an exact number. Adding or removing rows later is a snap.

FIGURE 9.1

This roster illustrates how neatly and clearly a table presents the information.

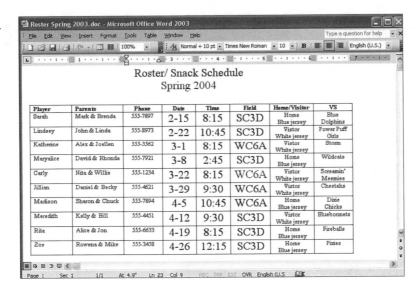

The easiest way to show you how tables work is to create a table that you can play around with as you go through this chapter. This will just be a sample table, so don't be too concerned if you make a few mistakes along the way.

There are several ways to create a table, and the method you use really depends on how complicated the table is and how steady your "mouse hand" is. Because you are creating just a basic table for this chapter's purposes, I'll show you two straightforward methods. The first is to use the Insert Table dialog box to enter a specific number of columns and rows. The second is to click and drag across a palette to select the number of rows and columns.

To create a table using the Insert Table dialog box, follow these steps:

1. Choose **Table**, **Insert**, **Table** to display the Insert Table dialog box (see Figure 9.2).

FIGURE 9.2

Type the number of rows and columns in the Insert Table dialog box.

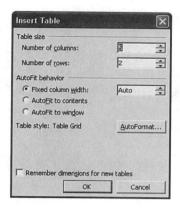

2. Change the number of columns and rows. For this example, enter **3** for the number of columns and **5** for the number of rows.

3. Click **OK** to create the table shown in Figure 9.3.

FIGURE 9.3

When you click OK, Word creates a table with three columns and five rows.

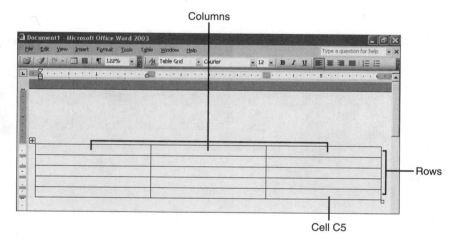

Tables look and function a lot like spreadsheets. In fact, the terminology is the same: Information is placed in *cells*, which are the intersections of *rows* and *columns*. Rows are labeled with numbers, and columns are labeled with letters. For example, in the table shown in Figure 9.3, the last cell (row 5, column C) is named cell C5. The first cell in any table is named A1.

That was pretty easy, wasn't it? Well, believe it or not, there is an even easier way to create a table: Simply click the **Insert Table** button on the Standard toolbar, and click and drag across the palette to select the number of rows and columns that you want to create.

Follow these steps to create a table with the Insert Table button:

1. Click the **Insert Table** button on the Standard toolbar to open the Table palette.

2. Click and drag across the palette to select the number of rows and columns that you want. For the sample table, drag across five rows and three columns (see Figure 9.4).

3. Release the mouse button to create the table (refer to Figure 9.3).

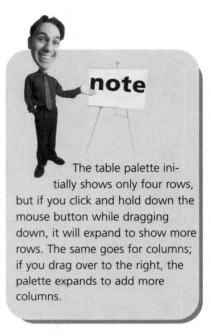

The table palette initially shows only four rows, but if you click and hold down the mouse button while dragging down, it will expand to show more rows. The same goes for columns; if you drag over to the right, the palette expands to add more columns.

Insert Table button   Table palette

FIGURE 9.4
Use the Insert Table palette to click and drag across the number of rows and columns that you want in your table.

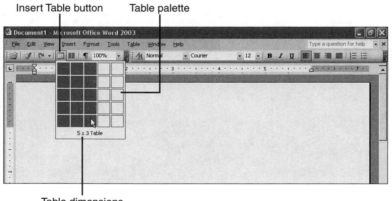

Table dimensions

Entering Text and Navigating in a Table

Appearances to the contrary, each cell in a table can contain more than one line of text. In fact, as you enter text, Word wraps all the words within the confines of the cell, adding lines to the row to accommodate what you type (see Figure 9.5). The remaining rows are not affected by the wrapped text so you can start to see how each row can be formatted independently of the others.

As you enter information in the table, remember that you can format it just as you would text in a document. You can change the font or font size; apply bold, italics, or underline; change to a different text color; align the entry within the cell; and so on.

There are several ways to navigate through a table, using both the mouse and the keyboard:

- Click anywhere in a table to move the insertion point.

tip

Don't forget you can use the Undo button if you make a mistake in either creating or modifying a table. Just click the **Undo** button or press **Ctrl+Z**.

FIGURE 9.5
Word wraps all the words within the boundaries of the cell and adds lines if necessary.

This row has two lines

These rows are not affected

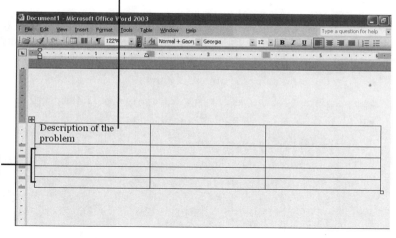

- Press the **Tab** key to move to the next cell to the right. When you reach the end of a row, pressing Tab moves you to the first cell of the next row. If you press Tab in the last cell of the last row, Word creates a new row for you.

- Press **Shift+Tab** to move back to the previous cell.

- Press **Alt+Home** to move to the first cell in the current row.

- Press **Alt+End** to move to the last cell in the current row.

tip

Because pressing Tab moves you to the next cell in a table, you might be asking yourself, "How do I enter a tab in a table?" It's simple. Just hold down the **Ctrl** key and then press Tab.

■ Press **Alt+PgUp** to move to the top cell of the current column. Note: Num Lock must be off for this key combination to work.

■ Press **Alt+PgDn** to move to the bottom cell of the current column. Note: Num Lock must be off for this key combination to work.

Working with the Structure

One of the biggest advantages of tables is that working with the information is easy. You can enter and edit text in a cell just as you do in a document. After you enter the information, you can manipulate it and format it to your heart's content. This section focuses on working with the structure of a table—adding rows and columns, adjusting column widths, moving and copying information, and joining and splitting cells.

Adjusting the Column Widths

When you create a Word document, certain default settings are in place. Likewise, default settings are in place for tables:

■ The rows and columns are evenly spaced.

■ The contents of the cells do not have any special formatting.

■ Single lines separate the cells of the table.

■ No special border appears around the table.

■ The tables are full-justified (tables extend from the left margin to the right margin).

The real beauty of Word tables is that you can easily make all kinds of adjustments to these default settings. When you make changes to the shape, size, and number of table cells, columns, and rows, you are editing the layout of the table or the table structure.

Say you don't necessarily want evenly spaced columns or rows. After all, you don't need the same amount of space for a phone number as you do for a name, right?

Let me show you how to adjust the column widths. (I'll describe how to change some of the other features later in this chapter.)

tip

If the ruler is displayed, you can also adjust the column widths by clicking and dragging the column markers. There is an additional neat trick with this method. If you hold down the **Alt** key while you drag the markers, the column width measurements are displayed on the ruler.

To change column widths, do the following:

1. Position the mouse pointer over a line separating the two columns you want to change. The mouse pointer changes to a vertical bar with left and right arrows.

2. Click and drag the column separator line to the right or to the left, thus widening one column and narrowing the other (see Figure 9.6).

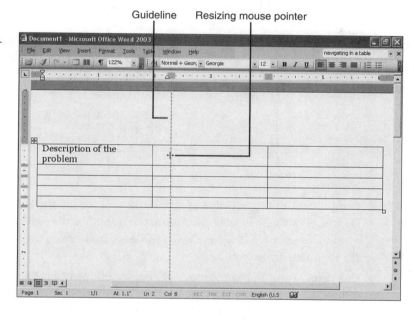

Guideline   Resizing mouse pointer

FIGURE 9.6

Click and drag column borders to change the widths of table columns.

3. When you reach the column widths that you want, release the mouse button.

You can repeat this process with other columns until your table looks just the way you want it. If you have already typed some text in the table, don't worry about it. Word automatically reformats the text within the new margins of the column.

Selecting Cells, Rows, and Columns

If you want to work with multiple cells, rows, or columns, you can select them in the table and work with them independently of the rest of the table. To select cells, rows, and columns, do the following:

■ **Cell**—Point to the left edge of a cell and wait for the thick arrow to appear (see Figure 9.7). Then click once to select the cell. Alternatively, triple-click in a cell (this method works best in Normal view).

FIGURE 9.7

When you see the thick arrow pointer, click to select a cell, row, or column.

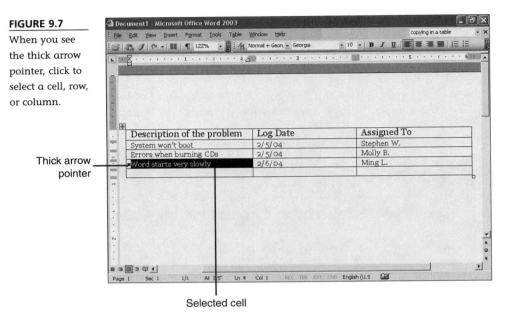

Thick arrow pointer

Selected cell

- **Row**—Point to the left edge of a cell and wait for the thick arrow to appear. Double-click to select the row. Alternatively, click to the left of the row. If you need to select more than one row, click and drag across the rows when you see the thick arrow pointer.

- **Column**—Point to the column's top border and wait for the thick arrow to appear. Click once to select the column. If you need to select more than one column, click and drag across the columns when you see the thick arrow pointer.

Adding Rows and Columns

A common problem in using tables is that you're never sure just how many rows or columns you're going to need. One easy way to add rows at the bottom of the table is to press the **Tab** key in the last column of the last row. However, rows and columns can also be added anywhere in a table with just a few clicks.

Follow these steps to add rows or columns to a table:

1. Position the insertion point where you want to add a new column or row.

2. Choose **Table**, **Insert**. Word displays the Insert menu (see Figure 9.8).

3. Choose **Columns to the Left**, **Columns to the Right**, **Rows Above**, or **Rows Below**. Word inserts the new column or row in the location that you have specified.

Toolbar buttons

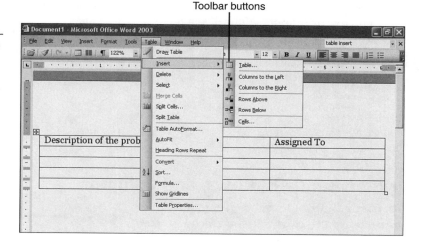

If you want to add more than one row or column, select the number of rows or columns in the table. Choose **Table**, **Insert** and then make your selection. Word inserts the rows or columns adjacent to the first row or column in the selection. If you don't like the location of the new rows and columns, choose **Undo** and try again.

Deleting Rows and Columns

Occasionally, you might overshoot the mark and end up with more rows or columns than you need. Rather than leave them empty, you can delete them from the table.

To delete rows or columns, do the following:

1. Click in the row or column you want to delete. If you want to delete multiple rows or columns, select them first.

2. Choose **Table**, **Delete** to open the Delete menu.

3. Choose **Rows** or **Columns**.

caution

Remember, when you delete rows or columns, the contents are also erased. Click the **Undo** button or choose **Edit**, **Undo (Ctrl+Z)** if you accidentally delete important data.

Personally, I like to use the context menus whenever I can. If my hand is already on the mouse, I find it faster to right-click and choose from the abbreviated menu than to click through the regular menus. If you right-click and choose **Delete Cells**, the Delete Cells dialog box appears (see Figure 9.9). Choose **Delete entire row** or **Delete entire column**. If you selected multiple rows or columns before opening this dialog box, they are deleted, even though the command makes it sound as if only one row or column will be deleted.

FIGURE 9.9
Use the Delete Cells dialog box to remove unneeded table rows or columns.

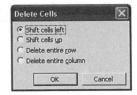

Moving or Copying Cells, Rows, and Columns

It's not uncommon to change your table structure after you've created it and typed in some information. Sometimes things are clearer after you see them laid out onscreen. Whatever the reason, moving or copying rows and columns in a table is a simple process.

The first step is to select the information that you want to move or copy. Refer to the section "Selecting Cells, Rows, and Columns" earlier in this chapter for a quick review if necessary.

To move selected cells, rows, or columns, follow these steps:

1. Select the cell(s), row(s), or column(s) you want to move.

2. Click the **Cut** button (or press **Ctrl+X**) or the **Copy** button (or press **Ctrl+C**) on the toolbar.

3. Click in the table where you want to insert the information.

4. Click the **Paste** button (or press **Ctrl+V**).

> **tip**
>
> You can also use the right-click menu to move, copy, and paste items. After you select the cell(s), row(s), or column(s), right-click in the selection and choose **Cut** or **Copy**. Right-click in the table where you want to move or copy the items and then choose **Paste**.

Joining and Splitting Cells

Another useful way to modify the layout of your table is to join cells together or split them apart. For example, you might want to make the entire top row of your team list a single cell to use as a title row. To do this, you need to join the cells in the top row.

Or you might decide that you need two separate pieces of information in place of one single cell. In this case, you need to split a single cell into two cells.

Follow these steps to join cells together:

1. Click in the first cell you want to join (for example, cell A1).
2. Click and drag the mouse to the last cell in the group you want to join (for example, D1).
3. Choose **Table**, **Merge Cells**. Word automatically joins the selected cells, combining any information that was in those cells into the new cell.

From now on, Word will treat the joined cells as a single cell. If you want to revert to the original cell division, you can choose **Undo** right away, or you can split the cells.

In some situations you need to create additional cells in a row or column. This capability is particularly useful if you're trying to create a special form.

To split a cell, follow these steps:

1. Position the insertion point in the cell you want to split.
2. Choose **Table**, **Split Cells**.
3. In the Split Cell dialog box, specify the number of columns (vertical cells) or rows (horizontal cells) you want.
4. Click **OK**.

Figure 9.10 shows an example of a form in which several cells have been joined, whereas others have been split.

Joined cell

FIGURE 9.10

You can join or split cells in a table to create useful table layouts, such as in a form.

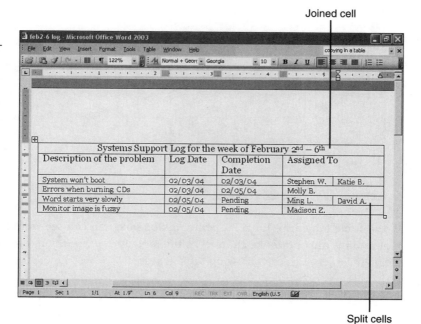

Split cells

Formatting the Table

You've learned about features that help you create the layout, or structure, of a table. But you also want your text to look good, and that's why it's important to learn how to format the different elements of a table. Sure, you can format the entries in much the same way as you would format text in a document, but you can do specific things to format text in a table. I'll start with the options that format an entire table and move on to formatting rows, columns, and cells.

Formatting the Entire Table

When you want to work with the entire table, you use the Table tab of the Table Properties dialog box to select a size and position for the table. You can also select how you want the text to wrap around your table.

Follow these steps to format a table:

1. Click in the table. If you don't, you cannot open the Table Properties dialog box.

2. Choose **Table**, **Table Properties** to open the Table Properties dialog box.

3. Click the **Table** tab to make changes to the entire table (see Figure 9.11).

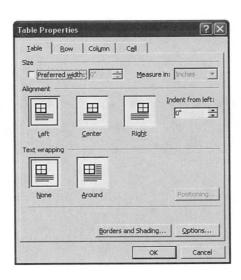

FIGURE 9.11
Use the Table tab of the Table Properties dialog box to set formatting for the entire table.

In the Table tab of the Table Properties dialog box, you can see what the current format settings are and make changes to the table format, position, or size. For example, you can change the following table features:

- **Table size**—Type a specific width for the table.

- **Table position**—Word tables stretch from margin to margin. You can also center, right-, or left-align a table instead. If you choose **Left**, you have an opportunity to specify how much you want the table indented from the left.

- **Text wrap**—Specify whether you want the text to wrap around the table. If you choose **Around**, additional options are available under the **Positioning** button.

tip

¶ If the cell row seems too high, check to see whether you have an extra hard return in any of the cells in that row. Delete the hard return, and the row will return to its normal height. Displaying the paragraph marks will make this easier to do. Click the Show/Hide ¶ button on the Standard toolbar.

Formatting Rows

As you've probably noted, Word automatically determines the amount of vertical space in a row based on the amount of text in its cells. The cell requiring the most vertical space sets the height for the entire row.

You can easily and quickly change a row's height by dragging the bottom line of the row up or down. Word displays a guideline showing the size the row will become when you release the mouse button (see Figure 9.12).

Resize mouse pointer   Guideline

FIGURE 9.12

You can easily change the height of a Word table row by dragging the horizontal line below the row.

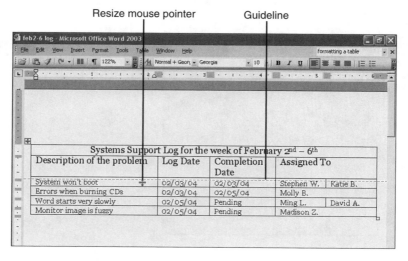

Sometimes you need to set a specific row height—for example, if you want to create a calendar in which all rows are the same height, regardless of the number of events on any given day.

To set a fixed row height, follow these steps:

1. Select the row or rows you want to format.

2. Choose **Table**, **Table Properties** to open the Table Properties dialog box.

3. Click the **Row** tab. Word displays options for formatting a row (see Figure 9.13).

4. Choose **Specify Height**, and in the text box, type the height of the row (for example, 1.0'' for a calendar row).

5. If necessary, open the **Row height is** drop-down list and choose **Exactly** or **At least** to control whether Word exceeds this height if you enter more text than the height will accommodate.

6. If you want to format another row, use the **Previous Row** and **Next Row** buttons to move to another row.

7. Click **OK** to apply the change and return to the table.

tip

If the vertical ruler is displayed, you can adjust the row height by clicking and dragging the row markers. There is also a neat trick with this method. If you hold down the **Alt** key while you drag the markers, the row height measurements are displayed on the ruler. The vertical ruler is displayed by default in Print Layout, so if you like using these shortcuts, you might prefer to work in Print Layout.

FIGURE 9.13

To alter the structure of a row, click the Row tab in the Table Properties dialog box.

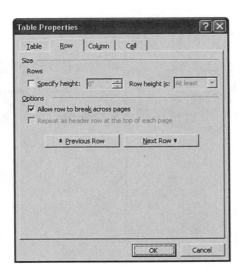

Sometimes you have table cells with a lot of text in them, or you have extremely long tables with many rows. In the Table Properties dialog box (refer to Figure 9.13), two options can help you deal with those situations:

■ **Divide a row across pages**—If you have cells with an unusually large amount of text, Word forces the entire cell to wrap to the next page. That can leave a lot of blank space. If, instead, you want to break the cell at the page break, enable the **Allow row to break across pages** check box.

■ **Create a header row**—If you create a table several pages long, you may want certain information (such as column headings) to repeat at the top of each page. Such rows are called *header rows*. To create a header row, first position the insertion point in the row you want to designate as a header row; then in the Table Properties dialog box, click the **Row** tab and enable the **Repeat as header row at the top of each page** check box.

Formatting Columns

At the beginning of the chapter, you learned how to adjust the column width by clicking and dragging the column borders. For situations in which you need to be very specific about your column widths, you can also enter a precise measurement in the Table Properties dialog box.

To set the column width for a column, follow these steps:

1. Click in the column.

2. Choose **Table**, **Table Properties**.

3. In the Table Properties dialog box, click the **Column** tab. Word displays the dialog box controls for formatting columns (see Figure 9.14).

FIGURE 9.14

To enter a precise column width, use the Column tab in the Table Properties dialog box.

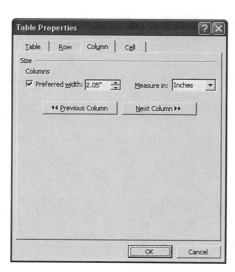

4. Enable the **Preferred width** check box.

5. Enter the width in the **Preferred width** text box or use the spinner arrows to adjust the width.

6. If necessary, move to another column by using the **Previous Column** or **Next Column** buttons.

7. Click **OK** to apply the change and return to the table.

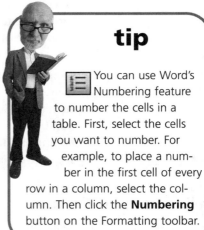

tip

You can use Word's Numbering feature to number the cells in a table. First, select the cells you want to number. For example, to place a number in the first cell of every row in a column, select the column. Then click the **Numbering** button on the Formatting toolbar.

Formatting Cells

Within cells, you format text as you normally do in a document. Simply select the text and add whatever attributes you want. Note, however, that you need to set a couple of options in the Table Properties dialog box.

To set the width of a cell, follow these steps:

1. Click in the cell or select a group of cells.

2. Choose **Table**, **Table Properties.**

3. In the Table Properties dialog box, click the **Cell** tab. Word displays the dialog box controls for formatting cells (see Figure 9.15).

FIGURE 9.15

To enter a precise cell width, use the Cell tab in the Table Properties dialog box.

4. Enable the **Preferred width** check box.

5. Enter a width for the cell or use the spinner arrows to adjust the width in the **Preferred width** text box.

6. If necessary, choose **Top**, **Center**, or **Bottom** to set the alignment for the text in the cell.

7. Click **OK** to apply the change.

If you want more control than merely setting the width of a cell, you can specify exact cell margins. You can do this for individual cells, or you can set default cell margins for the entire table.

Follow these steps to set exact margins for a cell or selected cells:

1. Click in the cell or select a group of cells.

2. Choose **Table**, **Table Properties.**

3. Click the **Cell** tab.

4. Choose **Options** to display the Cell Options dialog box (see Figure 9.16).

FIGURE 9.16

To enter precise cell margins, use the Cell Options dialog box.

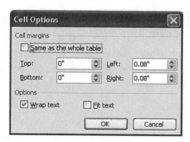

5. Disable the **Same as the whole table** check box.

6. Enter the cell margins in the **Top**, **Bottom**, **Left**, and **Right** text boxes.

7. Click **OK** when you're finished.

8. Click **OK** again to close the Table Properties dialog box.

To set default cell margins for the table, follow these steps:

1. Click in the cell or select a group of cells.

2. Choose **Table**, **Table Properties**.

3. Click the Table tab.

4. Choose **Options** to display the Table Options dialog box. This dialog has similar controls to the Cell Options dialog box.

5. Enter the cell margins (or click the spinner arrows) in the **Top**, **Bottom**, **Left**, and **Right** text boxes.

6. If necessary, enable the **Allow spacing between cells** check box and then type the spacing you want between the cells in the text box.

7. Click **OK** when you're finished.

8. Click **OK** again to close the Table Properties dialog box.

Formatting Lines, Borders, and Fill

Although the layout and content of your table are the most important, no one will take a close look if the table doesn't generate some interest. For example, you can easily change the lines around table cells so you can highlight important cells. Or you might decide to select a different border to make the table more attractive. Finally, perhaps you can add a fill to emphasize important information.

Before I explain how to use these formatting options, I want to show you how to completely automate the process. If you don't have time, or you don't care to learn the "ins and outs" of the formatting options, you can use AutoFormat to apply a table style that encompasses all these options.

Using AutoFormat

By default, single lines separate Word table cells and create a border around the table, but no other special formatting is assigned. To help you quickly add special line formatting, Word provides a nice collection of preset table styles.

To use AutoFormat to apply a table formatting style, follow these steps:

1. Position the insertion point anywhere within the table.

2. Choose **Table**, **Table AutoFormat**. Word displays the Table AutoFormat dialog box (see Figure 9.17).

3. Select a style in the **Table styles** list box. Word shows you what it looks like in the preview box. For example, if you select the **Table Classic 3** style, Word formats your table with a navy title bar, italicized column headings and shading, and line changes to set off the data (see Figure 9.18).

4. Choose **Apply**.

FIGURE 9.17

By default, Word uses a single-line border around each cell, also called a table grid.

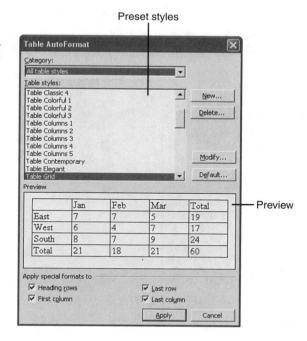

Preset styles

Preview

Changing the Lines

AutoFormat might be overkill, especially if all you want to do is change the line style for a few lines. You might just want to remove the lines, or change them to dotted or dashed lines for emphasis. Whatever the case, Word makes it easy to customize the lines in a table.

The default setting is for a plain, black 1/2-point border around each cell. You can change to a different type of line, a different thickness, or a different color. Furthermore, you can select exactly which sides of the cell you want to place the line.

To customize cell lines, do the following:

1. Select the cell(s) you want to change. For example, if you want to change the line beneath the cells in the first row, select all the cells in the first row.

2. Choose **Format**, **Borders and Shading**. Word displays the Borders and Shading dialog box (see Figure 9.19).

3. Choose from the following options:

   ■ Select a different line style from the **Style** list.

   ■ Choose a line color from the **Color** drop-down list.

■ Select a line thickness from the **Width** drop-down list.

■ Open the **Apply to** drop-down list and choose **Cell** if you want the line change applied to the cell(s) you have selected.

Selected style

FIGURE 9.18

When you select an AutoFormat style such as Table Classic 3, you apply a predefined set of attributes, lines, and fills to your table.

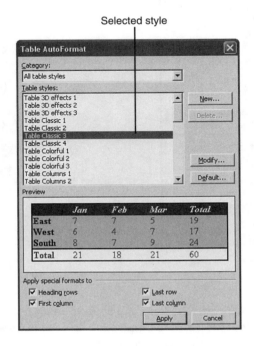

Remove the border completely

Turn lines on/off for different sides

FIGURE 9.19

Use the Borders and Shading dialog box to change lines and fills in Word table cells.

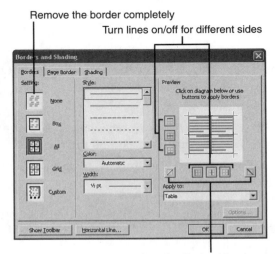

Insert a diagonal line in a cell

4. To remove lines from the sides of a cell or cells, click the buttons in the Preview area to turn lines on or off for different sides of a cell. The Preview sample shows you how the cell will look with your new settings (see Figure 9.20).

5. Click **OK** to close the Borders and Shading dialog box.

FIGURE 9.20

The Preview area in the Borders and Shading dialog box enables you to see the effect of your choice before applying it to your table.

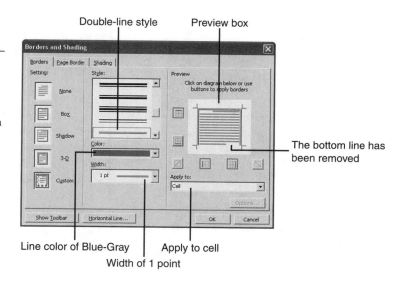

Double-line style   Preview box

The bottom line has been removed

Line color of Blue-Gray   Apply to cell

Width of 1 point

You may not want any lines at all. For example, you might want to organize your information but not have it look like a table. With all the lines removed, your text looks like you formatted into columns. The advantage of using tables over columns is that tables are so much easier to work with.

To remove all the table lines, follow these steps:

1. Right-click in the table and then choose **Borders and Shading**.

2. Click the **None** button.

3. If necessary, open the **Apply to** drop-down list and choose **Table**.

4. Click **OK** when you're finished.

When you remove the lines, you can't see the dimensions of each cell, or the table itself if it is empty! Table gridlines are helpful in this situation because they show you where the cells are, but they don't print. To turn on table gridlines, choose **Table**, **Show Gridlines**.

Changing the Fill Pattern

Fills are nothing more than color or shaded cell backgrounds. A fill color can be applied as a solid color, or in a pattern with foreground and background colors.

To add fill patterns to a cell, follow these steps:

1. Click in the cell where you want a fill. If you want to add a fill to more than one cell—for example, the entire first row of cells—select all the cells you want to change.

2. Choose **Format**, **Borders and Shading**.

3. Click the **Shading** tab to display the fill options (see Figure 9.21).

4. Select a fill color from the **Fill** palette.

5. Open the **Style** drop-down list and choose the level of shading or a fill pattern (scroll down). As usual, the Preview shows you how the cell will look when you apply the fill.

6. If you want to apply the shading to the entire table, open the **Apply to** drop-down list and choose **Table**.

7. Click **OK** to apply the fill pattern.

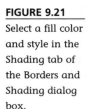

tip

The Tables and Borders toolbar has buttons for Line Style, Line Weight, Outside Border, and Border Color, and you can add other buttons to customize the toolbar. If you frequently work with tables, you can use the toolbar for quicker access to these features. Right-click a toolbar and then choose **Tables and Borders** from the list of toolbars. When you're finished, click the **Close** button to clear the toolbar off the screen.

FIGURE 9.21

Select a fill color and style in the Shading tab of the Borders and Shading dialog box.

Choose a fill color

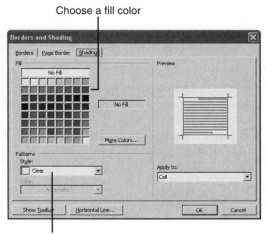

Choose a fill pattern

Choosing a Table Border

By default, a Word table has no border, so you can quickly improve its appearance by applying one of the border styles. Although the table appears to have a border, you are actually seeing the lines around the cells on the perimeter of the table.

To add a border around the table, follow these steps:

1. Right-click in the table and then choose **Borders and Shading**.

2. In the Borders and Shading dialog box, click the **Borders** tab.

3. Click the **Box** button in the **Setting** section if you want to apply a border only to the outside lines; click **All** if you want to apply the border style to the lines between cells; click **Grid** if you want to have thin lines between cells and the selected border style applied to the outside lines.

4. Choose from the following options:

   ■ Select a different line style from the **Style** list.

   ■ Choose a line color from the **Color** drop-down list.

   ■ Select a line thickness from the **Width** drop-down list.

5. Open the **Apply to** drop-down list and choose **Table**. The Preview area shows you how the border will look when you apply it to the table.

6. Click **OK** to apply the change and return to your table.

> **tip**
>
> If you plan to include text in a filled cell, it's best to use a light shade of gray, 10% or less, or a light color such as yellow. Otherwise, text won't show up very well.

Calculating Values

Word isn't a full-blown spreadsheet program, but for many different types of calculations, Word is definitely up to the task. For example, you might want to calculate totals for your company's latest fundraising effort. Word can do that and much more. In fact, users can construct small spreadsheets in Word and turn to Microsoft Excel only for larger, more complex spreadsheets. You might want to take a look at Que Publishing's *Absolute Beginner's Guide to Microsoft Office Excel 2003* by Joe Kraynak (ISBN: 0-7897-2941-5).

Using AutoSum

Suppose that your company is holding a canned food drive. You have a list of departments within your company, with a column indicating the stated goal and the actual number of canned food items donated. You want to calculate the total number of canned food items. Word has an AutoSum feature that quickly calculates a total for the cells above (column) or to the left (row) of the cell where the insertion point is located. Simply put, you click in the cell where you want the total, click the AutoSum button, and Word calculates the amount and places it in the cell. What could be easier?

You can create a formula that calculates a total as follows:

1. Position the insertion point in the cell where you want the total to appear.

2. If necessary, display the Tables and Borders toolbar. To do so, right-click a toolbar and then choose **Tables and Borders**.

3. Click the **AutoSum** button. Word calculates the total and places the result in the cell (see Figure 9.22).

AutoSum button

FIGURE 9.22

The AutoSum feature enables you to add a column or row of numbers.

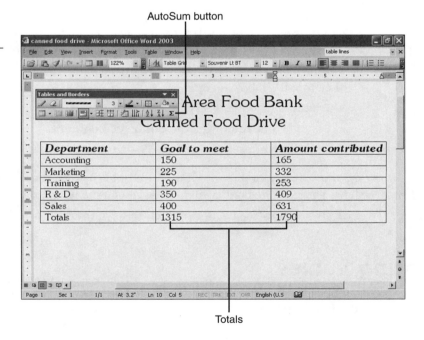

Totals

If you add or remove cells, or edit numbers in cells that are included in an AutoSum, you need to recalculate the total.

Just follow these steps to recalculate an AutoSum total:

1. Select the value in the cell where the results of the AutoSum are placed.

2. Press **F9** or click the **AutoSum** button on the Tables and Borders toolbar.

Inserting Formulas

AutoSum is a great feature, especially when you are frequently totaling numbers in a column. You can create spreadsheet-like formulas in a Word table to perform a variety of calculations on the figures.

The same math addition (+) and subtraction (–) operators that you learned in elementary school are used to build formulas in Word tables. An asterisk (*) is used as the multiplication symbol instead of the times sign (×), and the slash (/) is used as the division symbol instead of the dash with a dot above and below (÷). So, if you want to multiply two cells and divide by a third, your formula might look like this: C5*F14/A2.

Say you have a simple invoice in which you want to multiply the number of items sold by the cost of each unit. You create the formula in the cell where you want the result to appear and let Word take care of the rest. All formulas begin with an equal sign (=). This sign tells Word that the entry is a formula, not ordinary text.

Cell addresses are enclosed in parentheses. For example, if you want to add the values in cells B3 and D8, you would enter =SUM(B3,D8). Or if you want to sum the numbers in cells B3 through B11, you would type =SUM(B3:B11). Another example might be multiplying the value in cell A4 by .15, in which case you would enter =A4*.15.

> **caution**
>
> You can have problems using AutoSum if both the column and the row contain numbers. Adding the numbers in the column takes precedence. In other words, if you create an AutoSum in a cell that has numbers in the row to the left and in the column above, AutoSum will add the numbers in the column, not in the row.
>
> To force Word to add the numbers in the row, you have to use the SUM(LEFT) formula to add the numbers to the left. Also, the SUM function is unpredictable if one of the rows or columns in the formula is blank. You'll have to place a 0 in the empty cells so the SUM function isn't thrown off. See the section "Inserting Other Functions" later in this chapter for more information on inserting the SUM function.

You can insert a formula as follows:

1. Click in the cell where you want the result to appear.
2. Choose **Table**, **Formula** to display the Formula dialog box (see Figure 9.23).
3. Click in the **Formula** text box and erase the contents, leaving the equal sign.
4. Type the formula.
5. Open the **Number format** drop-down list and choose a format.
6. Click **OK** to place the formula in the target cell.

You can easily get mixed up, so if your formula doesn't work right the first time, just click **Undo** and try again. You'll get the hang of inserting formulas in no time.

FIGURE 9.23

Use the Formula dialog box to create and edit formulas.

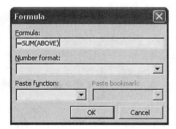

Inserting Other Functions

Okay, now things are getting technical. What's a function? It's nothing more than a word that describes a mathematical process. For example, SUM is a function that adds, or sums, all the values in a given group of cells.

Suppose, for example, that you now want to add all the extended prices on your invoice. You could use the AutoSum feature, but you can also use the SUM function. The SUM function is more flexible because you actually build the formula and indicate which cells to sum rather than let AutoSum figure out what you need.

Each function has one or more *arguments* in parentheses after it. The arguments are for cell addresses or numbers that you want to include in the calculation. Two or more arguments in a function are separated by commas like this: =AVERAGE(B1,B3,B5). If you want to calculate the average for consecutive cells, for example, you could type =AVERAGE(B1:B5).

To insert a function in a formula, follow these steps:

1. Click in the cell where you want the result to appear.

2. Choose **Table**, **Formula** to display the Formula dialog box (refer to Figure 9.23).

3. Click in the **Formula** text box and erase the contents, leaving the equal sign.

4. Open the **Paste function** drop-down list and select a function from the list (see Figure 9.24). Word inserts the function into the **Formula** text box. In the example shown in Figure 9.24, the insertion point is between the parentheses, indicating that the cell addresses for the cells that you want to average should be placed there.

5. Complete the formula by typing in cell addresses or numbers.

6. Open the **Number format** drop-down list and choose a format.

7. Click **OK** to place the formula in the target cell.

note

When you complete a formula by typing in the cell addresses and other information, pay particular attention to the format for the cell references.

Newly inserted function.

FIGURE 9.24

Functions, such as SUM, are simply shortcuts that enable you to make spreadsheet-type calculations.

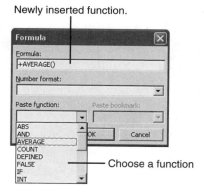

Choose a function

Sorting in a Table

You can rearrange the rows in a table by sorting the contents in a column alphabetically, or numerically, either in ascending or descending order. This capability can be helpful for arranging a list by last name, ZIP code, or item number.

If identical information appears in several rows of a selected column, Word arranges the rows in the order of the original table. In this situation, you might prefer to create a secondary sort that arranges those rows in the order that you prefer. For example, you want to sort by last name, but in the case of identical last names, you want the list sorted by first name. The primary sort would be for last name, and the secondary sort would be for first name.

A third sort can be done, but that's it. You can't sort by more than three levels in Word. If you need to create more complicated sorts, you're better off using Microsoft Excel.

For a quick, single-column sort, you can use the toolbar buttons. For more flexibility, you can use the Sort dialog box.

To sort with the toolbar buttons, follow these steps:

1. Display the Tables and Borders toolbar (right-click a toolbar and then choose **Tables and Borders**).

2. Select the column you want to sort by.

3. Click the **Sort Ascending** button or the **Sort Descending** button.

The toolbar buttons do a quick sort, but it's limited. You can sort by only one column at a time. To sort by more than one column and to create a combination ascending/descending sort, use the Sort dialog box.

Just follow these steps to sort with the Sort dialog box:

1. Click in the table that you want to sort.

2. Choose **Table**, **Sort** to open the Sort dialog box (see Figure 9.25).

Choose the type of sort

Choose a field (column)

FIGURE 9.25

You can set up a
multicolumn
sort in the Sort
dialog box.

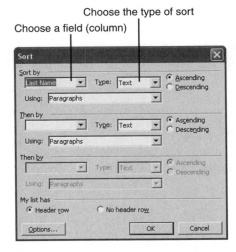

3. Click the **Sort by** drop-down list and choose a field, or column, to sort by.

4. If you're sorting numbers or dates, open the **Type** drop-down list and choose either **Numbers** or **Dates**.

5. If necessary, select **Ascending** or **Descending** to specify the direction of the sort.

6. If necessary, repeat steps 3–5 to set up a second and third sort sequence.

7. If you don't have a header row in the table, select **No header row**.

8. Click **OK** to sort the table.

Converting Text to a Table or a Table to Text

"*Now* you tell me about tables," you say. You've already created documents with rows and columns of data, but you would rather see this information in a table. Or the reverse—perhaps you want to convert a table list to a simple text list.

Fortunately, Word provides a simple method for creating a table from text formatted in tabular columns (columns with tabs between them). In fact, this capability may be one of the easiest yet most practical uses for tables.

Converting Tabular Columns to Tables

Suppose that you have a list of company employees that includes names, extensions, and cell phone numbers. Single tabs separate the three columns of data, as follows:

Weaver, Susan	1083	555-5117
Carter, Robert	1084	555-0092
Truluck, David	1080	555-3325

To convert data in tabular columns to a table, do the following:

1. Select all the text in the tabular columns to the end of the last line of data.

2. Choose **Table**, **Convert**, **Text to Table**. Word displays the Convert Text to Table dialog box (see Figure 9.26).

caution

Although converting tabbed text to tables is easy, the key to a successful conversion is making sure that a single tab separates the text columns. If, for example, you use more than one tab to separate some of the entries, Word adds extra cells in the table for the extra tabs. The result can be messy. If this is the case, use **Undo** to restore the text columns. Remove the extra tabs and try again.

FIGURE 9.26
When you convert text to a table, Word converts the tabs into columns.

3. Verify that the correct numbers of columns and rows are shown in the **Table Size** section.

4. Make sure that the **Tabs** option is selected in the **Separate text at** section.

5. Look at the options, make any necessary selections, and then click **OK**. Word converts your tabular columns of data into a table (see Figure 9.27).

Converting Tables to Text

At some point, you may want to use your table data in another format. For example, you need to export the information to a format that can be used in a database.

Follow these steps to convert a table to text:

1. Click in the table.

2. Choose **Table**, **Convert**, **Table to Text.** Word displays the Convert Table to Text dialog box, shown in Figure 9.28.

3. Make the necessary selection and then click **OK** to convert the table to text.

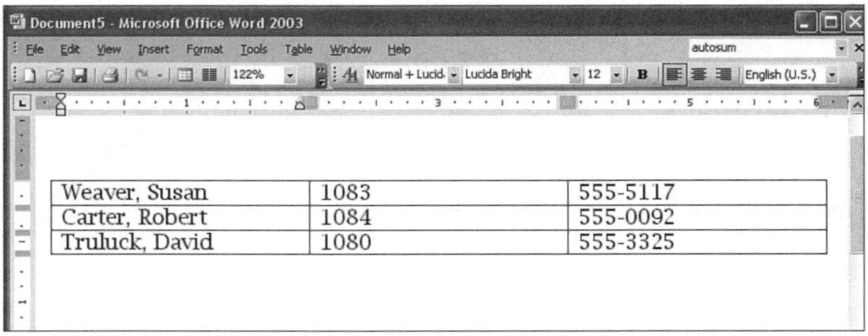

FIGURE 9.27

You might need to adjust the column width and other formatting to improve the layout of the data.

FIGURE 9.28

The Convert Table to Text dialog box enables you to convert tabular data to straight text.

THE ABSOLUTE MINIMUM

After reading this chapter, you now know how to

- Create tables by using the dialog box or by clicking and dragging across the Table palette.

- Move around in a table by clicking the mouse or by pressing Tab or Shift+Tab.

- Adjust column widths, add/delete rows and columns, and join or split rows/columns as you fine-tune the table structure.

- Format the table, rows, columns, and individual cells.

- Alter borders, lines, and fill to fit the situation and emphasize important parts of the table.

- Insert formulas to calculate values just like you would in a spreadsheet program.

- Convert an existing table into text or convert tabbed columns into a table. This way, if you already have content that you want in a table, you don't have to retype anything.

In the next chapter, you'll learn how to organize information into lists and outlines.

IN THIS CHAPTER

- Creating lists with bullets or numbers.
- Changing the bullet and number styles.
- Discovering how useful outlines can be and how easy they are to create and edit.
- Changing outline styles and how to collapse or expand outlines.

10

CREATING LISTS AND OUTLINES

Word is great for creating and editing paragraphs of text. But it's also well suited to creating structured lists and outlines that make it easy for the reader to quickly grasp the important items or ideas in your document. To illustrate, I could go on and on about various types of lists, including descriptions about each type. On the other hand, I could simply create a bulleted list, which I suspect you'll find quicker and easier to understand. Lists or outlines are perfect for

- To-do lists
- Meeting notes
- Legal documents
- Presentation materials
- Reports (academic, medical)
- Executive summaries

Working with Lists

For most of us, when we need to make a list, we type a number, enter the text, type the next number, enter more text, and so on. We have a nice list when we're done, but no way to rearrange the entries without renumbering everything. I don't know about you, but when I'm creating a to-do list, I just try to get everything typed in; then I go back and prioritize the items.

Word's list and outline features enable you to create lists and outlines that are automatically numbered as you create them. When you go back and start moving things around, the numbering is automatically updated. Creating lists the "manual" way doesn't make sense when you have an automatic method that is faster and more accurate.

Creating Bulleted and Numbered Lists

A *bulleted list* uses bullets, or symbols, to delineate the different levels in the list. The default bullet is a medium-sized solid black dot, but you can switch to a different type of bullet or select a certain symbol or clip art bullet.

You can create a list as you type, or you can apply the bullets to a list that you have already typed in. Either way, you have the same flexibility to change the bullet character without affecting the text in the list.

There are two ways to create a list while you type. You can use the toolbar buttons, or you can use the AutoFormat shortcut keys. The AutoFormat feature can be customized in the AutoCorrect Options dialog box (discussed in detail in Chapter 5, "Using the Writing Tools").

Follow these steps to create a bulleted or numbered list as you type:

1. Click the **Bullets** or **Numbering** button on the Formatting toolbar. Alternatively, type * to start a bulleted list or type 1. to start a numbered list; then press the **spacebar** or the **Tab** key.
2. Type your text.
3. Press **Enter** to add a new list item. Word inserts another bullet/number and a tab for you, so all you have to do is type the entry (see Figure 10.1).

FIGURE 10.1

When you start
a list, pressing
Enter automati-
cally adds a new
bulleted or num-
bered line.

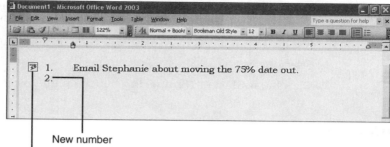

New number

AutoCorrect Options button

4. Type the item.

5. Repeat steps 2 and 3 until you finish the list and then press **Enter** one last
   time.

6. Press **Backspace** to erase the last bullet/number and to turn off the automatic numbering. You can also click the **Bullets** or **Numbering** buttons on
   the Formatting toolbar.

If the **AutoCorrect Options** button appears, click it to open a pop-up menu of the
following options (see Figure 10.2):

- **Undo Automatic Numbering**—Reverses the creation of an automatic bulleted or numbered list.

- **Stop Automatically Creating Numbered Lists**—Turns off the automatic
  creation of bulleted or numbered lists for this document.

- **Control AutoCorrect Options**—Opens the AutoCorrect Options dialog box
  where you can customize the options in the AutoFormat tab.

FIGURE 10.2

The AutoCorrect
Options button
provides a quick
way to undo or
turn off auto-
matic number-
ing.

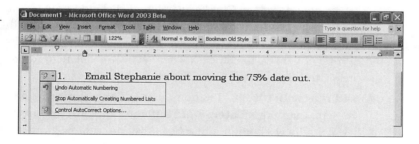

If you've already typed the text, you can easily turn it into an automatically bulleted or numbered list.

To apply bullets or numbers to an existing list, do the following:

1. Select the list.
2. Click the **Bullets** or **Numbering** button on the Formatting toolbar.

Editing Lists

It stands to reason that as soon as you complete a list of items, something will come up, and you'll need to rearrange the items. For just this reason, you need to know how to add or delete list items and how to add blank lines between the items. Lists can be combined into one big list. When you combine lists, the second list takes on the formatting from the first list, so keep that fact in mind when you start pulling lists together.

Here are a few of the more useful and important ways of modifying a bulleted or numbered list:

- **Add an extra blank line between list items**—Place the insertion point at the beginning of the line, press **Enter** to insert a new line, then move up to the new line, and backspace over the bullet or number, leaving the blank line.

- **Move and copy list items**—As you prioritize the entries, you'll move items around in the list. The wonderful thing about the automatic numbering is that no matter how often you rearrange the entries, the numbers are always consecutive. To move an entry, move the mouse pointer to the left of the entry until the pointer changes to an arrow pointing to the right. Double-click to select the item. Click and drag the selected item to a new place in the list, or hold down the **Ctrl** key when you click and drag if you want to copy the item (not move it). When you release the mouse button, the item is dropped into place and the numbers are updated. You can also press **Ctrl+C** to copy or **Ctrl+X** to cut, click where you want the item to appear, and then press **Ctrl+X** to paste.

- **Add a new list item**—Position the insertion point at the end of an existing list item; then press **Enter**. Word automatically inserts a new bullet or number. If you're working in a numbered list, notice how Word automatically inserts the correct number. Also, notice that if you add or delete a numbered item, Word adjusts all the numbers following the inserted item.

- **Remove a line**—Simply delete all the text on the line and press **Backspace** to delete the bullet or number. Press **Backspace** again to remove the blank space between the list items.

- **Turn off bullets or numbers**—When you're finished with the list, click the **Bullets** or **Numbering** button on the Formatting toolbar to turn off the automatic bulleted or numbered list.

Changing the Bullet or Numbering Style

Word makes it easy to change your mind, or to play around with the "look" of the list. You can change the bullet or number style even after you have created the list. There are a handful of numbering styles to choose from, some of which are also used for outlines. The default bullet style can be replaced with another type of bullet, another symbol, or a clip art bullet.

To change the bullet style for a list, follow these steps:

1. Select the list that you want to modify.

2. Choose **Format**, **Bullets and Numbering** to open the Bullets and Numbering dialog box.

3. Click the **Bulleted** tab to display samples of bullet styles (see Figure 10.3).

FIGURE 10.3

Click a sample to switch to a different bullet character or click Customize to access other characters.

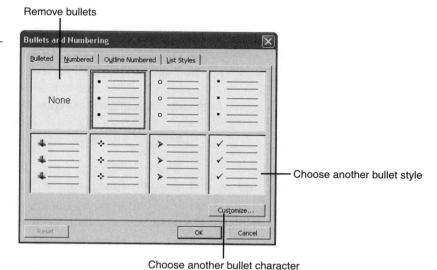

Remove bullets

Choose another bullet style

Choose another bullet character

4. To switch to a different style, click a sample page.

5. If you want to select a different bullet style, a symbol, or a clip art bullet, click **Customize** to open the Customize Bulleted List dialog box (see Figure 10.4).

6. Click **OK** when you're finished.

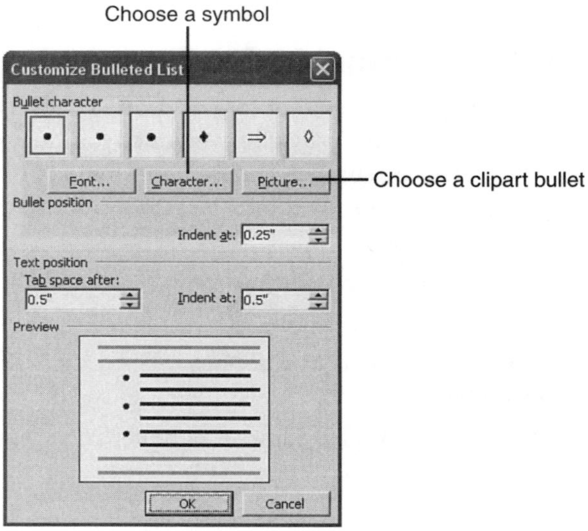

Choose a symbol

FIGURE 10.4

You aren't stuck with the default bullet; you can choose from a large collection of bullets, symbols, and pictures.

Choose a clipart bullet

If you have Internet access, choose **Picture** to access a huge collection of clip art bullets from the Web. Downloading the thumbnails may take awhile, so be patient as you wait for Word to populate the Picture Bullet dialog box. Select a bullet and click **OK** to add it to the list of bullet characters in the Customize Bulleted List dialog box.

To change the numbering style for a list, follow these steps:

1. Select the list that you want to modify.

2. Choose **Format**, **Bullets and Numbering** to open the Bullets and Numbering dialog box.

3. Click the **Numbered** tab to display samples of number styles (see Figure 10.5).

Remove numbers

FIGURE 10.5

Click a sample
to switch to a
different num-
ber character or
click Customize
to select another
numbering
style.

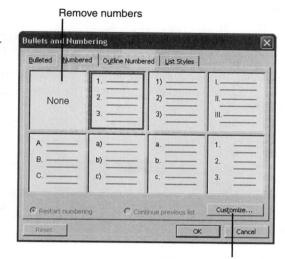

Choose another number style

4. To switch to a different style, click a sample page.

5. If you want to select a different number style, click **Customize** to open the
   Customize Numbered List dialog box (see Figure 10.6).

6. Click **OK** when you're finished.

Choose a number style

FIGURE 10.6

You can create a
new number for-
mat in the
Customize
Numbered List
dialog box.

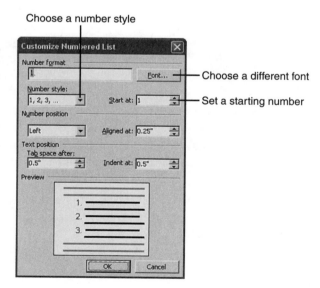

Choose a different font

Set a starting number

Working with Outlines

Outlines are a lot like lists, but they add another dimension of detail. For example, in a list, every item has the same relative importance (1, 2, 3, and so on). Outline items, on the other hand, are arranged in different levels of importance (1, 1a, 1b, 2, and so on). Consider the two lists shown in Figure 10.7. The second list's sublevels provide additional details about the major topics in the list.

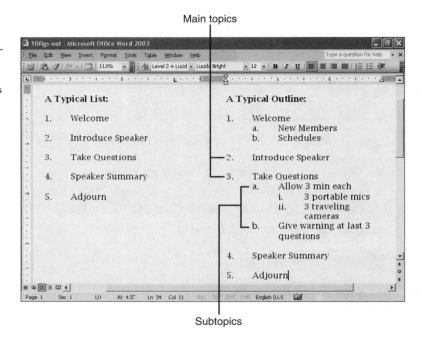

FIGURE 10.7

Outlines look a lot like lists, but outline sublevels provide more flexibility in organizing information.

Before you begin writing a lengthy document, take a few minutes to sketch out an outline to help you organize your thoughts. You can start out with a bare-bones outline, rearrange the items until you're satisfied, and then add the text later. As you work, you can switch to Word's Outline view, which focuses on the structure of the document.

When you create an outline in Outline view, Word uses the heading styles (Heading 1 through Heading 9). Heading 1 is used for main topics, Heading 2 for first-level subtopics, Heading 3 for second-level subtopics, and so on. You can also create outlines manually using the same techniques that you learned for creating bulleted and numbered lists.

Creating Outlines in Outline View

Outline view offers a unique view of a document. If you use either Word's heading styles or outline levels, you can use the Outline view to organize and revise your documents. The advantage of working in Outline view becomes clear when you work with highly structured documents that have headings formatted with Word's heading styles. You can easily collapse a document down to just the main headings, the main headings and one level of subheadings, two levels, three levels, and so on. You can rearrange the document by promoting or demoting headings. Entire chunks of a document can be moved around by cutting and copying the headings in Outline view.

When you switch to Outline view, paragraph formatting doesn't appear, so don't get upset if you don't see your formatting. Word indents each heading according to its level. The indentation appears only in Outline view; Word removes the indents when you switch to another view.

To switch to Outline view and create an outline, follow these steps:

1. Choose **View**, **Outline**. Word switches to the Outline view and displays the Outlining toolbar (see Figure 10.8). (You'll learn more about the toolbar buttons in the next section.)

Outlining toolbar

FIGURE 10.8

When you switch to Outline view, the Outlining toolbar is turned on automatically.

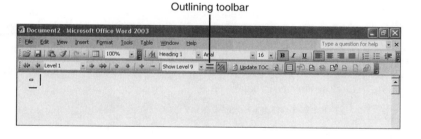

2. Type the first heading (refer to the outline in Figure 10.7 for sample text you can type). Word formats the text with a Level 1 heading style.

3. To insert the next heading, press **Enter**. If you want to insert a blank line, press **Enter** again.

4. Type the second heading. It is also formatted with a Level 1 heading style. Continue typing your main headings.

5. When you're ready to create a subheading, insert a blank line between headings.

6. Click the **Demote** button on the Outlining toolbar or press **Tab** to indent the line under the main heading (see Figure 10.9).

FIGURE 10.9
Subheadings are indented underneath the main headings.

Main heading   Subheading

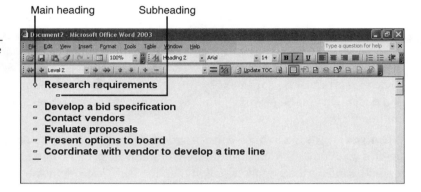

7. Type the first subheading. Notice that Word formats this text as a Level 2 heading style. You can continue to demote and create subheadings until you reach Level 9, the number of heading styles in Word.

8. Press **Enter**. Word inserts the next line at the same level as the preceding line.

9. Continue typing subheadings until you're finished with that section.

10. Press **Tab** or click the **Demote** button to move to the next lower level, or press **Shift+Tab** or click the **Promote** button to move up one level.

11. Continue typing and inserting headings until you finish the outline. Here is a quick reference of keystrokes:

    ■ Press **Enter** to add a new line.

    ■ Press **Enter** twice to insert a blank line between entries.

    ■ Press **Tab** to move to the next level.

    ■ Press **Shift+Tab** to return to a previous level.

12. Press **Enter** one last time and then press **Backspace** to delete the extra outline item and to turn off outlining.

When you're ready to switch back to a "normal" view of the document, open the **View** menu and choose another view mode. Alternatively, click one of the view buttons on the status bar.

Creating Outlines with the Outline Numbered Style

Creating outlines in Outline view is convenient, but it's a bit limited. If you want to change the style of the outline, you have to edit the heading styles. When you create an outline using the Outline Numbered style in the Bullets and Numbering dialog box, as shown here, you have a lot more flexibility to adjust the appearance:

1. Choose **Format**, **Bullets and Numbering** to open the Bullets and Numbering dialog box.

2. Click the **Outline Numbered** tab to display samples of outline styles (see Figure 10.10).

FIGURE 10.10

The Outline Numbered tab of the Bullets and Numbering dialog box shows the outline styles.

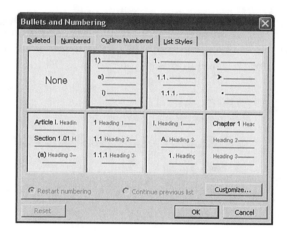

3. Click a sample page to choose the style you want.

4. Click **OK** to close the dialog box and insert the first number of the list in the document.

5. Type the first item and then press **Enter** to insert a new item.

6. Continue typing the list items, pressing **Enter** between each one.

7. To move to a lower level in the outline, press **Tab**; to move to a higher level in the outline, press **Shift+Tab**.

If you're feeling especially ambitious, you can create your own customized outline style. In the Bullets and Numbering dialog box, click the **Outline Numbered** tab, select a list format, and then click **Customize** to open the Customize Outline Numbered List dialog box (see Figure 10.11). Creating a custom style falls outside the scope of this book, so if you need help with this task, open the Assistance task pane and search for help. For more detailed information, get Que Publishing's *Special Edition Using Microsoft Office Word 2003* by Bill Camarda (ISBN: 0-7897-2958-X).

FIGURE 10.11

Create your own outline styles in the Customize Outline Numbered List dialog box.

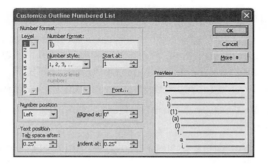

Using the Outlining Toolbar

Whenever you switch to the Outline view, Word displays the Outlining toolbar (see Figure 10.12). The buttons are valuable shortcuts that can save you lots of time and frustration. Buttons that are covered in this chapter include the following:

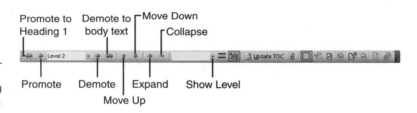

FIGURE 10.12

Use the buttons on the Outlining toolbar to adjust outline items.

   ■ **Promote to Heading 1**—Changes an outline item to a Level 1 heading.

   ■ **Promote**—Changes an outline item to a higher level (for example, a main heading rather than a subheading).

   ■ **Demote**—Changes an outline item to a lower level (for example, a subheading rather than a main heading).

   ■ **Demote to Body Text**—Changes an outline item to body text.

   ■ **Move Up**—Moves an outline item up in the outline.

   ■ **Move Down**—Moves an outline item down in the outline.

   ■ **Expand**—Displays lower level headings.

- **Collapse**—Hides lower level headings.

- **Show Level**—Expands or collapses an outline to show only a certain number of levels.

Changing the Outline Style

The default outline style in Word is the traditional outline style that you learned in high school. Other outline styles are available as well. Fortunately, Word makes it easy to change outline styles.

Just follow these steps to change to a different outline style:

1. Position the insertion point anywhere in the outline.
2. Choose **Format, Bullets and Numbering**. Word displays the Bullets and Numbering dialog box.
3. Click the **Outline Numbered** tab to switch to the outline styles (refer to Figure 10.10 if necessary).
4. Choose the outline style you want and click **OK**. Word automatically changes the outline style (see Figure 10.13).

FIGURE 10.13

The order of an outline does not change when you apply a different outline style.

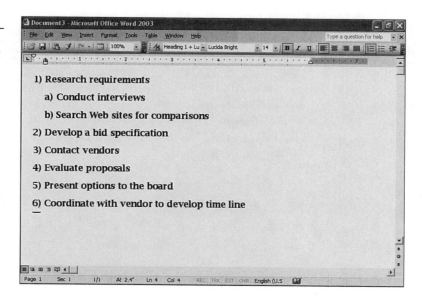

Editing an Outline

The greatest advantage of using outlines is the ease of adding, moving, or deleting outline items. If you are using a numbered outline, Word automatically numbers and renumbers everything so you don't have to worry about it. You can insert items in the middle of an outline, rearrange outline items, and promote/demote outline items, all in just a few quick steps.

Inserting Items in an Existing Outline

Say that you've decided to follow the advice of your middle school English teacher and create all the main topics of your outline and then go back to add subtopics and even sub-subtopics. When you go back to add the subtopics, you'll be adding items to an existing outline.

To add an outline item to an existing outline, do the following:

1. Choose **View**, **Outline** or click the **Outline View** button to switch to Outline view.

2. Position the insertion point at the beginning of the line (on the first letter of the text) where you want to insert a new entry.

3. Press **Enter**. Word adds a new line at the same level as the preceding line (see Figure 10.14).

FIGURE 10.14

When you insert a line in the middle of an outline, Word automatically inserts a new line at the same level as the preceding line.

New item ——

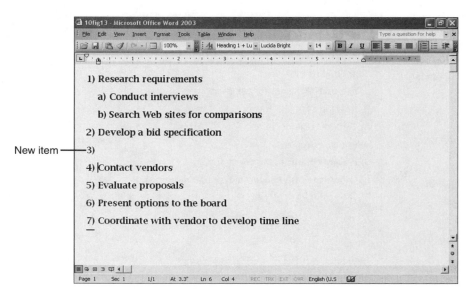

4. If you want to change the outline level of the new item, press **Tab** to move to the right or **Shift+Tab** to move to the left.

5. Type the text of the new outline item.

Rearranging Outline Items

Rearranging the items in an outline is also easy. For example, say you decide that item 5 really belongs after item 2, so you need to cut item 5 (and everything that falls beneath it) and move it under item 2. One easy method is to move an item using the Outlining toolbar. The other is to move an item by cutting and pasting.

Follow these steps to move an item using the Outlining toolbar:

1. Choose **View**, **Outline** or click the **Outline View** button to switch to Outline view.

2. Click on the item to be moved.

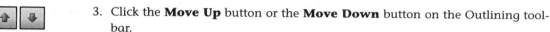

3. Click the **Move Up** button or the **Move Down** button on the Outlining toolbar.

To move an item along with its related subtopics, or to move several outline items at once, you simply select and then cut or copy the outline items.

Cut, copy, and paste outline items as follows:

1. Position the mouse pointer over the plus sign next to the item to be moved. The pointer turns into an four-sided arrow (see Figure 10.15).

FIGURE 10.15
Click in the left margin next to the outline items you want to select.

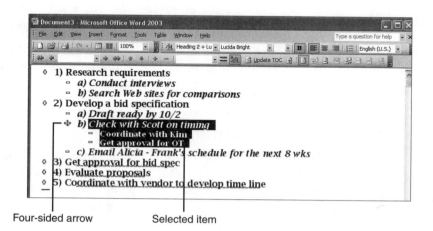

Four-sided arrow   Selected item

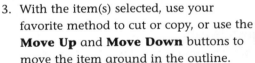

2. To select an outline item, click the plus sign. Word selects the entire outline item (refer to Figure 10.15).

3. With the item(s) selected, use your favorite method to cut or copy, or use the **Move Up** and **Move Down** buttons to move the item around in the outline.

4. If you opted for a cut or copy, move the insertion point to the beginning of the line where you want to paste the outline item(s); then use your favorite method to paste the item(s).

Note that when you cut outline items in a numbered outline, Word renumbers everything following those items, and when you paste them back, Word once again automatically adjusts the outline numbers.

tip

When you're ready to rearrange outline items, working with the items is much easier if you collapse the outline. Either use the **Show Level** drop-down list or click the **Collapse** button until you see only the headings that you need to rearrange. When you move/copy a heading, you are moving/copying that heading and everything underneath it. It's much easier to click and drag across a heading or two than it is to click and drag down half a page of outline items.

Promoting/Demoting Outline Items

You can also adjust outline levels by *promoting* or *demoting* outline items. For example, if you decide that a certain subtopic deserves the same importance as a main topic, you can *promote* it. In other words, you can change the numbering in a numbered outline from *a* to 1. Conversely, if you decide to reduce the importance of an item, you can *demote* it in the outline.

To promote or demote an outline item, follow these steps:

1. Position the insertion point on the item you want to promote or demote.

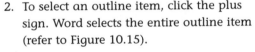

2. Click the **Promote** button or the **Demote** button on the Outlining toolbar.

Collapsing and Expanding Outlines

Word allows you to easily develop two or more different outlines from the same original outline. Say you need to prepare a test for your students that shows only the questions. However, you need a second, more detailed test with the answers to use for grading. All you have to do is create the full test or outline and then hide the sublevels (answers) that you don't want others to see. This process is called *collapsing* an outline. You can then print the collapsed copy of your test for the students and an expanded copy of the test for your use.

You can expand and collapse an entire outline or just parts of it. A plus sign next to an item indicates subtopics underneath. Just double-click the plus sign to expand that item, revealing the subtopics. Double-click the plus sign again to collapse an item.

To collapse and expand an outline, do the following:

1. Switch to the Outline view and display the Outlining toolbar.

2. Click on the item that you want to collapse and then click the **Collapse** button.

3. Click on the item that you want to expand and then click the **Expand** button.

You can also use the Show Level drop-down list to choose how many levels to display. To expand or collapse the outline to a certain level, follow these steps:

1. Switch to the Outline view and display the Outlining toolbar.

2. Open the **Show Level** drop-down list and choose the number of levels that you want to view (see Figure 10.16).

Show Level drop-down list

FIGURE 10.16

The Show Level drop-down list enables you to display only a certain number of levels or all levels.

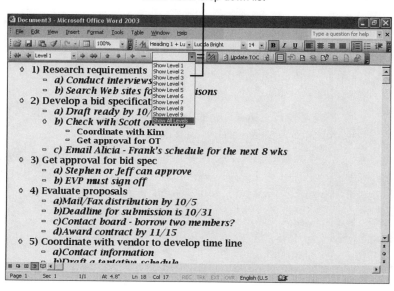

3. Click the number of levels you want to display—for example, **Show Level 3**. Word collapses the outline to display only the first three levels.

4. Open the **Show Level** drop-down list again and choose **Show Level 1** to display only the top level of headings (see Figure 10.17).

5. To display all levels again, repeat steps 1–3, choosing **Show All Levels**.

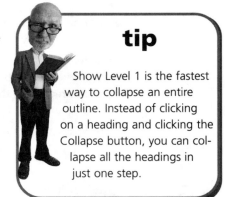

FIGURE 10.17

A collapsed outline shows only the major topics. The subtopics are still there; you just expand the outline to see them again.

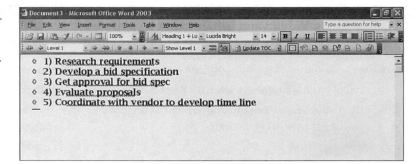

ABSOLUTE MINIMUM

After reading this chapter, you now know how to

- Create and edit bulleted lists.
- Add, remove, or move items in numbered lists. Switch to a different bullet or number style after you create a list.
- Use outlines, which give you the added dimension of subtopics. Change to a different outline style without affecting the order of the outline items.
- Edit outline items and collapse and expand your outlines.

In the next chapter—Chapter 11, "Working with Graphics"—you get to play with graphic images, lines, and other visual elements that spice up and enhance the content of your documents.

PART IV

ADDING VISUALS

...n-Age Thanksgiving Feast
November 20, 2003

Dear friends,

We feel grateful in just a little while for... when the best... work is behind. We prepare for a meal together as we keep from much food in... There is no question about it. It... raises the many members of... our home and the machinery of... through November...

To celebrate our event grows for 37 years our Nov-Age feast... we invite the entire A-to-Z to schools and Mr. Cambodia's classes invited to... parade... we... expected approximately 250 students.

11

WORKING WITH GRAPHICS

Most of us realize the importance of graphics in printed material. Graphics illustrate information in ways that words cannot. They are visually stimulating, they generate interest, and they spark curiosity. What better way to get the reader's attention? This chapter covers the Word features that allow you to create and edit graphics.

Simple things, such as a horizontal line to separate the letterhead from the body of a document, can be created in just seconds. Graphics from many sources, including the Internet, can be inserted into a Word document. Text boxes can be linked together so you can control how text flows across the boxes. All sorts of emphasis can be applied in the form of borders and fills. Last, but not least, you can insert a variety of shapes in a document with just a few clicks of the mouse, and you can create your own decorative logos and headings with WordArt toys.

Working with Horizontal Lines

Even users who don't work with graphics need to know how to insert a simple horizontal line. You see these lines in every type of document, from memos to schedules to fax cover sheets to expense reports. I'm creatively challenged, but I still like to use a simple line to separate sections of a form. Rest assured, you don't have to learn how to work with graphics just to place a line on a page. I'll show you how to insert graphic lines right now, and if you like, you can come back to the rest of this chapter when you are ready to play with pictures.

Inserting a Horizontal Line

Horizontal lines help the reader visually separate sections of your document. For example, when you create a fax cover sheet, you often separate the heading information (TO:, FROM:, FAX:) from the message area with a line that extends from one margin to the other. Most of us are content to use the simple black line that stretches from one margin to the next. As you'll see here, you can quickly insert a basic line, or you can take a few more seconds to create a customized line.

Follow these steps to insert a basic horizontal line:

1. Position the insertion point on the line where you want to create the graphic line.

2. Choose **Format**, **Borders and Shading** to open the Borders and Shading dialog box.

3. Click the **Borders** tab to display the Borders options.

4. In the Preview area, click the button that inserts a border at the bottom of the text or click the bottom border (see Figure 11.1).

FIGURE 11.1

Either click the button or click the border to insert a line under the text.

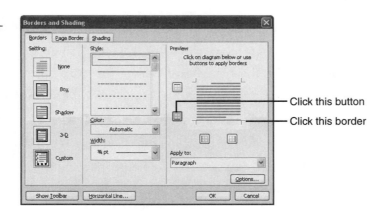

5. Click **OK**. Word inserts a thin black line (see Figure 11.2).

FIGURE 11.2

This thin horizontal line extends from the left margin to the right margin.

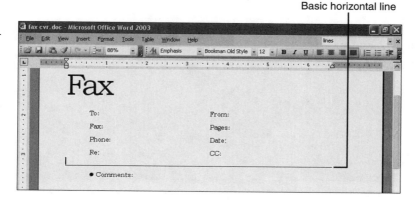

Basic horizontal line

Inserting Other Types of Lines

Okay, that's the quick and dirty way to create a line. Fast and easy—just a few clicks and you're done. There are lots and lots of different types of lines that you can create and insert into a document. If you've already read Chapter 7, "Working with Pages," you might remember using the Borders and Shading dialog box to add page borders. If you need a refresher, or if you didn't read Chapter 7, open the dialog box so that I can show you how to create different types of lines.

To create other types of horizontal lines, follow these steps:

1. Choose **Format**, **Borders and Shading** to open the Borders and Shading dialog box (see Figure 11.3).

2. Choose from the following options:

   ■ Scroll through the **Style** list box to see all the available lines and then click the one you want to use.

   ■ Click the **Color** button and then select a color for the border lines from the palette.

   ■ Open the **Width** drop-down list and choose a line width from the list.

3. Click **OK** when you're finished.

Choose a style

FIGURE 11.3

You can select a different type of line, color, and width in the Borders and Shading dialog box.

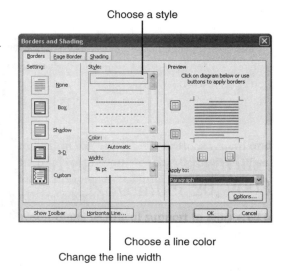

Choose a line color

Change the line width

Inserting Pictures

Now then, on to the fun stuff—inserting pictures into your documents! Word is very flexible and can incorporate graphics from many different sources. You have access to a large collection of clip art, both on the Office 2003 CD and online at the Microsoft Office Online site. You also can insert scanned images, graphics from the Internet, digital photographs, and files in a variety of formats.

Inserting Clip Art

The easiest place to start is with Word's own clip art images. You can use the techniques that you learn here to manipulate other graphic elements as well.

The Clip Art task pane puts everything you need at your fingertips. You can search for clip art images by using keywords or by browsing. If you don't have Internet access, you can restrict the search to the images on your local system.

To insert a clip art image in your document, do the following:

1. Click where you want to insert the picture.

2. Choose **Insert**, **Picture**, **Clip Art**. Word displays the Clip Art task pane (see Figure 11.4).

3. Type the keyword(s) that you want to use to search for clips in the **Search for** text box.

4. If you don't have Internet access, open the **Search in** drop-down list, open the **Everywhere** tree, and remove the check mark next to **Web Collections**.

Restrict search

Search by keyword Select media
types

FIGURE 11.4

The Clip Art
task pane gives
you access to
clip art, photos,
audio, and
video clips.

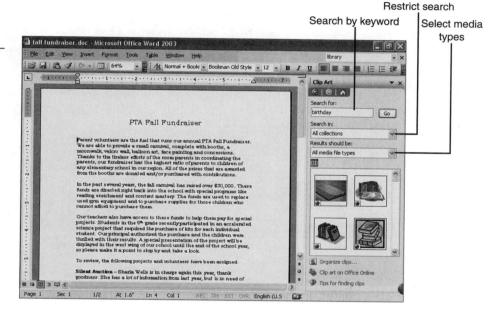

Restrict search

Search by keyword Select media
types

5. If you want to restrict the search to a particular type of media, open the
   Results should be drop-down list and deselect the media types that you
   want to exclude from the search.

6. Choose **Go** to search for the clip art. Word produces a thumbnail list of clip
   art images that are associated with the keyword(s) that you typed in (see
   Figure 11.5).

7. Scroll through the list of images. There may be a slight hesitation before the
   images are filled in, so be patient. If you want more room for thumbnails,
   click the **Expand Results** button to enlarge the window.

8. Click the image that you want to insert, and Word places it at the insertion
   point position (see Figure 11.6).

If you change your mind and want to insert another picture, press **Ctrl+Z** or click
Undo to reverse the insertion and try again. You can also click the image and press
Delete.

Keyword

FIGURE 11.5

The results of your search are displayed in the window. Scroll down to see more images.

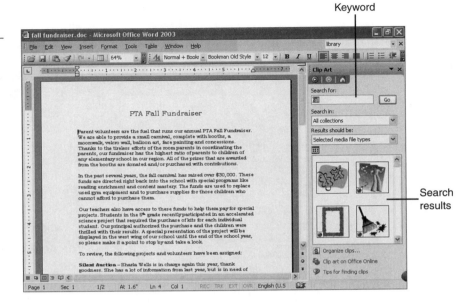

Search results

FIGURE 11.6

When you click an image in the thumbnail window, Word inserts the picture in the document.

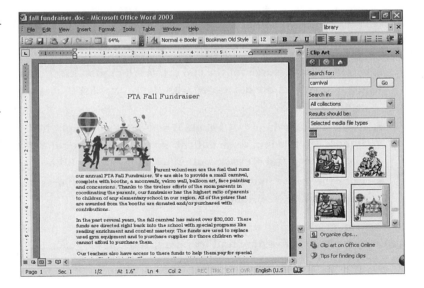

Using Other Types of Graphics

Word's clip art library is extensive and useful. But often the precise image you need just can't be found there. Fortunately, you can import almost any type of graphic, from almost any source. The Internet has a vast collection of free clip art that you can download and use freely in your documents. You can also convert graphics that were created in other applications to a format compatible with Word. Finally, if you have a printed copy of an image, you can scan it and insert it into a document.

Importing Graphics

Whether you use a graphic image created in another graphics program, a scanned graphic, or an image from the Internet, the procedure for inserting them is the same. Word capably imports a variety of graphics such as GIF, JPG, TIFF, or BMP formats. For a complete list of the different types of graphic files that you can use in Word, search the help topics for "graphics file types Word can use."

> **tip**
>
> You can also place a clip art image in your document by dragging it from the Clip Art task pane and dropping it into your document at the precise location where you want it. I've noticed that the image is larger when I insert it this way, but resizing it is easy enough.

To import a graphic from another format, all you have to do is insert the image, and Word takes care of the rest. If, for some reason, it doesn't recognize a graphic format, you get a message, and you must find another format for the image you want. Before you try to find another format, make sure you have all the graphics filters installed. If you aren't sure, run the Word Setup program and install the additional graphics filters.

To import a graphic image, follow these steps:

1. Click where you want to place the graphic image.

2. Choose **Insert**, **Picture**, **From File**. Word displays the Insert Picture dialog box (see Figure 11.7). It resembles the Open dialog box, and you use it the same way to locate and insert a graphic image that you've saved to your disk. You may have to browse to locate the file you want.

FIGURE 11.7

You can insert nearly any kind of graphic image, including scanned images or graphics from the Internet.

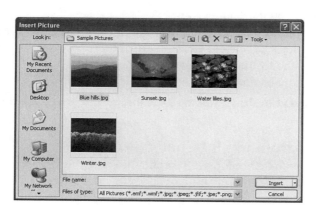

3. Select the file you want to use and click **In_s_ert**. Word converts the file and inserts it into your document.

Using Images from a Scanner

Any image, black-and-white or color, can be scanned and inserted into a document. The quality of the scanned image is directly related to the quality of the scanner. If you aren't satisfied with the scanned image, you might consider paying a print shop to scan the image for you.

Follow these steps to scan an image directly into your Word document:

1. Position the insertion point where you want the image.

2. Choose **Insert**, **_P_icture**, **From _S_canner or Camera**.

3. If you have more than one device connected to your computer, select the device you want to use. The Insert Picture from Scanner or Camera dialog box appears (see Figure 11.8).

4. If you are scanning the image, and you want to show the image onscreen, choose **_W_eb Quality**. For an image that you want to print, choose **_P_rint Quality**.

5. If you are obtaining the image from a digital camera, you'll probably want to customize the settings before you insert the image. In this case, choose **_C_ustom Insert** and follow the instructions that come with the device you are using.

6. Choose **_I_nsert** to scan, or obtain, the image and insert it in the document.

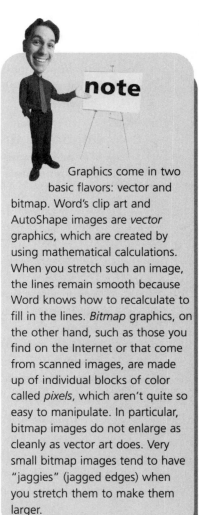

note

Graphics come in two basic flavors: vector and bitmap. Word's clip art and AutoShape images are *vector* graphics, which are created by using mathematical calculations. When you stretch such an image, the lines remain smooth because Word knows how to recalculate to fill in the lines. *Bitmap* graphics, on the other hand, such as those you find on the Internet or that come from scanned images, are made up of individual blocks of color called *pixels*, which aren't quite so easy to manipulate. In particular, bitmap images do not enlarge as cleanly as vector art does. Very small bitmap images tend to have "jaggies" (jagged edges) when you stretch them to make them larger.

Using Images from the Internet

You can even use images you obtain from the Internet. But first, a word of caution: Just because you *can* use Internet images doesn't necessarily make it *legal*. Copyright laws apply to Internet graphics just as they apply to print graphics. Depending on how and where your document will be used, you may need to seek permission before you use an Internet image in your document. Most sites have a user agreement or rules of use statement, so track that down and take a look.

FIGURE 11.8

Select the quality of the image you want to insert in the Insert Picture from Scanner or Camera dialog box.

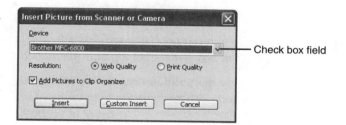

Check box field

To download an Internet image and use it in a Word document, do the following:

1. Locate an image using your Internet browser; then right-click the image you want to download.

2. In Netscape, choose **Save Image As**, or in Internet Explorer, choose **Save Picture As**.

3. Browse to the location where you want to save the file (for example, `c:\My Pictures\happyface.jpg`). The name of the file can be changed, but not the file type (Save as type).

4. Click **Save** to save the image.

5. Switch to Word and choose **Insert**, **Picture**, **From File**.

6. Browse to the location where you saved the image, select the image, and click **Insert**.

> **tip**
>
> If you want to add this image to the Microsoft Clip Organizer, enable the **Add Pictures to Clip Organizer** check box. The Clip Organizer helps you catalog photos, sounds, videos, drawings, and other types of media files. Click **Organize Clips** in the Clip Art task pane to open the Microsoft Clip Organizer.

Word converts the image from the Internet format (`.gif` or `.jpg`) and places it in the document. See Figure 11.9 for an example of an Internet image, at both normal and enlarged sizes. In this case, notice that enlarging the image caused it to become distorted. If you need to use this image in a larger size, you can try editing it in another application.

FIGURE 11.9

Small bitmap images downloaded from the Internet may have jagged edges if you try to enlarge them.

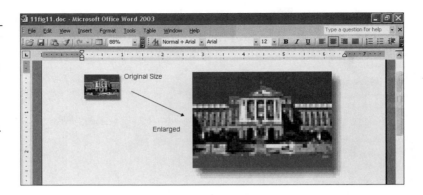

USING MICROSOFT PICTURE MANAGER TO EDIT PICTURES

The Picture Manager, which comes with Microsoft Office 2003, can be used to adjust brightness and contrast, color, and cropping. You can also rotate and flip an image as well as correct for red eye. I use it to resize pictures and compress them so I can send them via email and post them on the Internet.

Choose **Start**, **(All) Programs**, **Microsoft Office**, **Microsoft Office Tools**, **Microsoft Picture Manager** to start the application. Refer to the Picture Manager help topics for more information. For more detailed help with Word 2003, consult Que Publishing's *Special Edition Using Microsoft Office Word 2003* by Bill Camarda (ISBN: 0-7897-2859-X).

> **tip**
>
> When a document contains many graphics, they slow down scrolling and make editing more difficult. You can temporarily replace the graphics with picture placeholders, and Word displays an outline of the picture instead. Choose **Tools, Options** and then click the **View** tab. Enable the **Picture placeholders** check box in the Show section. If you want to hide objects created with the drawing tools, such as WordArt and AutoShapes, clear the **Drawings** check box.

Moving and Sizing Images

Rarely, if ever, does Word insert an image exactly where you want it, in the exact size that you need. Therefore, the next thing you need to learn is how to move and size the image.

Before you can change the size or position of an image, you have to select it. How? Just click it. When you do, a rectangle appears around the picture. The rectangle has eight black boxes called *sizing handles*. If you click elsewhere in the document, you deselect the graphics box and the handles disappear. When you click an image, you select the object, and the sizing handles reappear.

Follow these steps to move an image:

1. Click *once* on the image to select it; the sizing handles appear (see Figure 11.10).

Sizing handle

FIGURE 11.10

When you click
an image, sizing
handles appear
around it.

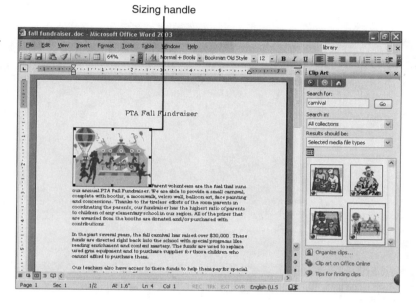

2. Position the mouse pointer over the image; then click and drag the image to the new location. You'll notice a different mouse pointer; this is the move pointer (see Figure 11.11). Also, a dotted insertion point marks where the image will appear when you release the mouse button.

3. Release the mouse button to drop the image.

In the case of the sample image in Figure 11.11, the problem is that the image is way too big. You can quickly change the size of a graphic image by clicking and dragging one of the sizing handles.

To resize a picture, do the following:

1. Select the image and then move the mouse pointer to one of the corner sizing handles until the pointer turns to a two-way arrow. This arrow is called a *resizing pointer* (see Figure 11.12).

tip

Dragging the corner sizing handles keeps the image proportional. If you want to distort an image, drag the top, bottom, or side sizing handles. You can produce some interesting effects with this method.

2. Click and drag the sizing handle toward the center of the image to make it smaller, or away from the center to make it larger.

3. Release the mouse button. You might need to make some adjustments to the location of the image as described previously.

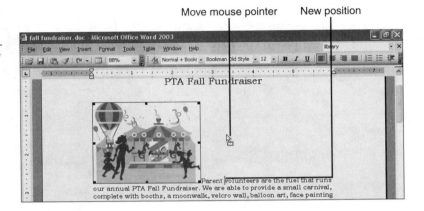

FIGURE 11.11

When you move an image, Word displays a move mouse pointer.

FIGURE 11.12

To resize a graphic image, click and drag the sizing handles.

The next section goes into more detail, but a short mention of the drawing canvas is important here. A drawing canvas is created when you insert a drawing object into a document. This canvas creates a frame around the object or objects and separates them from the rest of the document. You can move and resize drawing objects within the drawing canvas just as you would if they were outside the canvas. An object can be enlarged independently of the canvas, or they can be enlarged together. See the section titled "Working with the Drawing Canvas" later in this chapter for more information.

Working in Text Boxes

You can add labels and titles to drawings with text boxes. A text box can contain one or more paragraphs and can be formatted just like you would format any other piece of text, with paragraph and font settings.

Text boxes can be layered on top of, or behind, an image to achieve different results. You can also link text boxes together and control the flow of text across pages. Text boxes work the same as boxes around any other image, so you use the same techniques to move, resize, and enhance with borders and fills.

Creating Text Boxes

When you insert a text box, a drawing canvas is automatically placed around it. The drawing canvas is designed to help you arrange drawing objects, so it really comes in handy when your drawing involves more than one element or shape. When you insert a picture, a drawing canvas isn't automatically placed around it, but you can add a picture to an existing canvas by clicking and dragging it into the canvas.

To create a text box, follow these steps:

1. Position the insertion point where you want the text box to appear.

2. Choose **Insert**, **Te_x_t Box**. Word opens the drawing canvas and turns on the Drawing toolbar. A crosshair pointer appears within the canvas (see Figure 11.13).

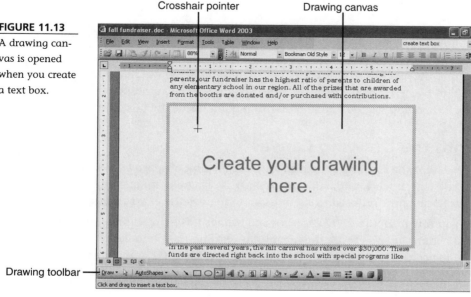

FIGURE 11.13

A drawing canvas is opened when you create a text box.

3. Click and drag inside the drawing canvas to create a text box of the size and position that you want. When you release the mouse pointer, Word creates the text box (see Figure 11.14).

4. Type the text you want. You can change the font style, size, color, or other attributes just like you would with regular text. You can also apply paragraph formatting.

5. When you're finished editing the text content of the box, click in the drawing canvas to deselect the text box.

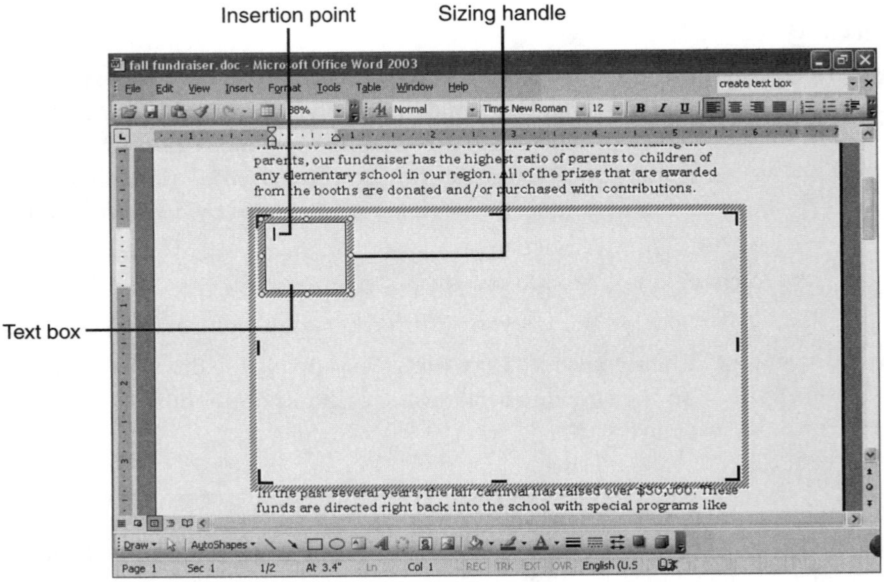

FIGURE 11.14

Click and drag the crosshair pointer to create a text box inside the drawing canvas.

If, after the text box is deselected, you want to make some changes to the text, you need to select the box first. When a text box is selected, a border appears around the box. When you see the blinking insertion point inside the box, you can edit the text.

Working with the Drawing Canvas

Notice that the drawing canvas takes up quite a bit of space on your screen, and if you deselect it (click in the document text), it also takes up quite a bit of space in your document. You need to size it down to remove the extra whitespace.

As you saw in Figure 11.14, the drawing canvas has sizing handles as well. The top and bottom handles resize the height, the left and right handles resize the width, and the corner handles resize the height and width at the same time.

To resize the drawing canvas, click and drag a sizing handle. Then release the mouse button.

When you hover over a sizing handle, you see a new resizing pointer. As you click and drag this pointer, a dotted guideline appears to illustrate the new boundaries of the drawing canvas. In the sample document, I'm clicking and dragging the corner handle to resize the drawing canvas up and to the left (see Figure 11.15). I'm doing this because I want to wrap text around this text box later.

If you would prefer to work without a drawing canvas, you can press **Escape** when it appears to dismiss it. Or you can disable the feature completely. Choose **Tools**, **Options**, click the **General** tab, and then disable the **Automatically create drawing canvas when inserting AutoShapes** check box. You can also click and drag objects out of the drawing canvas and then delete the canvas.

> ## tip
>
> You may find that the text box isn't big enough to hold the text that you type, so some of the text drops down below the box boundary. Don't panic. The text is still there; you just can't see it. When you resize the box, you'll be able to see the rest of the text.
>
> You can turn on a feature that automatically adjusts the size of a text box (or AutoShape) to accommodate the text. Select the text box and then choose **Format**, **Text Box**. Click the **Text Box** tab and then enable the **Resize AutoShape to fit text** check box.

Working with Linked Text Boxes

When you read a newspaper, you notice that articles on the first page are continued on later pages. In magazines, for example, articles are broken up and placed on several different places (and usually buried in the ads). Linked text boxes are used when you need to divide text between multiple pages, or when you want to position text side by side on page. In either case, you can control where the text is placed and how it flows across page breaks.

To create linked text boxes, follow these steps:

1. If necessary, switch to the Print Layout view.
2. Click where you want to start the columns.
3. Choose **Insert**, **Text Box**.
4. Click and drag the crosshair pointer to define the first text box.
5. Repeat steps 2–4 to insert additional text boxes where you want the text to flow. They might be scattered across several pages or grouped together on consecutive pages.
6. Scroll back to the first text box.
7. Click the border of the text box to select it.

New boundary   Old boundary

FIGURE 11.15

Click and drag a
sizing handle to
resize the draw-
ing canvas.

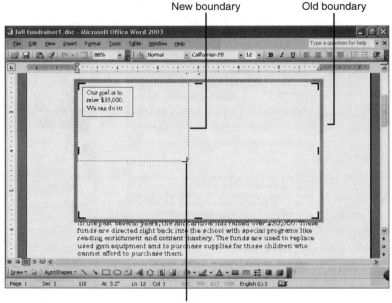

Resize pointer

8. If the Text Box toolbar isn't already displayed, right-click the toolbar and choose **Text Box** (see Figure 11.16).

9. Click the Create Text Box Link button. The mouse pointer turns into a pitcher (see Figure 11.17).

10. Click the text box that you want to flow into to create a link. When you click the text box, the pitcher pointer disappears.

11. Repeat steps 7–10 to create links for all the text box columns that you created. Each set of linked text boxes (one column) is called a *story*.

Now you know how to create a story! I want to quickly cover some of the things you can do. You must do everything from Print Layout view; if you need to, switch to that view now (choose **View**, **Print Layout**).

Now you can do the following:

- **Navigate through a story**—Select one of the text boxes in a story. On the Text Box toolbar, click the **Next Text Box** button to move down to the next text box or the **Previous Text Box** button to move up to the previous text box.

- **Move or copy a story**—Select the first text box (click a border) in a story. Hold down the **Shift** key and select each additional text box that you want to move or copy. Click the **Cut** or **Copy** buttons. Move to the location where you want to place the story. Click the **Paste** button.

FIGURE 11.16
The Text Box toolbar has buttons to create and break text box links.

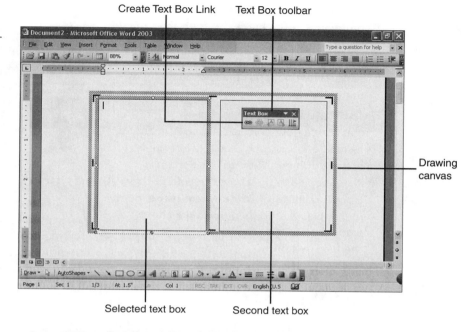

Create Text Box Link   Text Box toolbar

Drawing canvas

Selected text box   Second text box

FIGURE 11.17
With the new pitcher pointer, click in the text box on the next page.

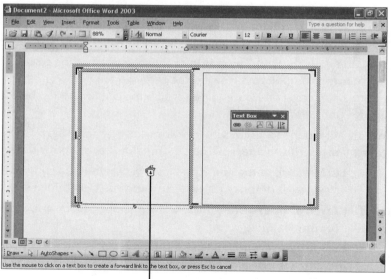

Pitcher pointer

■ **Break a text box link**—Select the text box that you want to break out from the story. On the Text Box toolbar, click the **Break Forward Link** button. Text appears in the selected text box, but the text boxes following it are empty.

■ **Use AutoShapes in stories**—Just for fun, you can lay out your text using AutoShapes instead of a boring old box. Select the text box(es) that you want to place in an AutoShape. On the Drawing toolbar, click **Draw**, point to **Change AutoShape**, point to a category, and then select the shape you want. AutoShapes are covered in detail in the next section, so stay tuned!

> **note**
>
> Linked text boxes enable you to create sets of columns where the text flows downward to the next page rather than jumps into the next column. This type of column is called a *newspaper* column. Linked text boxes are often referred to as *parallel* columns because each section of text remains parallel to the next one.

Inserting AutoShapes

Are you ready to explore your artistic side and create works of art? Okay, maybe not, but at least you can create your own graphic shapes—such as boxes, circles, stars, arrows, or even smiley faces—and insert them into your documents.

You can access the shape tools in a couple of ways, but the easiest is to click the **AutoShapes** drop-down arrow on the Drawing toolbar. Word then displays a palette of choices (see Figure 11.18), which include line styles, basic shapes, block arrows, and callout styles.

Word's AutoShape tools fall into three basic categories. Although each has similar characteristics, you create, edit, and manipulate each slightly differently:

■ **Lines**—Each of the line types has a beginning and end, and you can include arrow heads or tails to them. These include lines and connectors.

■ **Closed shapes**—These include basic shapes, block arrows, flowcharts, and stars and banners.

■ **Callout shapes**—These are similar to closed shapes, but you can type text in them to make it easier to create callouts, which are like speech or thought bubbles found in cartoons.

FIGURE 11.18

The shape tools are organized into categories on the AutoShapes button on the Drawing toolbar.

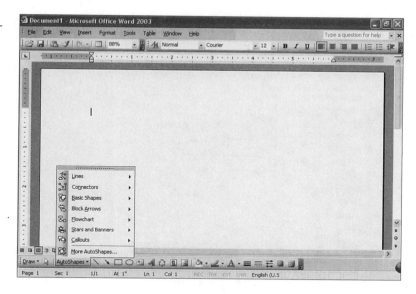

Adding Line Shapes

Suppose that you want to draw a line that points from some text to a graphic image in your document or a line that points to the next page so your reader knows that the text continues. You can select a line shape to quickly draw a horizontal line or arrow.

Follow these steps to draw a simple line:

1. Click the **AutoShapes** button.
2. Click **Lines** and then select the basic line from the palette (see Figure 11.19). A drawing canvas is inserted, and the mouse pointer changes to a crosshair pointer.
3. Position the crosshair pointer where you want the line to start.
4. Click and drag to the opposite end of the line (see Figure 11.20).
5. Release the mouse button to end the line.

   ■ If you're creating a curved line, click once to start the line, click again to change directions, and double-click to complete the line.

   ■ Freeform drawing works just like drawing with a pencil. Click and drag to draw. Double-click to release with a freeform; just release with scribble.

Notice the edit points at each end of the line. If you want to adjust the length or angle of the line, you can click and drag one of these circles. You can also hover

over the line until the four-sided arrow pointer appears. Click and drag this pointer to move the line.

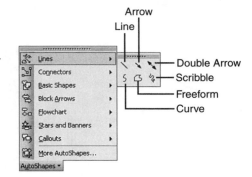

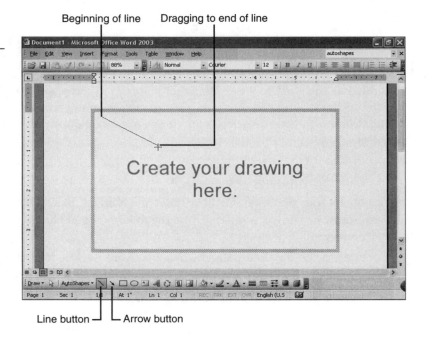

You can create lines with an arrow at the bottom or on both ends of your document. Arrows are helpful if you want to draw the reader's attention to a specific area of a graphic image or text.

To draw a line with an arrow on one or both ends, do the following:

1. Click the **A_utoShapes** button.

2. Click **Lines** and then select the **Arrow** or **Double Arrow** from the palette (refer to Figure 11.19). A drawing canvas is inserted, and the mouse pointer changes to a crosshair pointer.

3. Position the crosshair pointer where you want the line to start.

4. Click and drag to the opposite end of the line.

5. Release the mouse button to create the line and add the arrows.

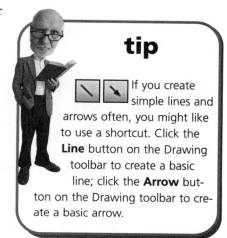

tip

If you create simple lines and arrows often, you might like to use a shortcut. Click the **Line** button on the Drawing toolbar to create a basic line; click the **Arrow** button on the Drawing toolbar to create a basic arrow.

The connectors are similar to lines, but more options are available. Select the connector from the **Connectors** palette; then click and drag to create. Some of the connectors have additional sizing handles that you can click and drag to change the angle of the curves or lines. The advantage of using connectors is that when you rearrange objects that are joined with a connector line, the connectors "stick" to the objects and move with them.

Adding Closed Shapes

The line ends of closed shapes come together, as in a circle, so the inside area is closed. These shapes have thin single lines; some components have light gray elements. Word includes more categories of closed shapes than any other AutoShape. Basic Shapes, Block Arrows, Stars and Banners, and Flowchart are all closed shapes. The way you create closed shapes is a bit different from the way you create lines and connectors.

To create a closed object shape, follow these steps:

1. Click the **AutoShapes** button on the Drawing toolbar.

2. Select one of the closed shape categories. Figure 11.21 shows the shapes in the Stars and Banners category.

3. Click a shape. I'll use a five-point star as an example.

4. Move the crosshair pointer to a corner of the area you intend to fill with the shape (for example, the upper-left corner).

5. Click and drag the crosshair pointer to the opposite corner (for example, the lower-right corner). Continue holding down the mouse button while you move the pointer, until you have exactly the right size and proportions. If you accidentally release the mouse button, click **Undo** and try again.

FIGURE 11.21

The shapes in
the Stars and
Banners cate-
gory are all
closed shapes.

Five-point star

6. Release the mouse button to place the shape in the document (see
Figure 11.22). Note the glyph, which is used to change the style of a graphic
shape.

Sizing handle   Glyph

FIGURE 11.22

Use the glyph
and sizing han-
dles to create
just the right
look.

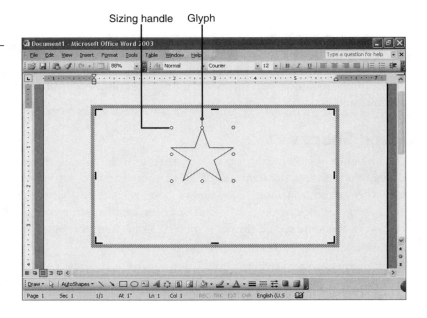

If the object has a glyph—small green-colored circles—you can rotate the shape.
Click and drag the glyph to rotate the shape. The sizing handles (and yellow glyphs
when available) are used to manipulate the shape. For example, on the five-point
star, you can drag the sizing handles to create a skinny starfish look or a fat sheriff's
star look. You can move shapes by pointing to the shape and waiting for the four-
sided arrow to appear. When it does, click and drag the shape to a new location.

Adding Callout Shapes

You may not even know that the "speech bubble" you often see in cartoons is also called a *callout*. Callouts are similar to closed shapes and are created in the same way. The difference is that Word creates a text box inside the closed shape, where you can type text to go along with the callout.

Follow these steps to create a callout shape:

1. Click the **A<u>u</u>toShapes** button on the Drawing toolbar.

2. Click **<u>C</u>allouts** to open the list of callout shapes (see Figure 11.23).

3. Select a callout shape.

tip

You can type text into most of the AutoShapes if you know the secret password. Just kidding. All you have to do is right-click an existing AutoShape and then choose **Add Te<u>x</u>t**. The insertion point is now inside the AutoShape, so you can type whatever you want. Click in the document when you're finished.

FIGURE 11.23

A callout is a closed object shape with a text box so you can type text in the bubble.

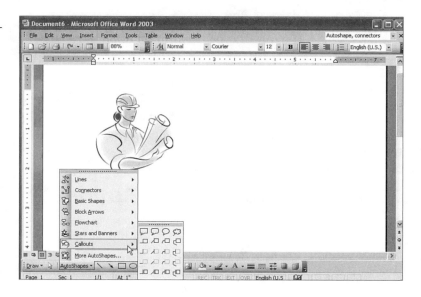

4. Press **Escape** to dismiss the drawing canvas.

5. Move the crosshair pointer above and to the left of the position where you want the callout to appear.

6. Click and drag the crosshair pointer to the opposite corner. Continue holding down the mouse button while you move the pointer, until you have exactly the right size and proportions. If you accidentally release the mouse button, click **Undo** and try again.

7. Release the mouse button to place the callout in the document. Click and drag the callout shape to make minor adjustments to the placement.

8. To fill in the callout text, click in the box and type text as you would in any text box (see Figure 11.24).

9. Select the callout shape and notice the new yellow glyph at the end of the callout pointer. You can click and drag this glyph to make it point where you want.

FIGURE 11.24

You may need to expand the size of the callout shape to accommodate the text box.

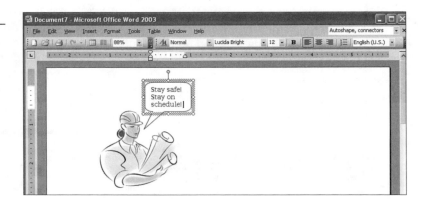

You might need to play around a bit with the sizing handles and glyphs until the shape looks exactly the way you want. If you change your mind and want to try another shape, just choose **Undo** until the shape is gone and try again. After you've finished your shape, you can add a border or fill color (discussed in the next section).

Setting Border, Wrap, and Fill Options

As you have seen, pictures and drawing objects (that is, AutoShapes, scanned images, text) are like containers that you place in a document. The way the text flows around pictures and drawing objects is called *wrap*. A picture or drawing object can also have a visible border, and it can be filled with a pattern or color.

For simplicity, I'll refer to pictures and drawing objects as simply *graphics* in this section.

Wrapping Text Around Graphics

You can control the flow of text around a graphic in several different ways. By default, Word text moves down to make room for graphics, but you can change the settings to have the text appear around, in front of, or behind the graphic (see Figure 11.25).

Square   Tight   Behind Text   In Front of Text

FIGURE 11.25
Wrapping text means making room around the graphic for the text that surrounds it.

In Line With Text

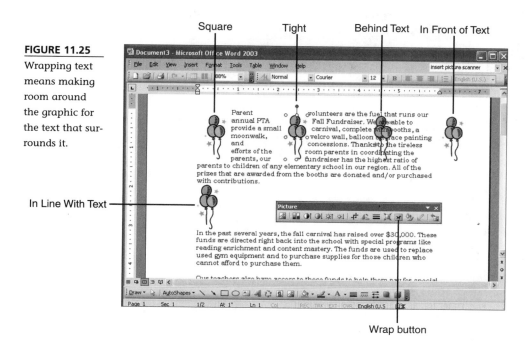

Wrap button

To change how text wraps around a graphic, follow these steps:

1. Select the graphic.

2. Choose **Format** to open the Format menu. Word displays an option for the type of graphic you have selected (that is, Picture, AutoShape, Text Box).

3. Choose the option that matches the graphic you have selected.

4. Click the **Layout** tab in the resulting dialog box to display the wrap options (see Figure 11.26).

5. Choose one of the options and then click **OK**.

Adding a Border

If you really want to set off your graphics, you can put a border around them. By default, text boxes are created with a single line border. You can switch to a more decorative border in just a few steps.

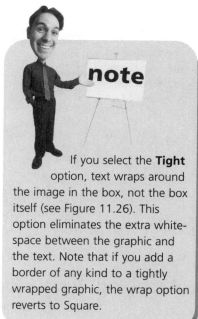

note

If you select the **Tight** option, text wraps around the image in the box, not the box itself (see Figure 11.26). This option eliminates the extra whitespace between the graphic and the text. Note that if you add a border of any kind to a tightly wrapped graphic, the wrap option reverts to Square.

FIGURE 11.26

The Layout tab contains the options to control the flow of text around a graphic.

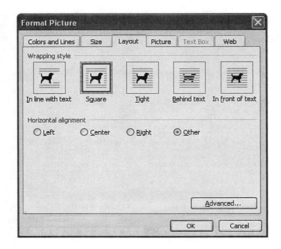

To add or edit the border around a graphic, do the following:

1. Right-click the graphic that needs a border.

2. Choose **Borders and Shading**. Word displays the Borders dialog box (see Figure 11.27).

FIGURE 11.27

Select a line style, color, and width from the Borders dialog box.

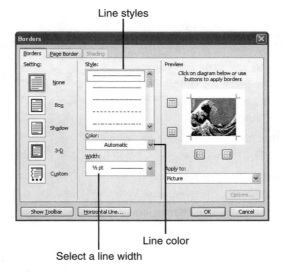

3. Select a line style from the palette. Word adds an outline around the graphic (see Figure 11.28).

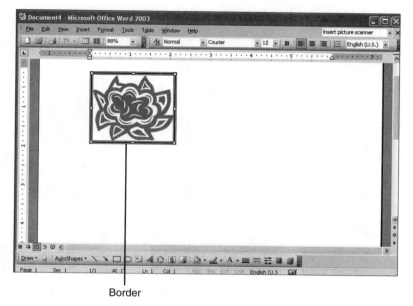

Border

Adding a Fill

For a different effect, you can provide a background pattern or color to your graphic, whether or not you use a border. You might want to add a shaded background behind a clip art image or to text in a text box. If you have access to a color printer, you can use colors; otherwise, the shading is done in shades of gray. There is a huge selection of backgrounds to choose from. You can use gradients, textures, patterns, or pictures.

Follow these steps to select a fill color:

1. Click the graphic to select it.

2. Click the drop-down arrow next to the **Fill Color** button on the Drawing toolbar. Word displays a palette of fill colors (see Figure 11.29).

3. Click a fill color to add it to the graphic. If you don't like it, choose **Undo** and try again.

Now, back to the fill patterns. You don't have to be an artist to create some pretty amazing effects with fill patterns. My personal favorite is gradient shading, which has a gradual shift from dark to light. You can also use a variety of textures, such as marble or tissue paper; geometric patterns, such as horizontal brick or plaid; and pictures that serve as an attractive background.

FIGURE 11.29

Select a prede-
fined color or
create your own
custom color
with the Fill
Color options.

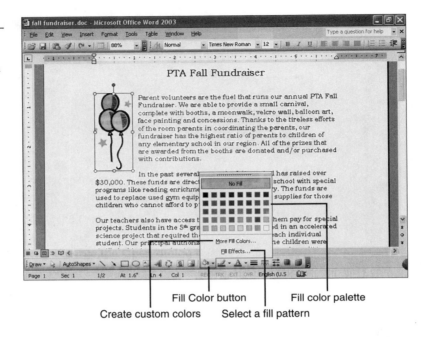

Create custom colors   Fill Color button   Select a fill pattern   Fill color palette

To select a fill pattern, follow these steps:

1. Click the graphic to select it.
2. Click the drop-down arrow next to the **Fill Color** button on the Drawing toolbar.
3. Choose **Fill Effects** to open the Fill Effects dialog box (see Figure 11.30).

Click a tab to select a pattern

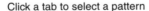

FIGURE 11.30

Gradient shad-
ing is just one of
many fill pat-
terns you can
apply to a
graphic.

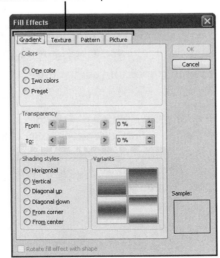

4. Click the tab for the type of pattern you want to use and then make your selections.

5. Click **OK** to add the selected pattern to the graphic.

Creating WordArt

If you've ever wondered how professional printers come up with the decorative text that they use for signs, banners, and letterhead, you're about to find out. The WordArt feature enables you to create text in a variety of different shapes and with many different effects. Figure 11.31 shows a few examples of WordArt.

FIGURE 11.31

Text can be distorted into shapes, and a variety of effects can be applied.

To insert WordArt in a document, follow these steps:

1. Choose **Insert**, **Picture**, **WordArt**, or click the **WordArt** button on the Drawing toolbar. The WordArt Gallery dialog box appears (see Figure 11.32).

2. Click one of the styles and then click **OK**. The Edit WordArt Text dialog box appears (see Figure 11.33).

3. Type the text you want to use.

4. Change the font or font size and apply bold or italics if you like.

5. Click **OK** to insert the WordArt object in the document.

The style that you start with is only the beginning. You can make all sorts of changes to the shapes, fill, rotation, text wrap, and alignment. The quickest way to make these changes is to use the buttons on the WordArt toolbar (see Figure 11.34).

FIGURE 11.32

Select one of the
WordArt styles
to begin.

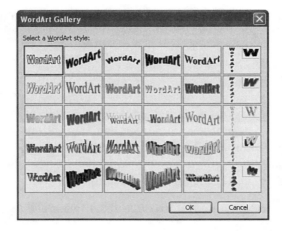

FIGURE 11.33

You enter the
text and choose
a font and font
size in the Edit
WordArt Text
dialog box.

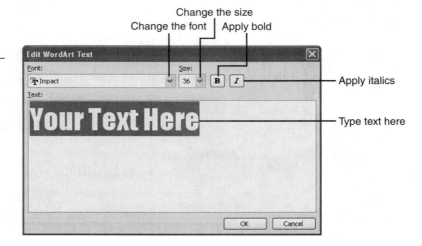

If you have any problems when you work with pictures and drawing objects, a great
troubleshooting guide is available in Word Help with a list of frequently asked questions (and answers, of course). Search Help for "troubleshoot graphics."

FIGURE 11.34
The WordArt toolbar has buttons for customizing every aspect of the WordArt object.

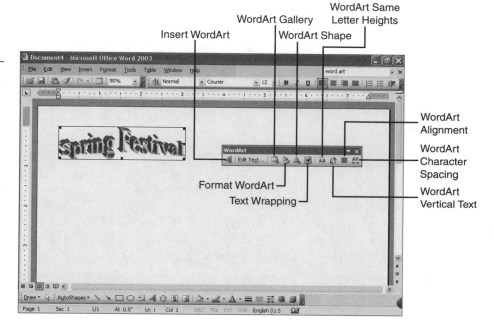

THE ABSOLUTE MINIMUM

After reading this chapter, you now know how to

- Add a simple black line.
- Add clip art and other graphics to your document and then resize and move them to achieve just the right effect.
- Identify the different types of graphics that you can use in your Word documents.
- Work with text boxes just like you would any other graphic and place them anywhere on the page, even on top of other text or graphic images.
- Use AutoShape to create your own graphic shapes, such as lines, arrows, boxes, and even callouts.
- Add a border around a drawing object or text box, use a fill pattern, and set a wrap option so the text wraps around the graphic the way you want it to.
- Use the WordArt feature, which gives you total design control over decorative text.

In the next chapter, you'll learn how to use data from other sources in your Word documents.

- Using cut, copy, and paste to transfer information from other applications into Word.

- Taking advantage of the Office Clipboard to store more than one clip at a time.

- Using Object Linking and Embedding to insert information.

- Working with files that are not in Word document (.doc) format.

- Saving documents so they can be opened in earlier versions of Word.

12

USING DATA FROM OTHER SOURCES

Microsoft Word 2003 is an amazing program by itself, but when you use it together with the other Microsoft Office applications, it becomes a very powerful application. You can use the specialized Office programs for other tasks and then incorporate that information into a Word document. Use Excel for your reporting, Outlook for scheduling, FrontPage for your Web work, Project for project data, PowerPoint for your presentations, and so on.

Because Word can open files in Hypertext Markup Language (HTML) format, you can save Web pages and open them in Word for editing. You can also save existing documents in HTML for posting on your company intranet or the Internet. Additional converters are available for files that are not in the most common formats.

Copying Information Between Applications

Word can do many things, but it can't do everything. You occasionally have to switch to another application for a project. You can have the best of both worlds because you can pull that information into a Word document. You can do a simple copy and paste operation to transfer one item at a time, or you can use the Office Clipboard to copy multiple items and then paste them in as needed.

Using Cut, Copy, and Paste

Using the same techniques you learned in the "Moving and Copying Text" section in Chapter 3, "Editing Documents," you can copy information from another program and paste it into Word. The system Clipboard acts as a "go-between," temporarily holding the cut or copied information until you can paste it into a document.

To move or copy a single selection between programs, follow these steps:

1. Open the source program (for example, Microsoft Excel).

2. Select the information you want to move or copy.

 3. Click the **Cut** or **Copy** button to cut or copy the selection. Alternatively, press **Ctrl+X** to cut the text or **Ctrl+C** to copy it.

4. Switch back to Word.

5. Position the insertion point where you want the information to appear.

 6. Click the **Paste** button (or press **Ctrl+V**) to paste the selection.

When you do a simple cut or copy, you use the system Clipboard to hold the information until you can paste. Also called the Windows Clipboard, this feature holds one piece of information at a time. When you exit Windows, the Clipboard is cleared.

Using the Office Clipboard to Copy Multiple Selections

The Office Clipboard can also hold more than one selection, so if you need to copy several passages of text, you can copy all of them at one time and paste them when you're ready instead of switching back and forth between the applications for each copy and paste operation. When you're ready to paste, you can insert the clips in whatever order you like.

To cut or copy multiple selections to the Office Clipboard, do the following:

1. Choose **Edit**, **Office Clipboard** to open the Office Clipboard in the task pane and activate it for use in other Office programs. An Office Clipboard icon is added to the taskbar.

2. Select a section of text or an image in Word, or switch to another application and select the information you want to cut or copy.

3. Either cut or copy the selection.

4. Select another section of text or an image. You can switch to another application to do this. As long as you see the Office Clipboard icon on the taskbar, you can copy items to the Office Clipboard.

5. Either cut or copy the selection.

6. Repeat steps 3 and 4 to store additional selections.

7. Switch to the Word document into which you want to paste these items. The clip items are shown in the Office Clipboard as a short section of the selected text or a thumbnail of an image (see Figure 12.1).

note

The Office Clipboard can hold only 24 clips. When you cut or copy a 25th item, the first item in the Clipboard is removed to make room for the new one.

Internet Explorer icon

Number of clips in the Clipboard

FIGURE 12.1

The clips that you have saved appear in a list in the Office Clipboard.

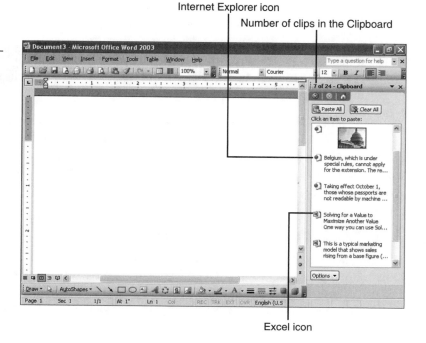

Excel icon

8. Click in the document where you want the information inserted.

9. Click the item that you want to insert in the Office Clipboard. The item is inserted and the Paste Options button appears. If you click this button, you see a pop-up list of Paste Options (see Figure 12.2).

FIGURE 12.2

When you paste a selection, you can choose from several options to transfer the information.

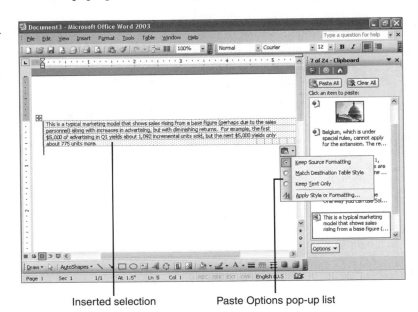

Inserted selection Paste Options pop-up list

10. If necessary, select one of the paste options; otherwise, click in the document to close the list. You might, for example, want to make the selection match the formatting you already have in place.

That's the quickest way to place information into Word, and believe me, you'll use these techniques over and over again. You can copy and paste information from intranet or Internet pages and review the documents offline or share them with a colleague. You can also copy and paste address information from your Outlook address book.

Using OLE to Link Information Together

One way to share data between Office applications is to copy and paste, but with Object Linking and Embedding (OLE), you can do more. You can *link* data between two programs so that if the data changes in the originating program, it is automatically updated in Word. Linking is very important if you use data that requires constant updating, such as spreadsheets or databases.

You can also *embed* the information in a document with a pointer to the application that created it. Embedded information can be edited from within Word; all you have to do is double-click it. Word creates an editing window with all the menus and toolbars from the originating program.

The main difference between linking and embedding is that linked information maintains an active connection between the data in the Word document and the data in the original application. When you embed something in a Word document, you forgo a link to the original data, but you maintain a connection to the application. This means you can make changes to the data in Word without affecting the information in the original file.

In either case, all you have to do to edit the data is double-click it. Word starts the other application and integrates it into the document window so you can revise the data without ever leaving Word.

Linking Data

You can create a link in Word in two ways: You can use the Paste Special feature or the Insert Object feature. Paste Special should be used when you want only a portion of a file; Insert Object should be used when you want to link to an entire file. Either way, when you double-click the information, you can edit it and have those changes reflected in the Word document.

To create a link with Paste Special, follow these steps:

1. Switch from Word to the other program and select the information to which you want to create a link.

2. Click the **Copy** button or press **Ctrl+C** to copy the information.

3. Switch back to Word and choose **Edit**, **Paste Special** to display the Paste Special dialog box (see Figure 12.3).

FIGURE 12.3

The Paste Special dialog box contains a list of possible formats that you can choose.

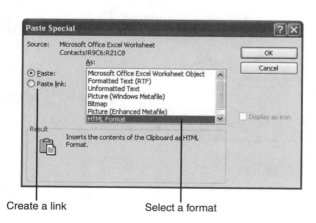

Create a link   Select a format

4. Select the format that you want to use to insert the information in the **As** list. For example, if the information is coming from Excel, select **Microsoft Office Excel Worksheet Object**.

5. Choose **Paste link**. The selected information is copied into the Word document (see Figure 12.4).

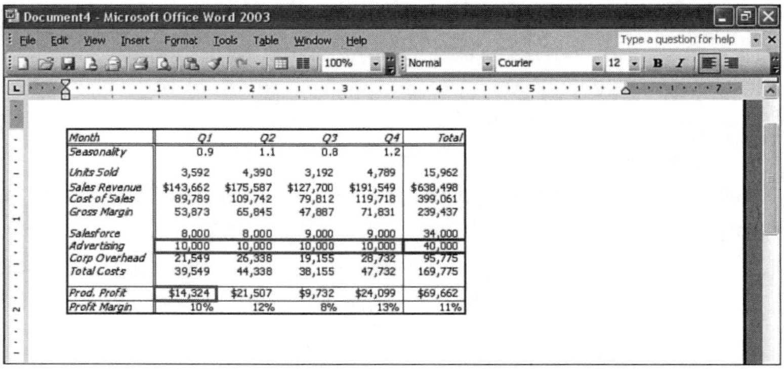

FIGURE 12.4

A link to a selected portion of an Excel spreadsheet has been created in this Word document.

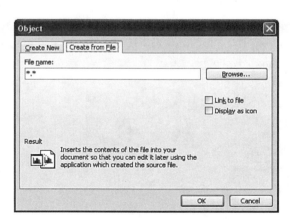

To create a link to a file with Insert Object, do the following:

1. In Word, choose **Insert**, **Object** to display the Object dialog box. You'll read more about using this dialog box in Chapter 18 on the Web, "Using Charts, Diagrams, and Equations."

2. Click the **Create from File** tab (see Figure 12.5).

FIGURE 12.5

Select the file with which you want to establish a link in the Create from File tab of the Object dialog box.

3. Click the **Browse** button to browse for the file.

4. Select the file and then choose **Insert**.

5. Place a check mark next to **Link to file**.

6. Click **OK**. Word inserts the information into the Word document (see Figure 12.6).

FIGURE 12.6

A link to an Excel spreadsheet has been inserted in this Word document.

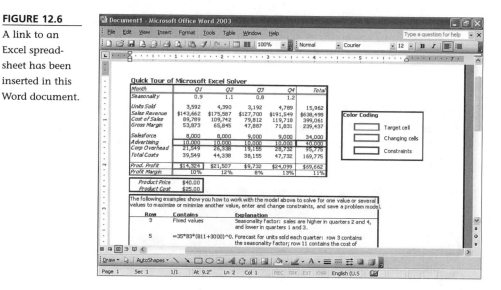

Now you've created a link to the data. Any changes that are made to that data are reflected in the Word document. Keep this point in mind: You can't edit the data in Word independently of the data in the original file; they are one and the same.

If you plan to share your documents with linked objects, remember that the recipients must have access to the files for the objects; otherwise, they cannot edit them in the Word document.

Embedding Data

The steps to embed data are similar to the steps to link data, so these two sections look almost identical. Still, it's important to break out the instructions for linking and embedding because these procedures are not usually done together.

Here again, you can use either Paste Special or Insert Object to embed data in Word. Paste Special should be used when you want only a portion of a file; Insert Object should be used when you want to embed an entire file. Either way, when you double-click the information, you can edit it and have those changes reflected in the Word document.

Follow these steps to embed data with Paste Special:

1. Switch from Word to the other program and select the information that you want to embed.

2. Switch back to Word and choose **Edit**, **Paste Special** to display the Paste Special dialog box (refer to Figure 12.3).

3. In the **As** list, select the entry with "Object" in the name. For example, if the information is coming from Excel, select **Microsoft Office Excel Worksheet Object**.

4. Choose **Paste**. The selected information is copied into the Word document.

To embed a file with Insert Object, do the following:

1. In Word, choose **Insert**, **Object** to display the Object dialog box.

2. If necessary, click the **Create New** tab. A list of object types from programs on your system that support OLE appears in the **Object type** list (see Figure 12.7).

FIGURE 12.7

The Create New tab of the Object dialog box contains a list of supported object types that you can choose.

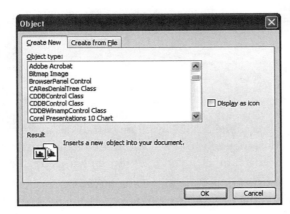

3. Select the type of embedded object you want to create.

4. Click **OK**.

Now you've embedded an object in a Word document. This information is *not* connected to the original data. The only "connection" is between the data and the application that created it. In other words, you can edit the data from within Word. Your changes do not affect data in any other file. You use this option when you need to include information contained in files that others don't have access to.

Editing OLE Objects

There! You just created an OLE object in a Word document. That wasn't as hard as you thought it would be, was it? Now, this is why you went to the trouble: Say you need to revise some of the figures in an Excel spreadsheet OLE object. Rather than closing your document, starting Excel, making the changes in Excel, switching back to Word, and reopening the document, you can do your editing from inside Word, thanks to OLE.

To edit an OLE object, follow these steps:

1. Double-click the object to launch the originating application. If the object is linked, and you have that application installed on your system, Microsoft Office starts it and opens the file (see Figure 12.8). If the object is embedded, you can edit the information from within Word with the appropriate toolbars and menus.

FIGURE 12.8

When you double-click an OLE object, the originating application is opened so you can make your changes.

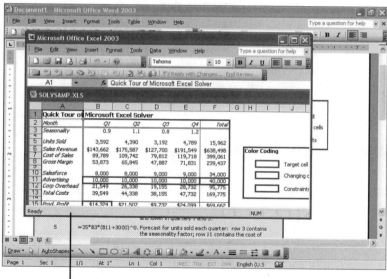

Microsoft Excel is started and the file is opened

2. When you are finished with your edits, close the application and save your changes, or click elsewhere in the document if the object is embedded. When you return to Word, you see that your changes are reflected in the OLE object.

Working with Files in Other Formats

With the increased popularity of sharing documents through email attachments, you never know what you're going to get in your Inbox. You might be lucky enough to get a Word file, but is it in a format that is compatible with Word 2003? What about WordPerfect documents? And Web pages?

Word uses file converters to convert files into a form that can be read in Word. The most commonly used converters are installed by default, and more can be installed if necessary. Word can open and save files in many formats, in addition to the default `.doc` format, without the use of a converter. Documents that were created in earlier versions of Word can be opened directly in Word 2003; all data and formatting are preserved.

The following files can be opened and saved in Word without a converter:

- **`.doc`**—The default Word document format
- **`.dot`**—Word template format
- **`.htm`, `.html`**—Web pages
- **`.mht`, `.mhtml`**—Web archive format
- **`.xml`**—Extensible Markup Language format
- **`.rtf`**—Rich Text Format (most programs can open and read this format)
- **`.txt`**—Plain text, no formatting

Installing Additional File Converters

If you need to open a file that is not in one of the formats listed in the preceding section, Word prompts you when you try to open the file. You are told that the converter isn't available, and you have an opportunity to install it. Have your Microsoft Office 2003 CD ready.

To install additional converters, follow these steps:

1. Close all programs.
2. Choose **Start**, **Control Panel**, **Add or Remove Programs**.
3. Select **Microsoft Office 2003** or **Microsoft Office Word 2003** from the list.
4. Choose **Change**.
5. When the install wizard starts, choose **Add or Remove Features**.
6. Place a check mark next to **Choose advanced customization of applications** and then choose **Next**.

7. Click the plus sign next to **Office Shared Features**.

8. Click the plus sign next to **Converters and Filters**.

9. Click the plus sign next to **Text Converters**.

10. Click the drop-down arrow next to the converter you want to install and then choose **Run from My Computer**.

11. Choose **Update**.

Saving Documents for Use in Older Versions of Word

Microsoft Office Word 2003 can open documents created in earlier versions of Microsoft Word without losing any data or formatting. However, the trick is to make it easy for users with older versions of Word to open and edit your Word 2003 documents.

> **note**
>
> If you choose to save your file in a format that would result in the loss of content or features, Word displays a message and provides a list of content or features that will be lost. You can either continue and accept the loss, or cancel and save to a different format.

For Word 2002, Word 2000, and Word 97, the procedure is fairly straightforward: Just save your Word 2003 documents in the Word document (*.doc) format. For Word 97, you can turn off those features that aren't supported in that version.

To turn off features not available in Word 97, follow these steps:

1. Choose **Tools**, **Options** to open the Options dialog box.

2. Click the **Save** tab to display those options (see Figure 12.9).

3. Enable the **Disable features introduced after** check box to activate the drop-down list.

4. Click the drop-down list arrow and choose **Microsoft Word 97**.

5. Click **OK**.

For Word 6.0 or Word 7.0/95, you can do two things. First, save documents with the Word 97-2003 & 6.0/95-RTF converter. When you do this, Word searches through the document and replaces formatting that isn't supported in Word 6.0 or Word 7.0/95 with formatting that is supported in those versions. A dialog box shows you what formatting will change.

FIGURE 12.9

When you are working on a document for use in Word 97, it's a good idea to turn off those features that aren't supported.

Furthermore, for documents that are saved in this format, Word automatically makes unavailable features that are not supported by Word 6.0 and Word 7.0/95. This makes it easier for you to create documents that look the same in Word 6.0 or Word 7.0/95 as they did in Word 2003. This converter is included in Microsoft Office 2003 and can be installed using the steps for installing additional conversion files (see "Installing Additional File Converters" in the previous section).

If you are creating a new document for someone with Word 6.0 or Word 7.0/95, you can turn off the features that aren't supported in those versions so you don't accidentally use them.

To turn off features not available in Word 6.0 or Word 7.0/95, follow these steps:

1. Choose **Tools**, **Options** to open the Options dialog box.
2. Click the **Save** tab.
3. Enable the **Disable features introduced after** check box to activate the drop-down list.
4. Click the drop-down list arrow and choose **Microsoft Word 6.0/95**.
5. Click **OK**.

THE ABSOLUTE MINIMUM

After reading this chapter, you now know how to

- Use the same cut, copy, and paste techniques that you learned in Chapter 3, to transfer information from other applications into Word.

- Copy and paste multiple clips using the Office Clipboard's capability to store more than one selection at a time.

- Incorporate data from other applications into your Word documents using the Object Linking and Embedding feature.

- Work with files that are not in Word document (*.doc) format.

- Install additional file converters from the Microsoft Office 2003 CD.

- Save documents that can be edited by users with earlier versions of Word.

In the next chapter, you'll learn how to use the Merge feature to generate mass mailings, complete with envelopes and labels.

PART V

AUTOMATING YOUR WORK

IN THIS CHAPTER

- Using the Mail Merge task pane to create a letter, create an address list, and merge the two together.

- Creating envelopes and labels with contact information from the address list.

- Editing, sorting, and filtering the address list entries.

- Using information from many different types of data sources in a mail merge.

- Inserting specific merge fields into a main document.

- Troubleshooting problems with the results of a mail merge.

13

SETTING UP A MAIL MERGE

What is a mail merge? you ask. It is the process of merging information from two different sources into one document. A typical mail merge consists of a letter and a list of addresses that you combine to create a stack of personalized letters and envelopes.

You define the *main document*, which is the document you want to send out, and a *data source*, which contains the information that you want to insert. The main document is just a regular document with merge fields in it. The merge fields act as markers for the information from the data source.

Word automates the process of setting up a mail merge with new features in the task pane. You can easily have a stack of letters and envelopes or labels in a matter of minutes.

Creating a Form Letter

The most common use of a merge feature is to create form letters. So, Microsoft changed the name of its merge feature from Mail Merge to Letters and Mailings. And…you're going to love this…Word 2003 has a great new Mail Merge task pane that walks you through the entire process of setting up a mail merge. You can't skip a step or go off in the wrong direction because the whole thing is presented to you in a series of steps.

The options in the task pane walk you through creating the main document and the data source, and then merging the two together. After you've created your letters, generating envelopes and labels is a piece of cake.

If you want to use an existing document as the main document, you can open it now, or you can browse for it later. Otherwise, create a new document and type any text that you need to precede the information that will be inserted during the merge.

> **note**
>
> The main document is the place where you want to set up all the formatting for the merged documents. For example, you definitely don't want to put punctuation or formatting in the data source; otherwise, it is duplicated over and over again.

To create a letter, follow these steps:

1. Choose **Tools**, **Letters and Mailings**, **Mail Merge** to display the Mail Merge task pane (see Figure 13.1).

2. Choose **Letters** and then click **Next: Starting document** (at the bottom of the task pane). The Select starting document page appears (see Figure 13.2).

3. Choose one of the following:

   ■ If you have a document onscreen, select the **Use the current document** radio button.

   ■ To start from a template, select the **Start from a template** radio button. In the middle section, click the **Select template** button to open the Select Template dialog box. Locate the template that you want to use, select it, and then click **OK**.

   ■ To browse for a document, select the **Start from existing document** radio button. In the middle section, click the **Open** button to display the Open dialog box. Locate the file you want to use, select it, and then choose **Open**.

Select a document type

FIGURE 13.1
The Mail Merge
task pane walks
you through the
process of creat-
ing a mail
merge.

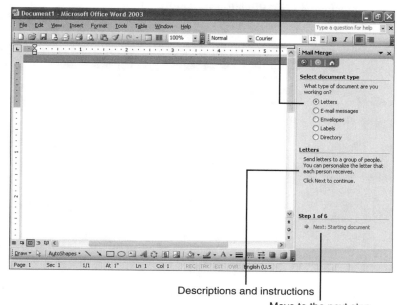

Descriptions and instructions

Move to the next step

Selecting a starting point for the document

FIGURE 13.2
Make the choice
to use the cur-
rent document
or start with an
existing docu-
ment in the
Select starting
document page.

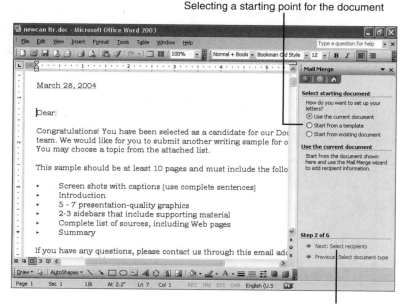

Move to the next step

4. Click **Next: Select recipients** (at the bottom of the task pane). The Select recipients page appears (see Figure 13.3).

Create a new list

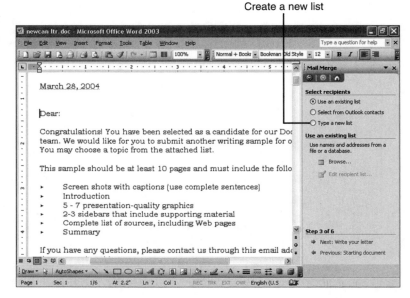

5. For now, choose **Type a new list**. I'll cover using an existing list and Outlook contacts later.

6. In the middle section, click **Create**. The New Address List dialog box appears (see Figure 13.4).

7. Type the title or press **Tab** to move to the First Name entry.

8. Type the first name, press **Tab** to move to the Last Name entry, and then type the last name.

9. Type the address information for the first person, pressing **Tab** to move to the next entry or **Shift+Tab** to move to the previous entry. You can also use the **up-** and **down-arrow** keys.

10. Click **New Entry** to create a blank entry form. Continue creating address list entries until you have entered your entire list.

11. Choose **Close** when you're done. The Save Address List dialog box appears in the File name text box.

12. Type a name for this address book and then choose **Save**. The Mail Merge Recipients dialog box appears (see Figure 13.5).

13. For now, leave all the entries selected. I'll show you how to rearrange the list and exclude recipients later. Click **OK**.

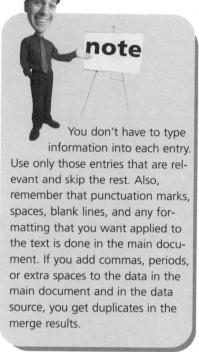

You don't have to type information into each entry. Use only those entries that are relevant and skip the rest. Also, remember that punctuation marks, spaces, blank lines, and any formatting that you want applied to the text is done in the main document. If you add commas, periods, or extra spaces to the data in the main document and in the data source, you get duplicates in the merge results.

FIGURE 13.5

The Mail Merge Recipients dialog box contains tools to help you locate, arrange, and select recipients.

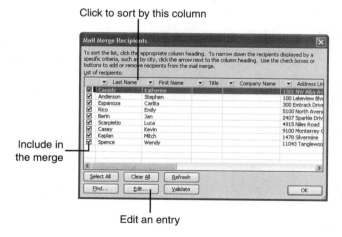

Click to sort by this column

Include in the merge

Edit an entry

14. Click **Next: Write your letter** in the task pane to move to Step 4 of 6. The Write your letter page appears (see Figure 13.6).

Insert the salutation

Insert the address block

FIGURE 13.6

The options in the Write your letter page allow you to insert the address block, salutation, electronic postage, and a bar code.

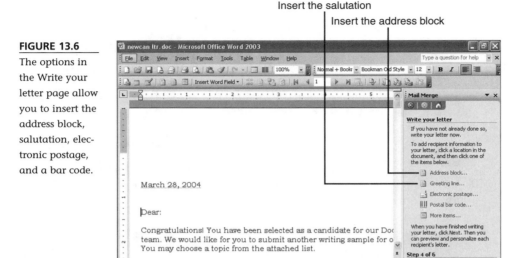

15. Position the insertion point where you want to insert the address block and then click **Address block**. The Insert Address Block dialog box appears (see Figure 13.7).

FIGURE 13.7

Select the format that you want to use for the recipient's address in the Insert Address Block dialog box.

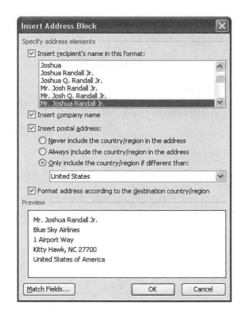

16. Choose from the following options:

   - **Recipient's name**—Select a format for the recipient's name or deselect the **Insert recipient's name in this format** check box if you don't want to include the recipient's name in the address block.

   - **Company name**—Deselect the **Insert company name** check box if you don't want to include the company name in the address block.

   - **Postal address**—Select the appropriate option for the country/region information under the **Insert postal address** check box.

17. Click **OK** when you are satisfied with the appearance of your address block in the **Preview** area. Word inserts a merge field for the address block (see Figure 13.8).

FIGURE 13.8

An address block merge field is inserted in the main document.

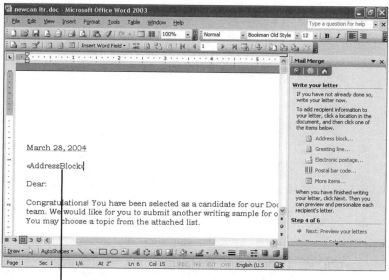

Address block field

18. Position the insertion point where you want to insert the greeting and then click **Greeting line**. The Greeting Line dialog box appears (see Figure 13.9).

19. Open the drop-down lists and select the preferred greeting line, including a greeting line for invalid or missing recipient names.

20. Click **OK** when you are finished creating the greeting line. Word inserts the merge field for the greeting line. Notice that if you click the field, it appears shaded (see Figure 13.10).

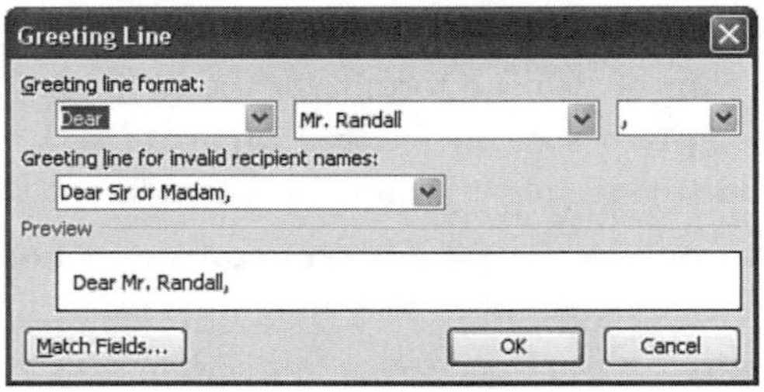

FIGURE 13.9

Open the drop-down lists and build an appropriate salutation for your letters in the Greeting Line dialog box.

FIGURE 13.10

All Word fields appear shaded when you select them.

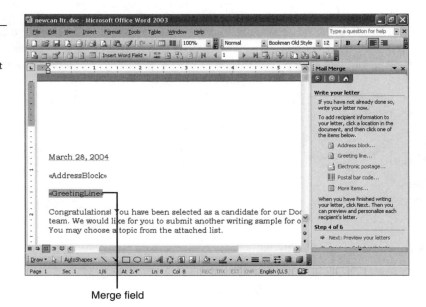

Merge field

21. To keep things simple, assume that's all you need for now. I'll come back to this later in the discussion on inserting specific fields to further personalize the letters. Choose **Next: Preview your letters**. The merge is performed, and the letters are displayed in the document window (see Figure 13.11).

22. Choose **Next: Complete the merge** to move to the last step. The Complete the merge page appears (see Figure 13.12).

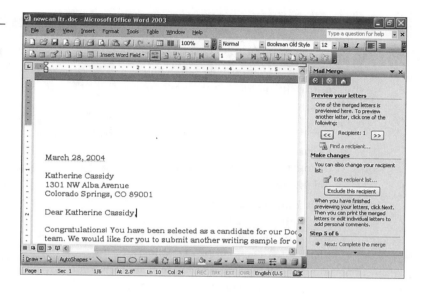

Print the letters

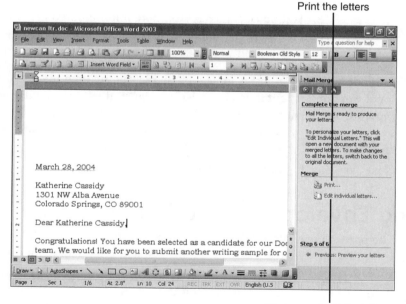

Review and edit the letters

23. You are one step away from finishing, so hang in there! The merge results shown in the document window are a representation of how the letters will look when you finalize the merge. You haven't done that yet. Choose one of the following options:

   ■ **Print**—Select this option to send the results of the merge directly to the printer.

   ■ **Edit individual letters**—Select this option if you want to send the results of the merge to a new document, where you can make adjustments to the letters. In the Merge to New Document dialog box, choose **All** and then click **OK**. When you're done, you can print your letters, fax them, or email them. See Chapter 3, "Editing Documents," for more information on emailing and faxing documents from Word. If things don't look the way they should, this is your opportunity to discard the results, make corrections, and try again.

tip

This tip may seem obvious, but you don't need to save the results of a merge. If you save the merge results, you are saving the same information twice, which eats up valuable disk space. Remember, you can always repeat the merge operation and reproduce the letters.

Congratulations! You just completed a merge! Setting up a merge might seem like a lot of work at first, but if you consider how much time you would spend creating a separate document for each individual address entry, it's time well spent. I also want to point out that you can reuse the address list over and over again, so once you've created that file, you don't have to repeat these steps.

Next, you need to print some envelopes or labels so you can mail your letters.

Creating Envelopes and Labels

The process of creating envelopes and labels is similar to creating letters. You start by setting up the envelope type or label size and use the Mail Merge task pane to work through the steps.

Because you've already created a stack of letters, it stands to reason that you will be using an existing address list to create envelopes and labels. For that reason, the following section includes information on selecting an existing address list.

Creating Envelopes

If you prefer printing directly onto envelopes rather than printing out labels and sticking them on, you can create an envelope as the main document and merge that with a data source, creating a stack of envelopes for the stack of letters you created earlier.

There are a couple of ways to go about this process. You can start from a blank document and select the envelope type from the Mail Merge task pane, or you can create the envelope first and use it for the merge.

To create merged envelopes, do the following:

1. Choose **Tools**, **Letters and Mailings**, **Mail Merge** to display the Mail Merge task pane (refer to Figure 13.1).

2. Select the **Envelopes** radio button and then click **Next: Starting document**. The Select starting document page appears. Figure 13.13 shows how the task pane will look when you start from a blank document. If you have already created the envelope, the Use the current document option will be available.

tip

If you want to use your return address on the merged envelopes, set it up before you start the merge. From a blank document, choose **Tools**, **Letters and Mailings**, **Envelopes and Labels** and then enter your return address in the **Return address** text box. Choose **Add to Document** and then choose **Use the Current document** in the Mail Merge task pane. For more information on creating envelopes, see "Creating Envelopes and Labels" in Chapter 4, "Learning Basic Formatting Techniques."

FIGURE 13.13

The Select starting document page contains options to choose an envelope size, work from the current document, or open an existing document.

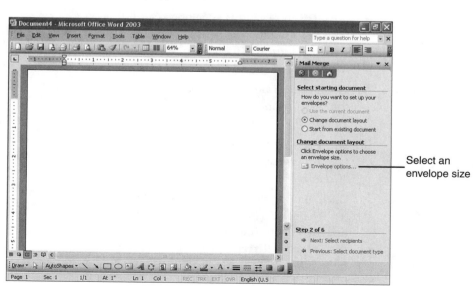

Select an envelope size

3. Click **Envelope options** to display the Envelope Options dialog box (see Figure 13.14).

4. If the envelope size that you use is already displayed in the **Envelope size** drop-down list, you don't have to do anything. Otherwise, click the drop-down list arrow and select an envelope size.

FIGURE 13.14

Select an envelope size and set the font for the return and delivery addresses in the Envelope Options dialog box.

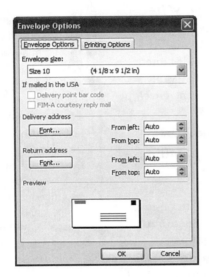

5. If necessary, click the **Font** buttons to set the font for the return and delivery addresses.

6. Click **OK** to select this envelope size and return to the Mail Merge task pane. The envelope form is displayed in the document window (see Figure 13.15).

7. Click **Next: Select recipients** to display the Select recipients page (refer to Figure 13.3).

8. Select **Use an existing list**. If you want to type a new list, refer to steps 5–13 in the "Creating a Form Letter" section.

9. Click the **Browse** button to search for the list. The Select Data Source dialog box appears. If you have already opened a list, the **Select a different list** option will be available, so you can switch to another list.

note

The Select Data Source dialog box functions just like the Open dialog box, so if you need to move to another folder or drive, use the techniques you learned in the section titled "Navigating Through Drives and Folders" in Chapter 2, "Finding and Opening Documents."

Envelope form

FIGURE 13.15
When you select
an envelope
size, Word dis-
plays an enve-
lope form in the
document win-
dow.

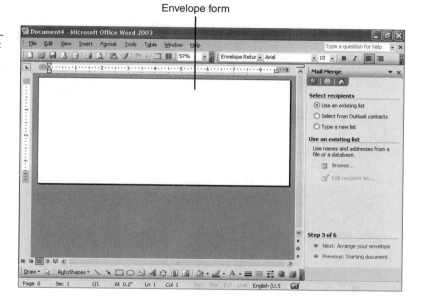

10. Select the address list to use in this merge and then choose **Open**. The
    Confirm Data Source dialog box appears (see Figure 13.16).

11. Select the source of the address list and then click **OK**. (If you created this
    address list, choose the (*.mdb) option.) The Mail Merge Recipients dialog box
    appears (refer to Figure 13.5).

FIGURE 13.16
You can confirm
the source of the
address list in
the Confirm
Data Source dia-
log box.

12. Remove the check marks next to names of individuals that you do not want
    to include in this mail merge and then click **OK**.

13. Click **Next: Arrange your envelope** to display the Arrange Your Envelope
    page.

14. Click in the lower half of the envelope to display the guidelines that mark the
    address block section (see Figure 13.17).

Click here to position the address block Insert the address block field

FIGURE 13.17
In Step 4 of 6 of the merge, you position the insertion point and then insert the address block field.

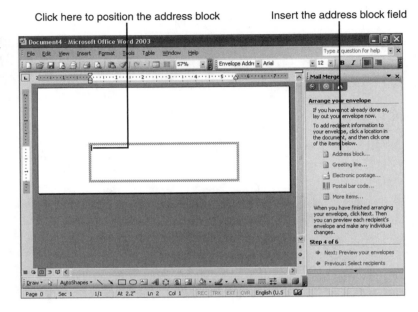

15. Click **Address block** to display the Insert Address Block dialog box (refer to Figure 13.7).

16. Choose from the following options:

    ■ **Recipient's name**—Select a format for the recipient's name or deselect the **Insert recipient's name in this format** check box if you don't want to include the recipient's name in the address block.

    ■ **Company name**—Deselect the **Insert company name** check box if you don't want to include the company name in the address block.

    ■ **Postal address**—Select the appropriate option for the country/region information under the **Insert postal address** check box.

17. Click **OK** when you are satisfied with the appearance of your address block in the **Preview** area. Word inserts a merge field for the address block.

18. Click **Next: Preview your envelopes** to display a preview of the merged envelopes (see Figure 13.18).

19. Click **Next: Complete the merge**.

FIGURE 13.18

The completed envelopes should have the address information formatted in an address block.

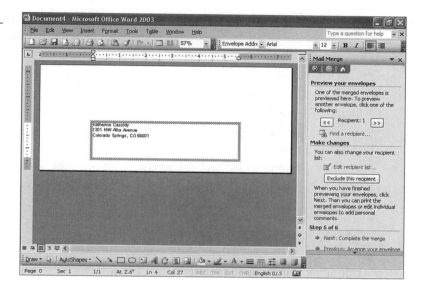

20. Choose one of the following options:

- **Print**—Select this option to send the results of the merge directly to the printer.
- **Edit individual envelopes**—Select this option if you want to send the results of the merge to a new document, where you can make adjustments to the envelopes. In the Merge to New Document dialog box, choose **All** and then click **OK**.

Creating Labels

The steps for creating merged labels are almost identical to those for creating merged envelopes, so if you are reading through each section, this information will seem repetitive. However, in my experience, users create envelopes *or* labels, not both at the same time. For this reason, I've decided to include a complete set of steps for labels.

caution

If the address information isn't formatted in an address block, you may have positioned the insertion point incorrectly when you inserted the address block field. Click **Previous: Arrange your envelopes**. Delete the AddressBlock field. Click in the lower half of the envelope to display a dashed rectangular area. Click in the upper-left corner of this rectangle and then insert the AddressBlock field again.

There are a couple of ways to go about this process. You can start from a blank document and select the labels from the Mail Merge task pane, or you can create the labels first and use them for the merge.

To create merged labels, do the following:

1. Choose **Tools**, **Letters and Mailings**, **Mail Merge** to display the Mail Merge task pane (refer to Figure 13.1).

2. Select the **Labels** radio button and then click **Next: Starting document**. The Select starting document page appears. If you have already created the labels, the **Use the current document** option will be available.

3. Click **Label options** to display the Label Options dialog box (see Figure 13.19).

FIGURE 13.19

Select a label product and then locate a product number in the Label Options dialog box.

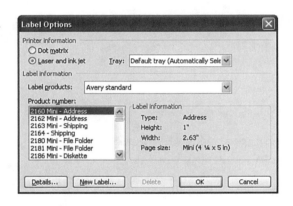

4. Select a product from the **Label products** drop-down list, select a label from the **Product number** list box, and then click **OK**. Word displays an empty label form, and you are ready to move to the next step, which is to select the recipients.

5. Click **Next: Select recipients** to display the Select recipients page (refer to Figure 13.3).

6. Select **Use an existing list**. If you want to type a new list, refer to steps 5–13 in the "Creating a Form Letter" section.

7. Click the **Browse** button to search for the list. The Select Data Source dialog box appears. If you have already opened a list, the **Select a different list** option will be available, so you can switch to another list.

8. Select the address list to use in this merge and then choose **Open**. The Confirm Data Source dialog box appears (refer to Figure 13.16).

9. Select the source of the address list and then click **OK**. The Mail Merge Recipients dialog box appears (refer to Figure 13.5).

10. Remove the check marks next to names of individuals that you do not want to include in this mail merge and then click **OK**. Word inserts fields in each label that will cause the merge to move to the next record at the end of every label (see Figure 13.20).

11. Click **Next: Arrange your labels** to display the Arrange your labels page.

12. Click in the first label.

13. Click **Address block** to display the Insert Address Block dialog box (refer to Figure 13.7).

14. Choose from the following options:

    ■ **Recipient's name**—Select a format for the recipient's name or deselect the **Insert recipient's name in this format** check box if you don't want to include the recipient's name in the address block.

    ■ **Company name**—Deselect the **Insert company name** check box if you don't want to include the company name in the address block.

    ■ **Postal address**—Select the appropriate option for the country/region information under the **Insert postal address** check box.

15. Click **OK** when you are satisfied with the appearance of your address block in the **Preview** area. Word inserts a merge field for the address block.

16. Click **Update all labels** to replicate the AddressBlock field to all the other labels (see Figure 13.21).

note

Just because your label type isn't listed in the Label Options dialog box doesn't mean that the definition doesn't exist. Check the layout (such as 3 columns by 10 rows) or the dimensions, and compare them to the definitions in the list. You will probably find an exact match (or at least a close approximation). For more information on selecting labels, see "Creating Envelopes and Labels" in Chapter 4.

note

The Select Data Source dialog box functions just like the Open dialog box, so if you need to move to another folder or drive, use the techniques you learned in the section titled "Navigating Through Drives and Folders" in Chapter 2.

Next Record field

FIGURE 13.20

The Next Record field is inserted into the second and subsequent labels.

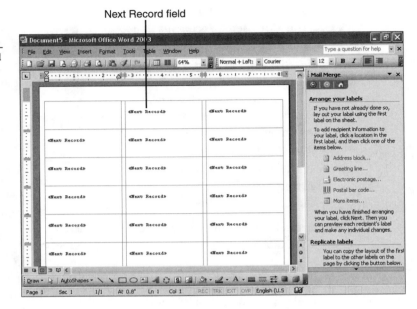

The AddressBlock code has been replicated

FIGURE 13.21

The Update all labels button replicates the characteristics of the first label to the other labels.

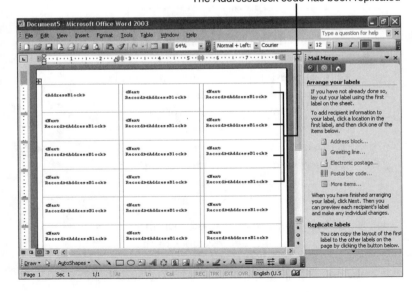

17. Click **Next: Preview your labels** to display a preview of the merged envelopes (see Figure 13.22).

18. Click **Next: Complete the merge**.

19. Choose one of the following options:

■ **Print**—Select this option to send the results of the merge directly to the printer.

■ **Edit individual labels**—Select this option if you want to send the results of the merge to a new document, where you can make adjustments to the labels. In the Merge to New Document dialog box, choose **All** and then click **OK**.

> **tip**
>
> If you want to customize the layout of the labels, set up the first label the way you want it to look and then click the **Update all labels** button in Step 4 of 6 in the Mail Merge task pane.

FIGURE 13.22

The completed labels should have the address information from each entry in the address list.

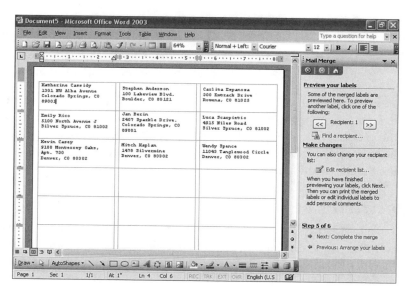

Working with Address Lists

The address list you created earlier is called a Microsoft Office Address List. This type of address list is useful for short lists that you don't use very often. For those names and addresses that you use often, you can make better use of your time by entering them into another electronic address book, such as the Outlook Contact List, or another data source, such as a Microsoft Excel worksheet or Access database. If you do this, you'll be able to use your contact information for a variety of purposes.

In either case, the contacts show up in the same Mail Merge Recipients dialog box that you saw in Figure 13.5, so I want to explain how to use the features in this dialog box.

tip

If the address information doesn't fit on the label, you can select a smaller font. Different fonts compress the letters closer together, so try using a different style if making the text smaller doesn't work for you.

Editing Entries

Anyone who maintains contact information knows that it is constantly changing and must be updated frequently. The entries in the address or Contact lists can be edited from the Mail Merge Recipients dialog box.

Follow these steps to edit an entry:

1. Select the entry and then click **Edit**. The entry is displayed in a dialog box that resembles the New Address List dialog box shown in Figure 13.4.

2. Make your changes and then choose **Close**. If you change your mind, click **Cancel** to close the dialog box without making any changes.

You may have already noticed this by now, but if you want to exclude an entry from the merge, you remove the check mark next to the name. A quick way to remove all the check marks is to click the **Clear All** button at the bottom of the Mail Merge Recipients dialog box. Likewise, the quickest way to select all the records is to click the **Select All** button.

Sorting Recipients

I don't know about you, but the first thing I needed to do was sort my list alphabetically. You may also want to sort by ZIP code or state to group certain entries together. Whatever the reason, sorting the entries is simple. I'll assume that you already have the Mail Merge Recipients dialog box open.

To sort entries in the list, do the following:

1. Click the column heading for the item you want to sort by. For example, click the Last Name column heading. The first time you click the column heading, the sort is in ascending order.

2. To sort the list in descending order, click the column heading again.

Filtering Out Recipients

It took me a few minutes to figure out why I would want to filter the list, but then it all made sense. If you want to mail information only to people in a particular city or state, you can filter out all the entries that do not fit certain criteria. In this example, you can filter out the entries that are *not* in a particular city or state. After you've filtered out the entries that you don't want to use, you can quickly select the entries that you do want to include and continue with the merge.

To filter out recipients, do the following:

1. Click the arrow on the column heading that you want to filter by (see Figure 13.23).

2. Select the entry that you want to use from the drop-down list. For example, select a city or state. Now, only the entries that contain that city or state are shown. Notice that when a list is filtered, the arrow in that column turns blue.

Now that you have a portion of the entries displayed, you can choose **Select All** to place check marks next to the entries, marking them for inclusion in the merge.

To display all the records again, click the arrow on the column heading and choose **(All)**.

FIGURE 13.23

The entries can be filtered by a common denominator in a specific column.

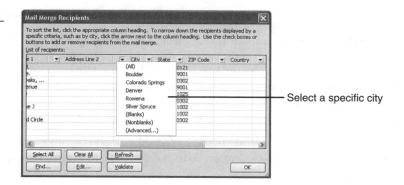

Selecting Other Data Sources

You can use a variety of data sources in a mail merge. The idea is that if you've already entered the information somewhere else, you can use it. Don't re-enter the information in an address list just for a mail merge. Your contact information might be in an Excel worksheet, an Access database, a Word table, an HTML file, or an electronic address book. Word allows you to connect to many different types of data sources for a mail merge.

You can use the following types of data sources:

- Microsoft Outlook Contact List
- Microsoft Excel worksheet
- Microsoft Access database
- Files from a single-tier, file-based database program for which you have installed an OLE-DB provider or ODBC driver
- HTML file that has a single table with column headings in the first row
- Microsoft Outlook Address Book
- Microsoft Schedule+ 7.0 Contact List
- Personal Address Book you created for use with Microsoft Exchange Server
- Address lists that were created with MAPI-compatible messaging systems, such as Microsoft Outlook
- Word documents that contain a table with column headings in the first row
- Text files that have data fields separated by tabs or commas and entries separated by paragraph marks

> **tip**
>
> Advanced sorting and filtering options are available in the Mail Merge Recipients dialog box. Click the arrow next to any column heading and choose **(Advanced)** from the drop-down list. Click the **Filter Records** or **Sort Records** tabs on the resulting dialog box to set up the type of query that you need. For more information on using these advanced sort and filter options, see Que Publishing's *Special Edition Using Microsoft Office Word 2003* by Bill Camarda (ISBN: 0-7897-2958-X).

In Step 3 of 6 in the Mail Merge task pane, you can select from your Outlook contacts. Choose **Select from Outlook contacts** and then click **Choose Contacts Folder**. Select your profile and then click **OK**. Select the Contacts list folder that you want to use; then click **OK** to open that list in the Mail Merge Recipients dialog box.

Within this step, you can also choose to use an existing list; then you can browse for that list. When you browse, you do so in the Select Data Source dialog box (see Figure 13.24).

Use the navigation techniques that you learned in Chapter 2 to locate the file you want to use. You must answer some questions before you can connect to the data source. There are too many variables to cover here, so if you get stuck, consult Word's help topics or consider purchasing Que Publishing's *Special Edition Using Microsoft Office Word 2003* by Bill Camarda (ISBN: 0-7897-2958-X), which goes into more detail.

Microsoft Office Address List

FIGURE 13.24

Browse for an existing contact list in the Select Data Source dialog box.

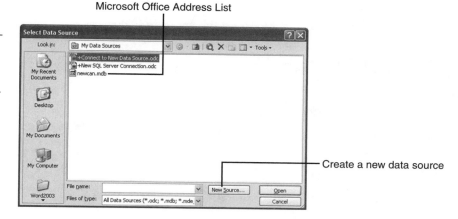

Create a new data source

Inserting Merge Fields into a Main Document

In the "Creating a Form Letter" section, the discussion was restricted to inserting the address block and greeting line fields into the main document, for the sake of simplicity. Inserting mail merge fields into a document is fairly simple, so for those situations in which you want to "embed" information in a document, you need to know how to insert fields outside the Mail Merge task pane.

In Step 4 of 6 in the Mail Merge task pane, when you insert the address block and greeting line fields, you have the option of inserting additional fields. Refer to Figure 13.6 and notice the **More items** option at the bottom of the list of merge fields.

To insert merge fields, follow these steps:

1. Click **More items** to display the Insert Merge Field dialog box (see Figure 13.25). In this example, the **Database Fields** radio button is selected. In your case, the **Address Fields** radio button may be selected, so the list of fields may be different.

2. Position the insertion point where you want the information to appear.

3. Select a field and then choose **Insert**, or double-click a field to insert it in the main document.

note

Speaking of working outside the Mail Merge task pane, you can use the Mail Merge toolbar to work on your own without the assistance of the task pane. Choose **Tools**, **Letters and Mailings**, **Show Mail Merge Toolbar**.

4. Choose **Close** to clear the dialog box.

5. Repeat steps 2–4 to insert the necessary fields.

Troubleshooting a Mail Merge

Unfortunately, the results of a merge might not
turn out the way you had planned. Don't worry;
with just a few minor adjustments, you can sort
things out. First, take a good look at the results
and see whether you can detect a pattern. Is the
state where the city should be? Are all the last
names missing, or just one or two?

You might decide to backtrack through your
steps in the Mail Merge task pane to fix the
problem, or you can just delete the merge results
and try again. If you decide to start over, close
the merge results document without saving.

If you have the same problem over and over,
start with the main document. Make sure that
you have the fields in the proper places. If you
need to change a field, select and delete it, and
then reinsert it. You can just save your changes
and try the merge again.

tip

In some cases, you won't
be able to locate the problem with your merge. In my
experience, I've been able to
resolve the problem in one of
two ways: by starting over
completely and doing the
exact same steps. For some magi-
cal reason, it works the second
time. Or, if just a few address
entries are affected, I can just
make the changes directly to the
mail merge results document.

If the problem occurs in only one or two entries, go straight to the data source and
look at the entries giving you trouble. Make sure that the right information is in the
correct field. You might have actually typed the State in the City field by accident.
Save your changes and try the merge again.

THE ABSOLUTE MINIMUM

After reading this chapter, you now know how to

- Use the Mail Merge task pane to create a letter with the information that you want to send out.
- Use the Mail Merge task pane to create a new address list.
- Use the Mail Merge task pane to merge the letter and the address list together, producing a series of personalized letters.
- Create envelopes or labels for a mass mailing.
- Edit address list entries to update contact information.
- Sort address list entries to group common entries together.
- Filter the address book entries to limit the number of recipients.
- Use data sources other than a simple address list.
- Troubleshoot problems with a mail merge.

In the next chapter, you'll learn how to use templates and wizards to build documents.

IN THIS CHAPTER

- Creating a new document with a template or wizard.

- Understanding how to protect yourself against macro viruses.

- Downloading template files from the Microsoft Office Online Web site.

- Creating a new template from an existing template, an existing document, or from scratch.

- Editing the default template to change the settings for all new documents.

- Transferring macros, toolbars, styles, and AutoText entries from one document/ template to another document/template.

14

USING TEMPLATES AND WIZARDS TO BUILD DOCUMENTS

Every document that you create in Word is based on a template. Up to this point, you've been using the `normal.dot` template, which is the default template in Word and contains all the initial settings for new documents. The default template is blank except for the initial settings. If you want to change the settings for all new documents, you edit the default template. From then on, all new documents will have those settings.

Wizards are little programs that take you by the hand and guide you through the creation of a new document. There are wizards to help you create letters, mailing labels, fax cover sheets, legal pleadings, memos, calendars, and a variety of other documents. You'll really appreciate how quickly you can put together a professionally designed document, ready to send out.

Using Word's Templates and Wizards

Templates are the most amazing time-saver. For those of us who are "graphics challenged," they provide an excellent base from which to create a variety of attractive, professionally designed business documents. You can easily edit them, so you can add your company name, address, and other personal information.

Wizards take the template concept one step further by stepping you through the process of creating documents based on templates. The wizard asks you a series of questions as you work through each step, and at the end, you have a finished document. The nice thing about wizards is that you can show them to new users and have them generating documents with confidence.

Creating a Document from a Template

When you create a new document based on a template, you can save the results just like you would any other document. With fax cover sheets, however, you will probably just print the document and not bother to save it.

To create a new document based on a Word template, follow these steps:

1. Choose **File**, **New**. The New Document task pane appears (see Figure 14.1).

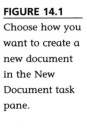

FIGURE 14.1
Choose how you want to create a new document in the New Document task pane.

Create an email message   New blank document

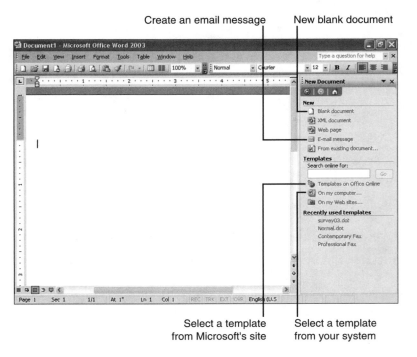

Select a template from Microsoft's site   Select a template from your system

2. For now, click **On my computer**. I'll show you how to get to the templates on Microsoft's site later. The Templates dialog box appears (see Figure 14.2).

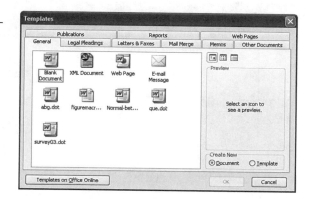

3. Click a tab to display a list of templates and wizards (see Figure 14.3).

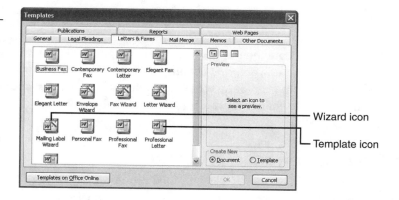

4. Select a template to display a thumbnail in the Preview section.
5. Double-click a template to open it in the document window. Figure 14.4 shows the Contemporary Fax template.

Filling in a document that is based on a template is fairly self-explanatory. Simply click the placeholders and fill in your information. The Contemporary Fax template has instructions in the comment area, but other templates do not include this information.

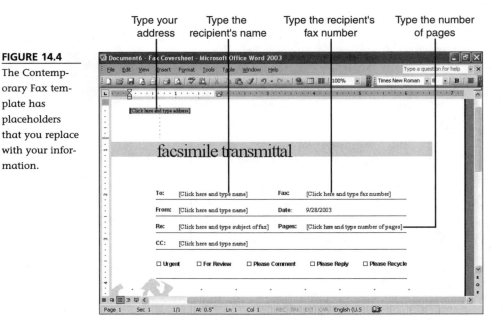

FIGURE 14.4

The Contemporary Fax template has placeholders that you replace with your information.

Many companies create their own set of templates and make them available on the company network so all company documents have a consistent appearance. The nice thing about using company templates is that when an address or phone number changes, the system administrators can modify them and the changes take effect immediately.

Creating a Document from a Wizard

Word has wizards that take you step by step through the creation of a document that you base in a template. Not every template has a wizard, but there are enough to get you started. When you start a wizard for the first time, you may see a brief message about installing the wizard. Some of the wizards are installed with the program, and others are installed by the Microsoft Windows Installer the first time you use them.

To create a new document with a wizard, do the following:

1. Choose **File**, **New**. The New Document task pane appears (refer to Figure 14.1).

2. Click **On my computer**. The Templates dialog box appears (refer to Figure 14.2).

3. Click a tab to display a list of templates and wizards. Figure 14.5 shows the templates and wizards in the Other Documents category.

4. Double-click a wizard to start it. Figure 14.6 shows the Calendar Wizard.

5. Click **Next** to start the wizard. The second page of the wizard appears (see Figure 14.7). Notice how the step you are working on is selected on the left side so you can get an idea of how many steps there are left to complete.

6. Make your selections and choose **Next** until you complete all the steps in the wizard.

7. Choose **Finish** to close the wizard dialog box so you can edit, print, or save the document you just created.

caution

In this case, you're using a template that came with Word Office 2003, so you can be relatively sure that it's safe.

However, if you get a message that alerts you about macros when you are using a template that didn't come from a trusted source, you should choose **Yes** to disable the macros. The template will probably not work correctly; this is to be expected. You should check into the sender of that template and assure yourself that it came from a respected source before you run the macros in it. The reason for extreme caution is that viruses can hide themselves in macros. By disabling the macros in a template, you are protecting your system from marauding macro viruses.

FIGURE 14.5

The Other Documents category has templates and wizards for calendars, agendas, and resumes.

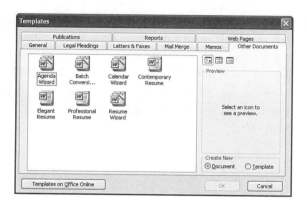

FIGURE 14.6

The Calendar Wizard walks you through the steps to create a monthly calendar.

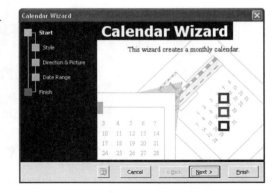

Step 2 is highlighted

FIGURE 14.7

The Calendar Wizard creates monthly calendars in a Jazzy, Boxes & Borders, or Banner style.

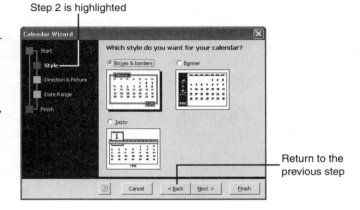

Return to the previous step

Protecting Yourself Against Macro Viruses

Before a template opens, you might see a macros message box explaining that the document contains macros, and if you don't know the source of the document, you might want to disable the macros. A macro is like a small program that you can create to repeat your actions. Some macros are malicious because they contain computer viruses, which can wreak havoc on your computer system. For this reason, it's a good idea to disable macros in documents that do not come from trusted sources.

If you're using one of the templates that shipped with Word, or a template from a trusted source, you can click **No**; you don't want to disable the macros. However, if you are unsure of the source, it's best to click **Yes** to disable the macros. Granted, the results won't be the same, but it's better to be safe than sorry.

You also can take some other steps to increase your level of security:

- Install antivirus software and download the latest virus definitions.

- Set the macro security level to high in Options. Choose **Tools**, **Options**, **Security**, **Macro Security**, **High**.

- Disable the **Trust all installed add-ins and templates** option in Options. Choose **Tools**, **Options**, **Security**, **Macro Security**, **Trusted Publishers**; then uncheck the **Trust all installed add-ins and templates** option.

Downloading Templates from the Office Online Site

Word 2003 includes a great collection of templates that you can use right away. However, you'll be pleased to know that hundreds more are available as a free download from the Microsoft Office site. The templates posted there are in response to user requests, so Microsoft is always adding to the collection. If you have Internet access, you can go to the Office Online site and download these templates from inside Word.

tip

Some of the templates are installed during a typical install, but others are available on the CD if you want to install them as well.

Choose **Start**, **Control Panel**, **Add/Remove Programs**. Scroll down and click the entry for **Microsoft Office 2003** or **Microsoft Office Word 2003** and then choose **Change**. Choose **Add or Remove Features**, **Next**, **Choose advanced customization of applications**, **Next**. Expand **Microsoft Office Word**, expand **Wizards and Templates**, and then select **More Templates and Macros**. Microsoft is always adding templates to its Microsoft Office site, so you can download additional templates from there.

Follow these steps to download additional templates from Office Online:

1. Choose **File**, **New**. The New Document task pane appears.

2. Click **Templates on Office Online**. Word launches your Internet browser and takes you to the Office Online site at Microsoft.com (see Figure 14.8).

3. Type key words to search for a template or scroll down to browse through the categories. The Business Legal Forms category has a Contracts and Agreements subcategory of templates (see Figure 14.9).

Search for a template

FIGURE 14.8

FIGURE 14.8
Hundreds of
templates are
available on the
Office Online
site, and more
are being added.

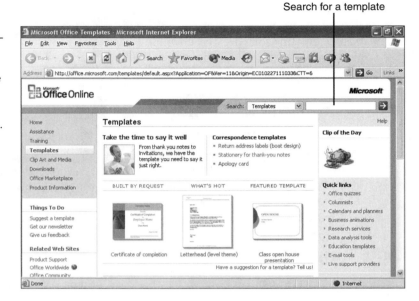

Total number of templates in category   Move to the next page

FIGURE 14.9
The templates
are organized
into categories
to make it easier
to locate just
what you are
looking for.

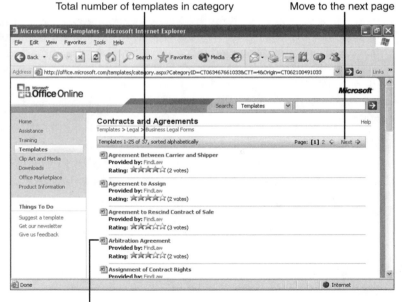

Word template

4. Click the template that you want to download. Detailed information about that template appears on a new page. The download size and the required version of Word are noted at the top, and a preview of the template is displayed below (see Figure 14.10).

Download size   Rating stars

FIGURE 14.10

The preview of the template can help you decide whether you want to download it.

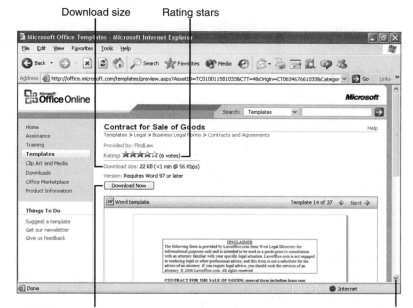

Click here to start the download   Scroll down to see the rest of the template

5. Choose **Download Now** to download the template. You'll have an opportunity to review the End-User License Agreement (EULA), which you will need to accept before the download will commence. You may see a message asking whether you want to install and run "Microsoft Office Template and Media Control." This application controls the downloading process, so choose **Yes**.

6. When the download is complete, choose **Continue**. Word loads the new template and displays a message about downloading and displaying links to additional resources for this template. Choose **Yes** or **No**. The next step is to save the template on your system.

7. Choose **File**, **Save As** so you can save the template to your system.

8. Open the **Save as type** drop-down list and choose **Document Template (*.dot)**.

9. Type a name for the template in the **File name** text box. Word automatically assigns the **.dot** file type.

10. Choose **Save**. The new template will now appear on the General tab of the Templates dialog box.

If you want to check the location of your templates, choose **Tools**, **Options** and then click the **File Locations** tab to display those options (see Figure 14.11). Take note of the path for the user templates.

FIGURE 14.11

The location of the templates is shown in the File Locations tab of the Options dialog box.

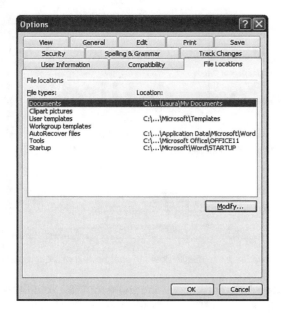

Creating New Templates

There are several ways to create a new template. You can use an existing template as a starting point, make the necessary changes, and then save the result as a new template. You can also convert an existing document into a template. This is the most popular method because you surely have form documents that you use over and over again. Last, but not least, you can start from scratch.

Creating a Template from Another Template

You can revise an existing template and then save your changes as a new template. You can use as your starting point one of your own templates or one of the templates that comes with Word, and then just make the necessary adjustments.

To create a new template from another template, do the following:

1. Choose **File**, **New**. The New Document task pane appears.
2. In the Templates section of the task pane, click **On my computer**. The Templates dialog box appears (refer to Figure 14.2).
3. Select the template that you want to start with.
4. Click **Template** in the Create New section.
5. Click **OK** to open the template for editing.
6. In the document window, make the necessary changes to the text and formatting.
7. When you are finished, choose **File**, **Save As**.
8. Type a new name for the template in the **File name** text box. You might want to choose a name that indicates you have personalized the template.
9. Choose **Save**.

You may have noticed that when you saved the new template, the Template folder was already open in the Save As dialog box, and **Document Template (*.dot)** was already selected in the **Save as type** box.

Converting an Existing Document to a Template

The most popular method for creating a template is to use an existing document. You're bound to have a handful of form documents that you use over and over. Fax cover sheets come to mind, but so do supply requests, time sheets, network maintenance bulletins, expense reports, newsletters, equipment checkout sheets, and so on.

To create a template from an existing document, follow these steps:

1. Open the document that you want to use as a starting point for the new template.
2. Remove any information that you do not want to appear in documents that are based on this template. In other words, alter the document so it is more "generic" and can be used to create new documents.
3. Choose **File**, **Save As** so you can save the template to your system.
4. In the **Save as type** drop-down list, choose **Document Template (*.dot)**.
5. Type a name for the new template in the **File name** text box.
6. Choose **Save**. The new template will now appear on the General tab of the Templates dialog box.

Creating a Template from Scratch

Creating a template from scratch is definitely a last resort. The other two options are much faster. Still, in some cases, starting from a blank page is more straightforward.

Follow these steps to create a template from scratch:

1. From a blank document, type in the text and set up the necessary formatting.

2. Choose **File**, **Save As** so you can save the template to your system.

3. In the **Save as type** drop-down list, choose **Document Template (*.dot).**

4. Type a name for the new template in the **File name** text box.

5. Choose **Save**. The new template will now appear on the General tab of the Templates dialog box.

> **tip**
>
> If you want to save a template so it appears under a tab other than the General tab, create a subfolder under the Templates folder and save the template there. The name of the subfolder will be the name of the new tab.

Customizing the Default Template

Every document that you create from a blank document is based on the default template. Word's default template is used when you create a document from scratch. If you want 1.25-inch margins, specific tab settings, and Century Schoolbook 12 point, you can make these changes to the default template so that they are in place for all new documents.

A word of caution: Make sure that you add only the elements that should be applied to all new documents. Otherwise, you defeat the time-saving purpose of using templates by forcing yourself to remove the unnecessary elements from all new documents.

Making a Backup Copy of the Default Template

Before you get started, make a backup copy of your default template. This step is very important. If you make unpleasant changes to your default template, the fastest way to recover is to revert to a backup copy.

To make a backup copy of the default template, follow these steps:

1. Choose **File**, **Open** to display the Open dialog box.

2. In the **Save as type** drop-down list, choose **Document Template (*.dot).** A list of the templates on your system appears in the window.

3. Right-click **Normal.dot** and choose **Copy**.

4. Right-click in the file list and choose **Paste**. The new file Copy of Normal.dot appears in the list. This is your backup copy.

Now, if you decide that you want to discard the changes you made to the default template, repeat steps 1 and 2 to display the list of templates. Right-click **Normal.dot** and choose **Delete**. Right-click **Copy of Normal.dot** and choose **Rename**. Edit the filename down to Normal.dot and press **Enter**.

Editing the Default Template

There are several ways to edit the default template. I've picked what I think is the simplest method to show you here.

Follow these steps to edit the default template:

1. Click the New Blank Document icon, or choose **File**, **New** and then select **Blank Document** from the New Document task pane.

2. Choose **Format**, **Styles and Formatting**.

3. In the Styles and Formatting task pane, you'll see that the Normal style is selected (see Figure 14.12).

FIGURE 14.12

The Styles and Formatting task pane shows a list of available styles for the document.

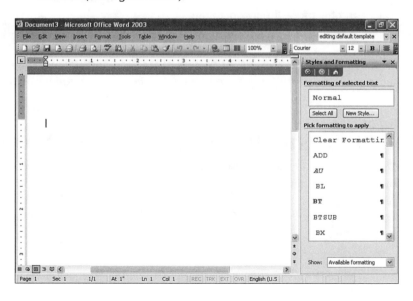

4. Move the mouse pointer over the top box (it has "Normal" in it). A drop-down arrow should appear.

5. Click the drop-down list arrow and choose **Modify**. The Modify Style dialog box appears (see Figure 14.13).

FIGURE 14.13

FIGURE 14.13

Use the controls in the Modify Style dialog box to make changes to a style.

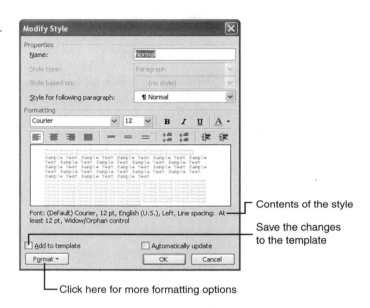

Contents of the style

Save the changes to the template

Click here for more formatting options

6. Using the options in the dialog box, make whatever changes you want to be in effect for all new documents.

7. Select **Add to template** and then click **OK**.

That's it! When you chose **Add to template**, you added your changes to the default template because that is the template you used to create the blank document. You can use this little trick on the other templates too, not just the default template.

Transferring Items to Templates and Documents

You may not realize it, but if you create AutoText entries, styles, macros, or custom toolbars, these items are stored in the template. You can copy these items from a template into another template or into a document, so if you have a guru in your office, you can take advantage of his or her expertise by transferring the guru's AutoText entries, macros, styles, and toolbars to your template(s) or document(s).

To copy items to another document or template, follow these steps:

1. Choose **Tools, Templates and Add-Ins**.

2. Click **Organizer** to display the Organizer dialog box (see Figure 14.14).

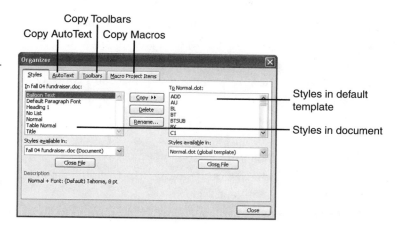

FIGURE 14.14

Use the Organizer to transfer customized items to other templates and documents.

3. Click the tab that corresponds to the item you want to transfer.

4. To copy items from a different template or document, click **Close File** to close the active document; then click **Open File** and select the template or document that you want.

5. Select the items that you want to copy in either list and then choose **Copy**. You can copy from the list on the left to the list on the right, or vice versa. It all depends on what you select first.

6. Choose **Close** when you are finished.

tip

Let's say you started by creating a document with the default template, but then you decide that you want to use some styles from another template. You do this by attaching another template to the document. Choose **Tools, Templates and Add-Ins**. Click the **Templates** tab and then choose **Attach**. Select the template you want. Choose **Open** and then click **OK**.

THE ABSOLUTE MINIMUM

After reading this chapter, you now know how to

- Convert existing "form" documents, such as invoices, expense reports, and company memos, into templates that you can use over and over again.
- Be especially cautious when opening templates from other sources because templates can contain macros.
- Download additional templates from Microsoft's Office Online site and add them to the list of templates in the Templates dialog box.
- Convert a document into a template.
- Edit any Word template so that you can add your company logo or any other customization to personalize them for your business.
- Edit and adjust the default template, which contains all the initial settings for new documents, for your preferences.
- Store customized elements such as macros, custom toolbars, styles, and AutoText entries in a document or template and transfer those items to a different document or template.

In the next chapter, you'll learn how to collaborate with co-workers and associates on documents.

IN THIS CHAPTER

- Working through a document, making revisions and adding explanatory comments.

- Reviewing a document and accepting or rejecting revisions.

- Customizing the display of revision marks and comment balloons.

- Comparing documents to automatically insert revision marks or to view the documents side by side.

- Taking advantage of the Word features that protect shared documents.

- Retaining previous versions of a file so you can revert to a previous copy.

15

COLLABORATING ON DOCUMENTS

One of the greatest advantages that electronic mail has brought to the table is the ability to share documents with people outside your local network. The editors of this book are scattered all over the United States, but you would never know it. We can send files to each other, make changes, and turn them around in a matter of minutes.

This is a great concept, after you work out ways to keep track of what changes are made and by whom. This is where Word's collaboration tools come into play. For example, the Track Changes feature makes it possible to show every change that a reviewer makes to a document. Protecting a document from unauthorized changes is another method to safely share information. When problems do arise, the Versions feature provides a safety net by allowing you to revert to a previous copy of the document.

Tracking Document Revisions

Doesn't it seem as though everyone has an email address? It does to me. I can collaborate on a writing project with people all over the world. All I have to do is attach a file to an email message and distribute it. It's when I have a handful of people working on the same document that keeping track of revisions can become a nightmare.

Thank goodness for the Track Changes feature. You use it to mark any revisions that are made to a document, whether the revision is an added word, a deleted sentence, or a revised phrase. Track Changes is used by reviewers and the author, or "owner," of the document. First, the author creates a document, turns on revision marks, and then sends the document to the reviewer(s). The reviewer inserts revisions and suggestions. Then, you (as the author) use the Track Changes feature to locate every revision, no matter how small. Each reviewer has a unique color, so revisions can be traced back to the person who made it. You can then accept or reject each individual change so you can retain control of the document.

Turning on Track Changes

If you want to make sure that any revisions are marked in a document you are sending out for review, turn on Track Changes and then save the document. Then, when the reviewer opens the document, Track Changes is automatically turned on, so all the reviewer's revisions and suggestions are clearly marked.

As the document's author, you need to understand how to toggle the Track Changes feature on and off so you can make changes that do not need to be reviewed by others.

To turn on Track Changes, follow these steps:

1. Choose **Tools**, **Track Changes** (**Ctrl+Shift+E**). The Reviewing toolbar is added to the top of the screen (see Figure 15.1).

2. Choose one of the following options to toggle the Track Changes feature on and off:

   ■ Press **Ctrl+Shift+E**.

   ■ Double-click the **TRK** indicator on the status bar.

> **tip**
>
> Word has a built-in feature that lets you email a document for review. To use this feature, choose **File**, **Send To: Mail Recipient (for Review)**. There are a lot of benefits to doing it this way. For one, you can create a list of recipients and have the file emailed to each recipient in that order. When a reviewer is finished with the file, it is sent to the next reviewer on the list. Something else: When you send a file out for review, the Reviewing toolbar is displayed and Track Changes is automatically turned on.

■ Click the **Track Changes** button on the Reviewing toolbar.

Reviewing toolbar   Track Changes button

Track Changes indicator

Marking Revisions

By default, each reviewer's changes show up in a different color. How does Word keep track of different reviewers? By looking at the user information in the User Information tab of the Options dialog box (choose **Tools**, **Options**). This informa-tion is shared by all the Office programs, so the changes you make to these settings will be reflected in other programs.

If two people share the same computer, they each need to update the user informa-tion when they start to work in Word so that their revision marks appear in different colors. Also, if you are sending the document out, you might want to add a note to remind reviewers to add this information before they start their review. Otherwise, you'll see the comments, but you won't know who they are from.

To mark revisions in a document, insert and delete text just as you would any other document. Inserted text appears in a different color. In Normal view, deleted text is shown in strikethrough (a line through the text). In the other views, deleted text is pulled into a balloon in the margin. Formatting changes are also flagged, and details are given in the balloon. If you hover the mouse pointer over a change, a ScreenTip appears with the reviewer's name, the date and time the change was made, and what the change was (see Figure 15.2).

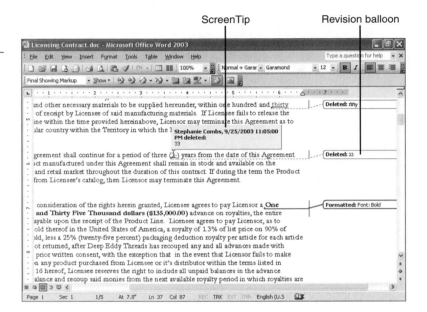

You can customize the color or effect that Word uses for revision marks. Choose **Tools**, **Options** and then click the **Track Changes** tab. The Track Changes tab has controls for insertions, deletions, and format changes (see Figure 15.3). You can also play around with the line that appears in the margin when a change has been made (changed lines).

Using the drop-down lists, make the necessary adjustments to the settings for the Markup and Balloons sections. Click **OK** when you're finished.

The revision balloons are a new feature in Word 2003. If you don't see them, first make sure you are viewing the document in Print Layout, Web Layout, or Reading Layout view; then adjust your zoom setting so you can view the margins on either side of the page.

FIGURE 15.3

The Track
Changes tab of
the Options dia-
log box controls
the appearance
of revision
marks.

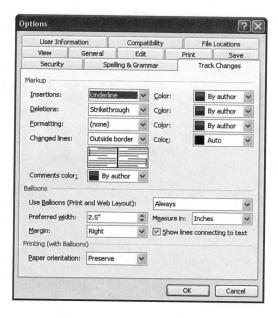

Adding Comments with a Revision

When multiple people work on the same document, it's common to include a comment to
explain a revision, so the author understands
why the change was suggested. Comments can
also be used to pose a question or make a sugges-
tion for a revision, without actually making the
revision in the text.

Comments complement the revision balloons that
you saw in Figure 15.2. They rest on top of them,
so you can easily read the comment and review
the revision. As you review a document and
accept or reject the changes, you can delete the
comments after you read them.

A line from the revision balloon points to the
location in the text where the change took place.
You can create a comment that points to a location in the text so the reader knows what is being
commented on.

caution

Here's a situation that
won't amuse you when it
happens: Say you are
reviewing a document,
and all of the sudden,
your changes disappear. The revision
marks are gone, and your changes
look just like regular text. What
happened?

You accidentally turned off the view
of the revision balloons and
comments. Choose **View**, **Markup**
to display these elements again.

Like revision balloons, comment balloons have different colors for different reviewers. In fact, your comment balloon is the same color as your revision balloon. Pretty nifty if you ask me.

To insert a comment, follow these steps:

1. Select the text or item that you want to comment on.

2. Choose **Insert**, **Comment** or click the **Insert Comment** button on the Reviewing toolbar. Word inserts an empty comment on top of the revision balloons. Your user initials are shown with the comment number (see Figure 15.4, shown in Print Layout).

3. Type the text of your comment. Keep it short and sweet.

4. When you're finished, click in the document text to move out of the comment.

Use the following techniques to work with comments:

- Move the mouse pointer over a comment to display a ToolTip with the name of the reviewer and the date and time the comment was inserted.

- To edit one of your comments, click in the comment and make your changes, or in Normal view, click the **Reviewing Pane** button to open the Reviewing pane, locate the comment you want to edit, and make your changes. You aren't allowed to revise any else's comments.

- To respond to a comment, click in the comment you want to respond to and then create a new comment. Type your comment in the new comment balloon or in the Reviewing pane.

- If you have a sound card and a microphone, you can record a voice message. On the Reviewing toolbar, click the **Insert Voice** button to use this feature. Your message is saved as a sound object in the comment. If you don't see the **Insert Voice** button on the Reviewing toolbar, you can add it yourself. Click the **Toolbar Options** button on the right side of the toolbar. Choose **Add or Remove Buttons**, **Reviewing**. Click the **Insert Voice** button to place a check mark next to the button and add it to your Reviewing toolbar.

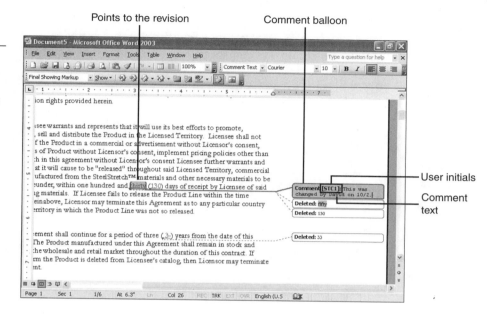

FIGURE 15.4

Comments
aren't designed
for long pas-
sages of text, so
try to be brief.

User initials

Comment
text

Reviewing a Document

As the document's author, you have complete control over which revisions are made
and which are discarded. As you review a document, each revision is highlighted.
You can accept or reject each change individually, or you can accept or reject all the
changes at once.

Furthermore, you can decide which revisions you want to look at. You might decide
to ignore the formatting changes so you can focus on the insertions and deletions.
Or you might want to review the comments from one particular reviewer. Remember,
as you work through a document, you can delete the comments after you read them.

To review a document and incorporate revisions, follow these steps:

1. Open the document with the revisions.

2. Right-click a toolbar and select **Reviewing**. Use the following buttons on the
   Reviewing toolbar to work through the document:

   - **Previous**—Click to move to the previous revision.

   - **Next**—Click to move to the next revision. Clicking this button starts the
     review process.

- **Accept Change**—Click the arrow to open a list of options (see Figure 15.5). Select to accept the current change, all visible changes, or all changes in the document.

FIGURE 15.5

Select to accept the selected change or to accept all the changes in the document without any further confirmation.

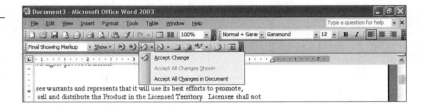

- **Reject Change/Delete Comment**—Click the arrow to open a list of options (see Figure 15.6). Select to reject the current change, all visible changes, or all changes in the document. Likewise, you can opt to delete all the visible comments or all the comments in a document.

FIGURE 15.6

The Reject Changes/Delete Comment button has a dual purpose: to reject revisions and to delete all comments.

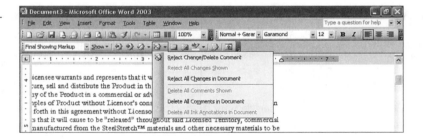

Here is another trick you should know about: Word has a Reviewing pane that you can use as an alternative to reading through the text. The Reviewing pane shows you all the revisions and comments in a separate window underneath the document window. You can accept or reject revisions and review and delete comments in the Reviewing pane.

To display the Reviewing pane, do the following:

1. Click the **Reviewing Pane** button on the Reviewing toolbar to open the Reviewing pane (see Figure 15.7).

caution

Be careful with the **Accept All Changes in Document** and **Reject All Changes in Document** options because you won't have an opportunity to review each change before you accept or reject it.

2. Scroll through the Reviewing pane to view the rest of the revisions and comments. Use the buttons on the Reviewing toolbar to accept or reject revisions.

Customizing the Display of Revisions and Comments

Something else that really comes in handy when you have a number of reviewers working on the same document is being able to customize the display of revisions and comments. You can elect to show only those revisions that were made by a particular reviewer so you can focus on one reviewer at a time. You can also select which revision marks you want displayed, so if you want to look only at comments, you can turn off everything else.

Reviewing pane   Reviewing pane button

The Reviewing pane gives you a larger workspace to work in.

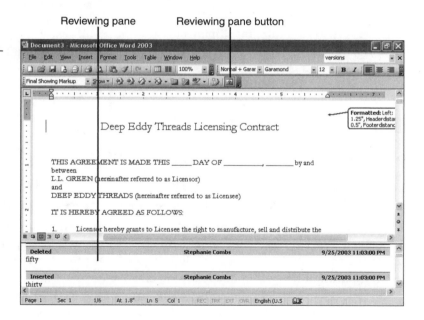

To show only those changes by a certain reviewer, do the following:

1. On the Reviewing toolbar, click the **Show** button. This opens a drop-down list of options (see Figure 15.8).

2. Select **Reviewers** to open a list of reviewers for this document.

FIGURE 15.8

The options on the Show button control what you see onscreen when you review a document.

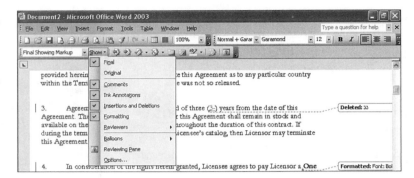

3. Clear all the check boxes except the one next to the reviewer that you want to concentrate on.

When you're ready to review revisions and comments made by the other reviewers, choose **All Reviewers** from the list of reviewers.

Another way to customize the display of a revised document is to limit what types of revisions you see. You might decide to focus only on the insertions and deletions so you can tackle the formatting later.

To remove a revision element from the display, clear the check mark next to the option in the **Show** drop-down list. For example, if you want to view only the insertions and deletions, clear the check marks next to **Comments**, **Ink Annotations** (for Tablet PCs), and **Formatting**.

> **tip**
>
> You can print a document with the revision and comment balloons included so you can review it later. Or you can just print a list of the changes (the output looks just like the Reviewing pane). In the Print dialog box (**File**, **Print**), select **Document showing markup** to print everything together, or **List of markup** to print only the changes, in the **Print what** drop-down list.

How would you like to be able to preview a revised document to see how things will look if you accept or reject the changes? You can, without disturbing the revisions at all. In the corner of the Reviewing toolbar, click the **Display for Review** drop-down list arrow. Choose from the following options:

- **Final Showing Markup**—Shows deleted text in the balloons, and the inserted text and formatting changes are shown embedded in the document text.

- **Final**—Displays the document as it would look if you accepted all the changes.

- **Original Showing Markup**—Shows the inserted text and formatting changes in the balloons. The deleted text stays embedded in the document text or in the document.

- **Original**—Displays your original document, before you accept or reject any changes.

Comparing Documents

Despite all the advantages that electronic file transfers can bring, you might be reluctant to distribute your documents electronically because of the possibility of accidental (or intentional) changes being made to the text. Even if you instruct someone to review the document using Track Changes, there is no guarantee that he or she will do it. Only by comparing the reviewed document to the original can you be sure that no unauthorized changes were made.

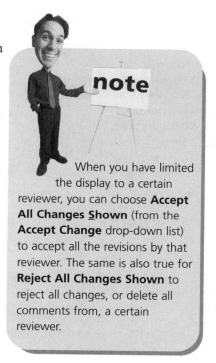

note

When you have limited the display to a certain reviewer, you can choose **Accept All Changes Shown** (from the **Accept Change** drop-down list) to accept all the revisions by that reviewer. The same is also true for **Reject All Changes Shown** to reject all changes, or delete all comments from, a certain reviewer.

Using the Compare and Merge Feature

The Compare and Merge Documents feature compares two copies of a document and inserts revision marks for you. If text has been added, it is displayed in red; if text has been deleted, it is moved into a revision balloon.

Follow these steps to compare and merge two documents:

1. Open the original document.

2. Choose **Tools**, **Compare and Merge Documents**. The Compare and Merge Documents dialog box appears (see Figure 15.9).

3. Locate and select the file with the revisions (or suspected revisions) in the list and then choose **Merge**.

4. You can now accept or reject the changes and then save the file.

By default, Word merges the two documents into a new document so you can work in it independently of your original. You may opt to save this new document, if you want to keep a record of the revisions.

FIGURE 15.9

Open the origi-
nal file first and
then select the
file that may
have been
changed in the
Compare and
Merge
Documents dia-
log box.

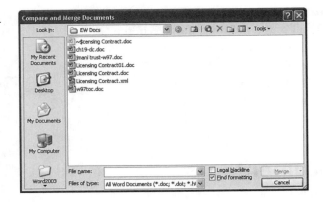

Comparing Documents Side by Side

Some documents are easier to review if you can look at them side by side. If you
have tables in your document, for example, you can see the changes more easily if
you compare them next to each other rather than having revision marks inserted.
For those situations in which you don't want to merge revisions into a single document, you can compare the two documents side by side.

To view two documents side by side, follow these steps:

1. Open the two documents.

2. Choose **Window**, **Compare Side by Side**. Word places the two document
   windows side by side (see Figure 15.10).

FIGURE 15.10

Sometimes it is
easier to review
two documents
if you can look
at them side by
side.

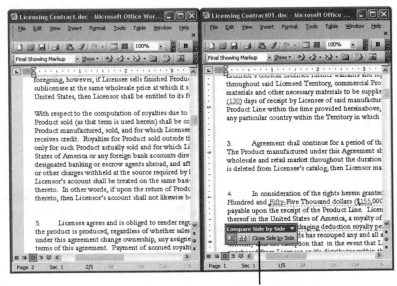

Compare Side by Side toolbar

3. The **Compare Side by Side** toolbar has two buttons that enable you to perform the following actions:

- **Synchronous Scrolling**—Turn on this option if you want to scroll through both documents at the same time. Click the button again to turn it back off.

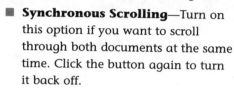

caution

The Compare and Merge Documents feature is designed to compare two documents in Word format. If you try to compare documents in two different formats, you will get unpredictable results.

- **Reset Window Position**—Click this button to reset the window positions back to where they were when you first started comparing documents.

4. Click the **Close Side by Side** button when you're finished with the documents.

Protecting Documents

Comparing documents and turning on Track Changes are two ways to make sure no one makes changes to your file without your consent. There are also other ways to protect your documents against unauthorized revisions.

Setting the Document as Read-Only

You can configure a document so it can be viewed, but not edited or printed. This type of protection is perfect for documents that you are posting on a company network for general use.

To open the document as read-only, do the following:

1. Open the document that you want to protect.

2. Choose **Tools**, **Protect Document** to display the Protect Document task pane (see Figure 15.11).

3. Select the **Allow only this type of editing in the document** check box. The drop-down list is now available.

4. Open the drop-down list and select **No changes (Read only)**.

5. Select **Yes, Start Enforcing Protection**. The Start Enforcing Protection dialog box appears (see Figure 15.12).

Enable this check box

FIGURE 15.11

The Protect Document task pane contains options that limit a reviewer's editing and formatting privileges.

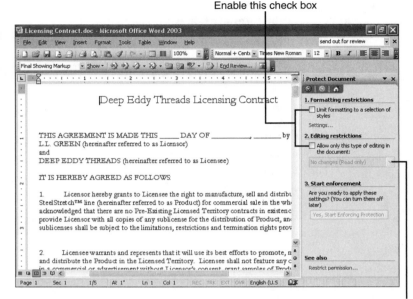

Select from this drop-down list

FIGURE 15.12

Set an optional password in the Start Enforcing Protection dialog box.

6. (Optional) Type a password in the **Enter new password (optional)** box and then confirm the password. To protect a document without a password, leave the password fields blank.

7. Click **OK** to clear the Start Enforcing Protection dialog box.

Allowing Only Tracked Changes or Comments

Say you are involved in a project with several other people, so you want to give them the right to add tracked changes and/or comments, but nothing else. You can set the document protection to allow only tracked changes or to only allow comments.

To allow reviewers to insert comments or tracked changes only, follow these steps:

1. Open the document that you want to protect.
2. Choose **Tools**, **Protect Document** to display the Protect Document task pane (refer to Figure 15.11).
3. Select the **Allow only this type of editing in the document** check box. The drop-down list is now available.
4. Open the drop-down list and select **Tracked changes**.
5. Select **Yes, Start Enforcing Protection**. The Start Enforcing Protection dialog box appears (refer to Figure 15.12).
6. (Optional) Type a password in the **Enter new password (optional)** box and then confirm the password. To protect a document without a password, leave the password fields blank.
7. Click **OK** to clear the Start Enforcing Protection dialog box.

To allow reviewers to insert only comments, do the following:

1. Open the document that you want to protect.
2. Choose **Tools**, **Protect Document** to display the Protect Document task pane (refer to Figure 15.11).
3. Select the **Allow only this type of editing in the document** check box. The drop-down list is now available.
4. Open the drop-down list and select **Comments**.
5. Select **Yes, Start Enforcing Protection**. The Start Enforcing Protection dialog box appears (refer to Figure 15.12).
6. (Optional) Type a password in the **Enter new password (optional)** box and then confirm the password. To protect a document without a password, leave the password fields blank.
7. Click **OK** to clear the Start Enforcing Protection dialog box.

When you prevent any changes to a document by setting it up as read-only, or if you specify that only comments can be inserted, you're not limited to an "all or nothing" assignment. Word lets you designate parts of the document as unrestricted.

1. Protect the entire document.
2. Go back and select the areas that you want to allow access to. When you select **No changes (Read only)** or **Comments**, you'll see an Exceptions section.

3. Click **More users** and then enter the usernames, separated by semicolons. If you want all users to have access, select **Everyone**.

4. Click **OK** and then enable the check boxes next to the names of the reviewers that you want to give editing privileges to. Continue selecting sections of the document and assigning users who can edit those sections.

5. Click **Yes, Start Enforcing Protection** when you're done.

6. Type a password in the **Enter new password (optional)** box and then confirm the password. To protect a document without a password, leave the password fields blank.

7. Click **OK**.

Limiting the Available Styles

In another situation, you might want to restrict formatting to a handful of styles to ensure that your company's standards are enforced.

To limit the number of styles available to a reviewer, follow these steps:

1. Open the document that you want to protect.

2. Choose **Tools**, **Protect Document** to display the Protect Document task pane.

3. Select the **Limit formatting to a selection of styles** check box.

4. Click **Settings** to display the Formatting Restrictions dialog box (see Figure 15.13).

FIGURE 15.13
Select only those styles that you want reviewers to use in the Formatting Restrictions dialog box.

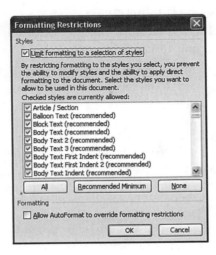

5. Remove check marks next to the styles you do not want to make available.

6. Add check marks next to the styles that you want to allow access to.

7. Click **OK**.

8. Select **Yes, Start Enforcing Protection**. The Start Enforcing Protection dialog box appears.

9. (Optional) Type a password in the **Enter new password (optional)** box and then confirm the password. To protect a document without a password, leave the password fields blank.

10. Click **OK** to clear the Start Enforcing Protection dialog box.

The **Your permissions** section appears in the Protect Document task pane (see Figure 15.14). This section contains buttons to help you locate the regions you are allowed to edit. You can also view the styles you can use.

FIGURE 15.14
When a document has protected regions, you'll see a Your permissions pane to help you locate the areas you can edit.

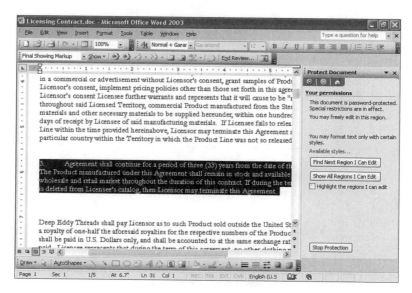

Protecting Documents with Passwords

Some people prefer to use the password approach because it offers a higher level of security. You can create a password to open a document and a password to modify a document. They are independent of each other, so you can have one or both set up.

Follow these steps to create a password for a document:

1. Open the document.

2. Choose **Tools**, **Options** to display the Options dialog box.

3. Click the **Security** tab to display those options (see Figure 15.15).

FIGURE 15.15

Create pass-words to open and modify doc-uments in the Security tab of the Options dia-log box.

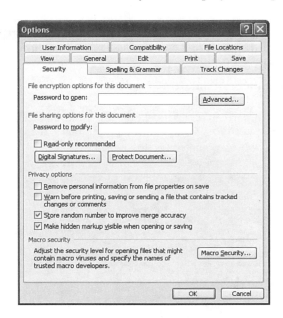

4. Choose from the following:

   - In the **Password to open box**, type a password and then click **OK**. In the **Reenter password to open** box, type the password again and then click **OK**.

   - In the **Password to modify** box, type a password and then click **OK**. In the **Reenter password to mod-ify** box, type the password again and then click **OK**.

caution

If you are having prob-lems opening a password-protected file, remember that pass-words are case sensitive. Make sure Caps Lock isn't on and try again. On the other hand, if you think that Caps Lock may have been turned on when you created the password, try typing it in all caps.

Protecting Documents with Information Rights Management

If you have Microsoft Office Professional Edition 2003 or Microsoft Office Word 2003, you can take advantage of the new Information Rights Management (IRM) features that are built into the new release. Information Rights Management allows you to create documents and then limit the access by assigning a set of permissions. There are three access levels:

- **Read**—Users with Read access can view a document, but they cannot edit, print, or copy it.
- **Change**—Users with Change access can view, edit, and save changes to a document, but they cannot print it.
- **Full Control**—Users with Full Control access can do anything that the author can do.

Users who receive documents with restricted permission must have Office 2003 (or later) on their computers; otherwise, they will not be able to open the documents. Microsoft offers a free IRM add-on program that works with Internet Explorer.

After you've opened a restricted document, you can view the permissions you have for the document in the Shared Workspace task pane. Simply click the **Status** tab and then click the **View my permission** link.

For more information on Information Rights Management, consult the Microsoft Office Word 2003 help topics, or consider picking up a copy of Que Publishing's *Special Edition Using Microsoft Office Word 2003* by Bill Camarda (ISBN: 0-7897-2958-X).

Retaining Previous Versions of a File

When several individuals are working on the same document, things can get a little confusing. Someone can get in a hurry and accidentally incorporate changes to the wrong file, or worse, delete text from the wrong document. Of course, you won't realize this until you've already saved your changes. That's when panic sets in as you frantically start searching your system for a clean copy.

The Versions feature can eliminate your panic and streamline the process of maintaining multiple copies of a document, within the same file. Here's how it works: You can manually save a copy of a file after you've made changes, or you can have Word automatically save a version of the document every time the file is closed. Law offices use this option frequently to keep a record of who made changes and when. The document's author then has the choice of versions to work from.

To save the current version of the document, follow these steps:

1. Choose **File**, **Versions** to open the Versions dialog box (see Figure 15.16).

2. Choose **Save Now** to open the Save Version dialog box (see Figure 15.17).

3. (Optional) Type a short description or explanation in the **Comments on version** text box.

4. Click **OK** to save the current version of the document.

tip

Enabling the Versions feature can result in some very large documents, so keep that in mind when you start using it on documents that you want to send via email.

FIGURE 15.16

Save a current version of the document in the Versions dialog box.

FIGURE 15.17

You can enter a short description or explanation for the version you are saving in the Save Version dialog box.

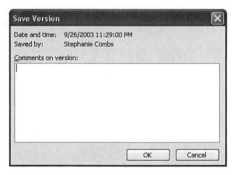

To automatically save a document on close, do the following:

1. Choose **File**, **Versions** to open the Versions dialog box.

2. Enable the **Automatically save a version on close** check box.

3. Choose **Close**.

To open a specific version of a document, follow these steps:

1. Choose **File**, **Versions** to open the Versions dialog box.

2. Select one of the versions in the list (see Figure 15.18).

3. To see the complete text of the comments for the selected version, click **View Comments**.

4. Choose **Open** to open that version for review.

tip

If, at some point, you want to be able to compare two versions of a document, you can switch to any one of the versions and save it as a separate file. Then you can compare the saved version file to the current version file and mark the revisions.

FIGURE 15.18
Each version of a document is listed in the Versions dialog box.

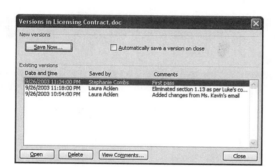

caution

If you save your document as a Web page, you'll lose all your version information. To preserve that information, save one copy of the document in Word format and then save another copy as a Web page.

THE ABSOLUTE MINIMUM

After reading this chapter, you now know how to

- Activate the Track Changes feature so all revisions are marked and identified.
- Review a document, adding revision marks and including explanations for your changes in comments.
- Go through a reviewed document to accept or reject the reviewer's suggestions and changes.
- Limit the number of items displayed onscreen so you can focus on a particular reviewer or a type of revision.
- Compare two documents and let Word automatically insert the revision marks for any changes.
- Compare documents side by side so you can locate changes without adding revision marks to the documents.
- Use Word's Document Protect features to prevent others from accidentally changing text and formatting.
- Use the Versions feature to retain previous versions of a document, so you can go back to a previous version or save a previous version to compare two copies of the file.

In the next chapter, you'll learn how to create and play macros to automate repetitive tasks. You'll have a chance to create two sample macros that you can use right away.

IN THIS CHAPTER

- Learning what a macro is and how it can save you time.

- Running macros that someone else has written.

- Creating your own macros for repetitive tasks.

- Creating two sample macros that you can use right away.

- Assigning macros to shortcut keys, toolbars, and menus.

- Protecting your system against macro viruses.

16

CREATING AND RUNNING MACROS

Macros are different from the other automation features in Word. The macro language is powerful. With a few exceptions, anything you can do in a document can be done in a macro. The nice thing about macros is that you don't have to learn the macro language to write your own macros.

If you think that macros are only for "techies," think again. They can be as simple as typing an address block or inserting a header. All you have to do is record your steps once. After that, you just run the macro.

What Is a Macro?

Stop and think for a minute. How much of your time is spent doing repetitive tasks? Do you type company name and address information all day long? Do you often insert page numbers at the bottom of every page? Do you repeat the same series of steps over and over again, setting up formatting for your documents? Are you responsible for maintaining a consistent appearance in company documents? If you answered "yes" to any of these questions, you will *love* the Macro feature.

A macro can be created to perform a series of steps. Those steps might take you several minutes to complete manually, but when you run the macro, the process takes only seconds. And equally important, every time you run the macro, the exact same steps are done. This means that the results are consistent and accurate.

Let me use a popular analogy to explain how a macro works. A camcorder records video and sound on a videotape, or memory card. You can turn on the recorder, record the video, and then turn off the recorder. The video that you recorded is there for you to access when you play back the tape. The same is true for creating a macro, except instead of recording video, you record actions taken on a document. You turn on the Macro Recorder, record your actions, and then turn off the Macro Recorder. Whatever you do between turning on the Macro Recorder and turning it back off is recorded in a macro.

Don't skip this chapter because you think only techies write macros. A macro can be simple: type a signature block, insert a page number, change to a different font, and so on. A macro can also be complex. Some macros ask questions and assemble documents based on the answers.

If you're lucky, your company maintains a standard set of macros for everyone's use, or you have some very good friends who are willing to share theirs. If this is the case, all you need to know is how to run their macros; so let's start there. I'll explain how to create your own macros later in the chapter.

Running Macros

Macros can be stored in a document or a template, so if someone is sharing macros, you'll get them through one of these files. If you are on a network, templates can be stored in a specific folder on the network. Standalone systems also have a template folder where you can save the template files. The template locations are specified in the Options dialog box. Choose **Tools**, **Options** and then click the **File Locations** tab. You will see locations for the user templates and workgroup templates. The workgroup templates folder is generally used as a method for gaining access to macros stored on a network. Your network administrator will be able to give you the location of the folder.

Before you run a macro, be sure that everything is in place first. If you are running a macro to add page numbers to a document, for example, you need to open the document first. Likewise, if the macro acts on selected text, select the text before you run the macro. Finally, if the macro creates a new document, you should start in a blank document.

To run a macro, follow these steps:

1. Choose **Tools**, **Macro**, **Macros** (**Alt+F8**) to open the Macros dialog box (see Figure 16.1).

Double-click a macro file to run it

FIGURE 16.1
In the Macros dialog box, you can select a macro to run or edit.

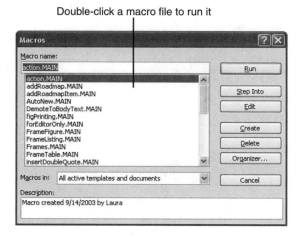

2. Double-click a macro, or select it and click **Run**.

Creating Macros

When you create your first macro, try to remember that you don't have to do it perfectly the first time. You can keep recording the macro over and over until you get it right.

Before you get started, grab a pen and jot down a rough sequence of events you need to go through so that you don't forget anything. For example, if you want to create a macro to insert a signature block, write down the closing that you prefer, make a note about the number of blank lines you want to allow room for a signature, and then jot down all the elements you want to include beneath the written signature.

You can record a macro in a blank document or an existing document. The next time you need to perform a certain series of steps, you can create your macro and accomplish your task at the same time, making your efforts more efficient.

To record a macro, do the following:

1. Choose **Tools**, **Macro**, **Record New Macro**. The Record Macro dialog box appears (see Figure 16.2).

note

If you store your macro in the `normal.dot` template file, it will be available to all new documents. If you only want to save the new macro with the current document, select it from the **Store macro in** list.

FIGURE 16.2

Type a name and select a location for the new macro in the Record Macro dialog box.

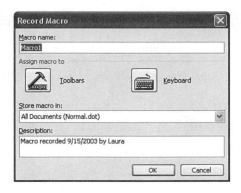

2. Type a name for the macro in the **Macro name** text box.

3. Select a location for your macro from the **Store macro in** drop-down list.

4. Click **OK**. The Stop Recording toolbar is displayed as a small palette, and the mouse pointer now has a tape icon attached to it (see Figure 16.3). That's the sign that you're currently recording a macro.

Stop Record toolbar

FIGURE 16.3
The tape icon
on the mouse
pointer shows
you that the
macro recorder
is on.

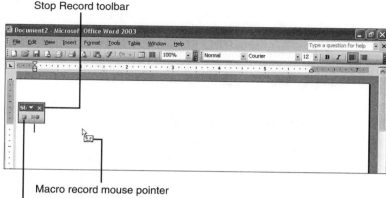

Macro record mouse pointer

Click here to stop recording

5. Type the text, use the menus and tool-bars, go through the dialog boxes, and make your selections. The macro records all your actions, whether you use the keyboard or the mouse. The only exception is that you have to use the keyboard to select text and to position the insertion point in the document window.

6. When you're finished, click the **Stop Recording** button. The Stop Recording toolbar disappears, and you are returned to a normal document window. The actions you took while you created the macro have been performed on the document, so you might or might not want to save those changes.

tip

You can easily pause recording a macro so you can type something in or perform some action that you don't want recorded. Simply click the **Pause Recording** button (on the Stop Recording toolbar). When you're ready to resume recording, click the **Resume Recorder** button.

To run the macro, follow the steps detailed previously in the "Running Macros" section. If you don't get the results you want, try again. You can use the same macro name and replace the original. It's probably faster just to re-create the macro than it is to learn how to use the Microsoft Visual Basic Editor. If you're interested in learning more about the Editor, check out Que Publishing's *Special Edition Using Microsoft Office Word 2003* by Bill Camarda (ISBN: 0-7897-2859-X).

Recording Two Sample Macros

The best way for you to learn how to write macros is "just do it." So, the following sections contain the steps to create two basic macros. Even if you don't think you will ever use the macros, take a few minutes and create them anyway. You'll learn a lot about the way macros work.

Creating a Signature Block Macro

A typical signature block is two lines down from the last line of a letter. A signature block generally contains a person's name, followed by four blank lines (or enough room for a signature), the person's title, and other identifying information. This might include an email address or direct line phone number.

You can create this macro in a blank document, or if you prefer, you can position the insertion point at the end of a letter. You can do double duty by creating your macro and inserting a signature block in the letter at the same time.

Follow these steps to create the sample signature block macro:

1. Choose **Tools**, **Macro**, **Record New Macro**.
2. Type the name `sigblock` in the **Macro name** text box.
3. If necessary, select a location for the macro in the **Store macro in** drop-down list.
4. Click **OK** to start the macro recorder.
5. Press **Enter** two (or three) times to insert two blank lines between the last line of the letter and the closing.
6. Type `Sincerely,` or `Warm regards,` or whatever closing phrase you prefer.
7. Press **Enter** four (or five) times to insert four blank lines.
8. Type your name and then press **Enter**.
9. Type your title and then press **Enter**.
10. Type your email address or phone number and then press **Enter**.
11. Click the **Stop Recording** button to stop recording the macro.

Now, open a blank document and run the macro you just created. Don't blink—if you do, you might miss seeing the macro run. Some macros run so quickly that it might seem as though the results appear out of thin air.

Creating a Document Identification Footer

This sample macro creates a footer that appears on every page of the document. The filename and location will be inserted against the left margin of the footer, in 8-point type. This type of document identification is popular, especially when you share documents on a company network. Anyone who receives a copy of the document knows where it can be found on the network.

To create a document identification footer, do the following:

1. Choose **Tools**, **Macro**, **Record New Macro**.
2. Type the name idfooter in the **Macro name** text box.
3. If necessary, select a location for the macro in the **Store macro in** drop-down list and then click **OK** to start the macro recorder.
4. Choose **View**, **Header and Footer**.

5. Click the **Switch Between Header and Footer** button on the Header and Footer toolbar to move down to the footer space.
6. Click the **Font Size** drop-down list arrow and choose **8**. If you want, change the font as well by clicking the **Font** drop-down list arrow and choosing a new font.
7. Click the **Insert AutoText** button on the Header and Footer toolbar.
8. Choose **Filename and path**.
9. Click **Close** to clear the Header and Footer toolbar and return the insertion point to the document window.

10. Click the **Stop Recording** button to stop recording the macro.

Now, open a document that you have already created. Run the idfooter macro to add a footer with the path and filename for the document. The footer will be visible only in Print Layout, so if necessary, switch to Print Layout to view the footer. Don't worry. You don't have to save the changes; this is just so that you can test your new macro.

Assigning Macros to Shortcut Keys, Toolbars, and Menus

If you find yourself running the same handful of macros over and over again, consider assigning them to a menu, shortcut key, or toolbar. You'll avoid repeating the menu commands to open the Macros dialog box and the process of selecting the macro from the list. I find myself using shortcut keys because my hands are already on the keyboard, so most of my macros are assigned to a keystroke combination. Your habits may be different, so choose whichever method is most convenient for you.

Assigning Macros to Shortcut Keys

When you create a new macro, you have the option of selecting a shortcut key in the Record Macro dialog box. If you didn't assign a shortcut key when you created the macro, you can do it later using the Customize dialog box.

To assign a macro to a shortcut key when you create the macro, follow these steps:

1. Choose **Tools**, **Macro**, **Record New Macro**.
2. Type the name of the macro in the **Macro name** text box.
3. Click the **Keyboard** button to open the Customize Keyboard dialog box (see Figure 16.4).

FIGURE 16.4
You can assign shortcut keys to menu commands, macros, fonts, AutoText entries, styles, or common symbols in the Customize Keyboard dialog box.

Current key assignment

Click here to insert the keyboard shortcut

4. Press the keystroke combination you want to use in the **Press new shortcut key** text box. For example, press **Ctrl+L**. If the shortcut key is already assigned, the current assignment is shown directly underneath the shortcut key that you typed in. At this point, you can either delete the shortcut key and try another combination, or you can go ahead and reassign it to this macro.

5. Choose **Assign** to assign the macro to the shortcut key.

6. Choose **Close** to clear the Customize Keyboard dialog box.

7. Choose **Close** again to clear the Customize dialog box.

To assign a macro to a shortcut key in the Customize dialog box, follow these steps:

1. Choose **Tools**, **Customize** to open the Customize dialog box (see Figure 16.5).

FIGURE 16.5

You can assign a macro to a shortcut key in the Customize dialog box.

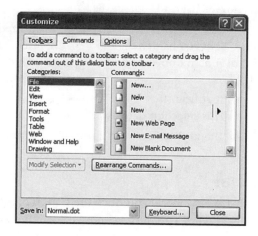

2. Click the **Keyboard** button to open the Customize Keyboard dialog box.

3. Scroll down through the **Categories** list and then select **Macros**. The list box on the right displays a list of available macros.

4. Select the macro you want to assign.

5. Click in the **Press new shortcut key** text box and then press the keystroke combination you want to use. If the shortcut key is already assigned, the current assignment is shown directly underneath the shortcut key that you typed in. At this point, you can either delete the shortcut key and try another combination, or you can go ahead and reassign it to this macro.

6. Choose **Assign** to assign the macro to the shortcut key.

7. Choose **Close** to clear the Customize Keyboard dialog box.

8. Choose **Close** again to clear the Customize dialog box.

If you decide later to remove a macro assignment, you can do so through the Customize Keyboard dialog box.

To remove a keyboard shortcut, follow these steps:

1. Choose **Tools**, **Customize** to open the Customize dialog box (refer to Figure 16.5).

2. Click the **Keyboard** button to open the Customize Keyboard dialog box.

3. Scroll down the **Categories** list and choose **Macros**.

4. Select the macro in the **Macros** list. The key assignment for that macro appears in the **Current keys** list box.

5. Select the keyboard shortcut from the **Current keys** list box. This selection activates the Remove button.

6. Click **Remove** to delete the keyboard shortcut (but not the macro).

tip

If you get a little carried away with your keyboard customization and decide that you want to start over, click the **Reset All** button in the Customize Keyboard dialog box to reset the keyboard shortcuts to their original assignments.

Assigning Macros to a Toolbar

Here again, when you create a new macro, you have the option of selecting a toolbar in the Record Macro dialog box. If you didn't choose a toolbar when you created the macro, you can do it later using the Customize dialog box. With either method, you need to make sure the toolbar is displayed first.

To assign a macro to a toolbar when you create the macro, follow these steps:

1. Make sure the toolbar is displayed onscreen.

2. Choose **Tools**, **Macro**, **Record New Macro**.

3. Type the name of the macro in the **Macro name** text box.

4. Click the **Toolbars** button to open the Customize dialog box (see Figure 16.6).

5. Click and drag the macro entry to the toolbar that you want to assign the macro to. A black guideline shows you where the macro button will be placed. A special mouse pointer shows you that you are dragging a command to the toolbar (see Figure 16.7).

FIGURE 16.6

The macro you are creating is shown in the Commands list box of the Customize dialog box.

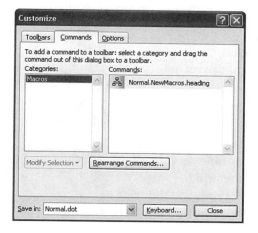

Special mouse pointer
Black guideline

FIGURE 16.7

Click and drag the macro button to a toolbar to assign the macro to that toolbar.

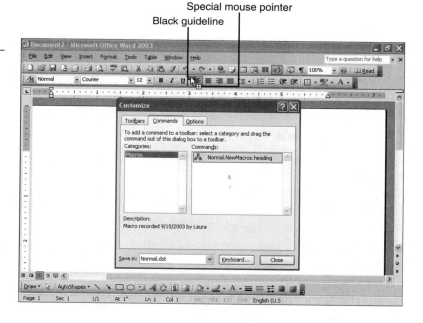

6. Choose **Close** to start recording the macro.

To assign a macro to a toolbar in the Customize dialog box, do the following:

1. Make sure the toolbar is displayed onscreen.

2. Choose **Tools**, **Customize** to open the Customize dialog box.

3. If necessary, click the **Commands** tab.

4. Scroll down through the **Categories** list and then select **Macros**. The list box on the right displays a list of available macros.

5. Select the macro you want to assign.

6. Click and drag the macro entry to the toolbar that you want to assign the macro to. A black guideline shows you where the macro button will be placed. A special mouse pointer shows you that you are dragging a command to the toolbar (refer to Figure 16.7).

7. Choose **Close** to assign the macro to the toolbar.

If you decide later to remove a macro button from a toolbar, you can click and drag it off the toolbar. First, display the Customize dialog box by choosing **Tools**, **Customize**. Next, hold down the **Alt** key; then click and drag the macro button down into the document window.

Assigning Macros to Menus

One last time! When you create a new macro, you have the option of assigning the macro to a menu from the Record Macro dialog box. If you didn't select a menu when you created the macro, you can do it later using the Customize dialog box. I know this is starting to sound like a broken record, but readers should be able to read just the steps for their preferred method.

To assign a macro to a menu when you create the macro, follow these steps:

1. Make sure the toolbar is displayed onscreen.

2. Choose **Tools**, **Macro**, **Record New Macro**.

3. Type the name of the macro in the **Macro name** text box.

4. Click the **Toolbars** button to open the Customize dialog box (refer to Figure 16.6). The macro you are creating is shown in the Commands list box.

5. Click and drag the macro entry to the menu that you want to assign the macro to. A black guideline shows you where the macro button will be placed. A special mouse pointer shows you that you are dragging a command to the menu (see Figure 16.8).

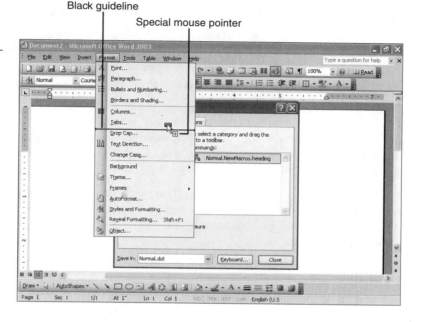

FIGURE 16.8

Click and drag the macro button to a menu to assign the macro to that menu.

Black guideline

Special mouse pointer

6. Choose **Close** to start recording the macro.

To assign a macro to a menu in the Customize dialog box, do the following:

1. Choose **Tools**, **Customize** to open the Customize dialog box.

2. If necessary, click the **Commands** tab.

3. Scroll down through the **Categories** list and then select **Macros**. The list box on the right displays a list of available macros.

4. Select the macro you want to assign.

5. Click and drag the macro entry to the menu that you want to assign the macro to. Don't release the mouse button; just let the menu open. A black guideline shows you where the macro button will be placed when you release the mouse button. A special mouse pointer shows you that you are dragging a command to the menu (refer to Figure 16.8).

6. Choose **Close** to assign the macro to the menu.

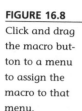

tip

If you decide later to remove a macro button from a menu, you can click and drag it off the menu. Choose **Tools**, **Customize** to open the Customize dialog box. Open the menu. Click and drag the macro off the menu.

Protecting Your System from Macro Viruses

We've all heard about the latest virus being unleashed on the Internet. Computer viruses spread rapidly in an environment of email messages with attached documents. The best protection you can have against viruses is a good antivirus program. Word has some built-in controls to help prevent further risk of virus infection in Word files.

A macro virus is a type of computer virus that is stored in a macro, either within a file, a template, or an "add-in," which is essentially a third-party utility that you can use with Word. To protect your system, you should increase your level of security and open files only from trusted sources.

Digital signatures are one way of identifying a trusted source. In Word, you can attach a digital signature to a macro that you want to share. Another way to identify a trusted source is to add the publisher of the macro to a list of "trusted publishers."

You can find more information on each of these topics in the Word 2003 Help topics. I encourage you to start there when you're ready to take these steps. For more detailed information, take a look at Que Publishing's *Special Edition Using Microsoft Office Word 2003* by Bill Camarda (ISBN: 0-7897-2859-X).

THE ABSOLUTE MINIMUM

After reading this chapter, you now know how to

- Use macros for repetitive tasks to save time and guarantee consistency.
- Run macros that someone else has created and given to you in a document or in a template.
- Create macros by using the two sample macros in this chapter as a guide.
- Assign macros to keyboard shortcuts, toolbars, and menus for easier access.
- Use Word's tools to combat macro viruses, which are becoming increasingly common.

In the next chapter, you'll learn how to save your documents in XML format.

17

WORKING WITH XML

Everyone is talking about the Extensible Markup Language, or XML. Why is it such a hot topic? XML is a standard language that was developed to improve online communications and data transfer between businesses. It has evolved into a method by which a company can leverage all the information that is contained in documents, spreadsheets, and presentations. That information can be "repurposed" and used along with information from other documents.

What does this mean to you? Simply that you can open an XML file and work with it without special training. You can also save one of your documents in XML format for someone else to manipulate. It's a high-tech concept that is moving down into the trenches, so even a beginner should know what it is and how to deal with it.

Understanding XML

Technically speaking, XML is a pared-down version of the Standard Generalized Markup Language (SGML), created especially for Web documents. It allows system administrators to create customized tags for their industry or business. These tags surround key pieces of information in a document. These key pieces can then be extracted and used in other applications.

XML files are plain text files, just like Hypertext Markup Language (HTML) files. The only difference is that HTML tags are predefined and XML tags are not. Someone has to define the tags that are going to be used, how they are to be used, and how they can appear in a document. This type of document definition is known as an *XML Schema*. Many professional groups, industries, and associations are developing XML Schemas to facilitate the sharing of data.

Word 2003 supports XML file formats, so you can open an XML document and work with it just as you would any other document. You can also save a document in XML format so the data can be extracted from it and used in other applications.

Let me give you an example of how XML can be used. Say you are working on a document that contains data someone else wants to extract and use in a database. That same data will be published on the company intranet and on the Internet. Furthermore, it must be in a format that can be downloaded to colleagues' PDAs. The XML format makes this possible by providing a standard means of identifying the different pieces of data.

The key is to realize that after you create the document and enclose the data in XML tags, that data can be reused over and over again. It can be extracted and used in a variety of applications, even those running on different platforms. XML is a "standard" that will allow programs to freely use XML information from a variety of different sources. The possibilities are endless. Modern businesses are only scratching the surface of the data processing power that XML brings to the table.

note

XML features, except for saving documents as XML with the WordML Schema, are available only in Microsoft Office Professional Edition 2003 or the standalone product of Word 2003.

Opening XML Documents

You open an XML document just as you would any other document. You can make it easier to find the document in the file list by limiting the file type to just XML.

To open an XML document, follow these steps:

1. Choose **File**, **Open** (**Ctrl+O**) to display the Open dialog box.
2. Click the **Files of type** drop-down list arrow and choose **XML Files (*.xml)**.
3. Locate the file and then select it.
4. Choose **Open** or double-click the file. Figure 17.1 shows an XML document in the document window.

Start tag   XML tag

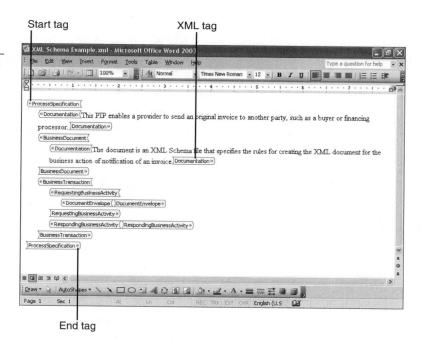

End tag

Notice in Figure 17.1 that XML tags come in pairs with a beginning and end tag. The XML document is contained within a pair of outer tags (in this case, the ProcessSpecification tag) and tags can be nested several layers deep. Each pair of XML tags encloses a data element. XML tags (such as the DocumentEnvelope tag in Figure 17.1) can be empty unless the Schema used requires that it contains data.

Saving XML Documents in the Special WordML Format

When you save a document as XML, Word can use its own XML schema, known as WordML, to apply XML tags that store information such as the file properties.

The special WordML Schema is intended to allow applications, other than Word, that recognize and use the WordML Schema, to display and use Word documents with formatting, structure, and content preserved.

These tags also define the structure of the document (that is, paragraphs, headings, and tables). Word employs the XML tags to store formatting and layout information. Word can also employ custom XML Schemas that allow you to save data from a document that has been marked using predefined XML tags. Custom schemas are generally developed by IT staff, or the resident expert, and then distributed to the users.

To save a document in WordML, do the following:

1. Open an existing document or create a new document.
2. Choose **File**, **Save As** to display the Save As dialog box.
3. Browse to and select a location to save the document.
4. Open the **Save as type** drop-down list and choose **XML Document (*.xml)** (see Figure 17.2).

FIGURE 17.2

This file is being saved as XML using the built-in WordML Schema.

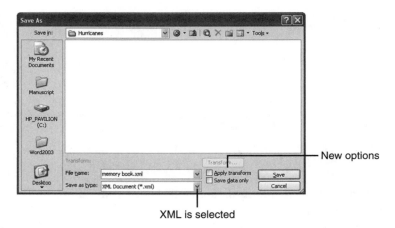

New options

XML is selected

5. To save as WordML only and preserve Word formatting, ensure the **Save data only** and **Apply transform** check boxes are not selected.
6. Type a name for the file in the **File name** text box.
7. Choose **Save**.

The saved WordML document, in XML format, can now be opened, with formatting preserved, in Word or any application that supports the WordML schema.

Attaching Schemas to Word Documents

Before you can mark up and save XML data from a Word document, you need to attach a Schema that defines the structure and content of the XML document. An organization may supply the Schemas, or you might have even created one of your own.

To attach a Schema to a Word document, do the following:

1. Open an existing document or create a new document.

2. Select **Tools**, **Templates and Add-Ins** and select the **XML Schema** tab.

3. Select the **Add Schema** button in the XML Schema tab of the Templates and Add-Ins dialog box (see Figure 17.3).

4. Browse to, locate, and select the Schema to be attached. XML Schemas have the .xsd file extension.

5. Choose **Open**.

6. Enter an alias for the Schema in the **Alias** text box of the Schema Settings dialog box (see Figure 17.4). Word will refer to the Schema by the alias that you enter.

7. Click **OK**. The newly attached Schema appears checked in the **Checked schemas are currently attached** section of the XML Schema tab. The check mark indicates that the Schema is currently active. You can make any attached Schema active by selecting its check box.

8. Click **OK** to close the Templates and Add-Ins dialog box. Figure 17.5 shows a Word document with an attached and active XML Schema.

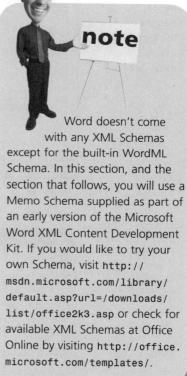

note

Word doesn't come with any XML Schemas except for the built-in WordML Schema. In this section, and the section that follows, you will use a Memo Schema supplied as part of an early version of the Microsoft Word XML Content Development Kit. If you would like to try your own Schema, visit http://msdn.microsoft.com/library/default.asp?url=/downloads/list/office2k3.asp or check for available XML Schemas at Office Online by visiting http://office.microsoft.com/templates/.

FIGURE 17.3

You can manage XML Schemas using the XML Schema tab of the Templates and Add-Ins dialog box.

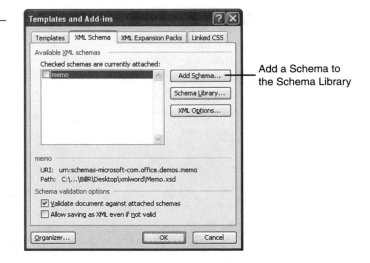

Add a Schema to the Schema Library

FIGURE 17.4

Assign a friendly alias to the XML Schema.

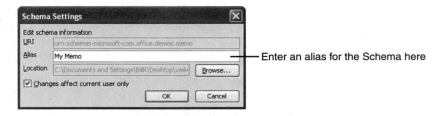

Enter an alias for the Schema here

FIGURE 17.5

The XML Structure task pane can be used to apply XML tags to data in the document.

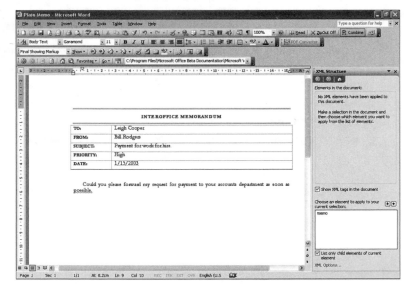

You use the XML Structure task pane to apply XML tags to the data in the document. You can display the XML Structure task pane, at any time, by choosing **View**, **Tas_k_ Pane** and then selecting **XML Structure** from the task pane's drop-down list.

Marking XML Data in a Word Document

After an XML Schema has been attached to a document and made active, you can mark data in the documents as XML according to the rules of the Schema. This allows extraction of the data from the document in XML format in a standardized way. The XML data can then be used in other applications that also support XML. Having data represented in a standard way, using XML and XML Schemas, allows for the easy interchange of data. Data, in XML format, is currently being used in such fields as medicine, science, law, engineering, and mathematics.

To mark data in a Word document as XML, do the following:

1. Ensure the Schema to be used is attached to the open Word document and is active. If in doubt, refer to the preceding section.

2. If necessary, display the XML Structure task pane by choosing **View**, **Tas_k_ Pane** and then selecting **XML Structure** from the task pane's drop-down list.

3. Place the cursor inside the body of the document. Alternatively, select the block of text that contains all the data that is to be marked using XML tags.

4. In **Choose an element to apply to your current selection** in the XML Structure task pane, select the XML tag that defines the type of document. This is the outermost (or parent) tag that encloses all XML data in the document and is applied first. In Figure 17.5, this is the memo tag. Prior to applying any XML tags, the outermost, or parent, tag should be the only tag listed in **Choose an element to apply to your current selection**.

5. At the **Apply to entire document?** prompt, choose to apply the tag to the entire document or to the selection only, depending on your choice in step 3. When the document is saved as XML data, text that is not marked using XML tags is not saved. So, don't worry if your selection in step 3 contains additional text.

   The outermost XML tag is now applied and the **Choose an element to apply to your current selection** section of the XML Structure task pane should now contain the list of XML tags to be applied to data within this outermost XML tag. Figure 17.6 shows the outermost memo tag applied to a Word document and the newly available XML child tags.

FIGURE 17.6

The XML Structure task pane contains a list of all the XML tags that can be applied to data in the document.

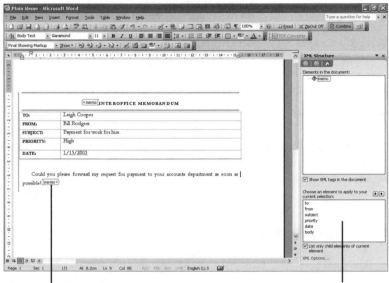

The outermost tag encloses all text that contains data to be marked as XML

This section now contains child XML tags to be applied to data in the document

6. In the **Elements in the document** section of the XML Structure task pane, select the uppermost tag applied to the document data in step 4. This way, you can view the child tags of the outermost tag in the bottom pane. In the example in Figure 17.5, we select the memo tag in **Elements in the document**.

7. Select the text in the document that you want to apply the appropriate tag listed in **Choose an element to apply to your current selection** in the XML Structure task pane. For the example shown in Figure 17.5, the first element is **to**, and we want to send our memo to Leigh Cooper. So, we select **Leigh Cooper** in the Word document.

> **note**
>
> The prompt in step 5 of the preceding steps appears only when you first apply the single outermost tag listed alone in **Choose an element to apply to your current selection**. This single tag defines the XML document and is applied first.

8. Select the tag in **Choose an element to apply to your current selection** that we want to apply to the selected text. In the memo example in Figure 17.5, we select the **to** tag to apply to the selected name Leigh Cooper.

9. Repeat steps 6–8 for each of the child tags of the outermost tag. Figure 17.7 shows the completed memo example.

FIGURE 17.7

The data in this
Word document
is marked as
XML with XML
tags.

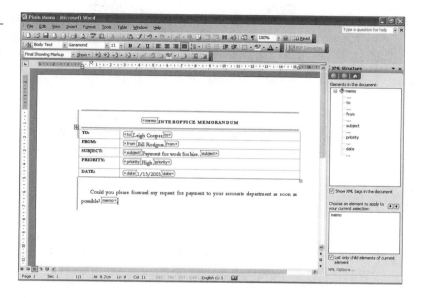

Notice in Figure 17.7 that the outermost memo tag in
the top section of the XML Structure task pane has a
question mark next to it. Notice also the squiggly
vertical lines in the document. These lines indicate
a problem with the document. Any attempt to save
this document as XML data will result in an error.
Right-clicking on the question mark provides information about the error. In this case, required content is missing from the document. Here, we forgot
to mark the *body* of the memo. We can correct this
error by selecting the text at the end of the document and marking it with the body tag.

Saving XML Documents

After data in a document is marked as XML according to the requirements of an attached Schema,
you can easily save the data as XML.

To save a document as XML data, do the following:

1. Choose **File**, **Save As** to display the Save As
   dialog box.

2. Browse to and select a location to save the document.

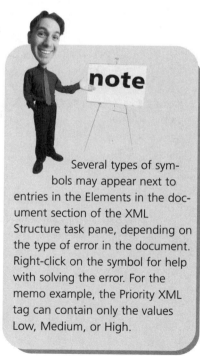

note

Several types of sym-
bols may appear next to
entries in the Elements in the document section of the XML
Structure task pane, depending on
the type of error in the document.
Right-click on the symbol for help
with solving the error. For the
memo example, the Priority XML
tag can contain only the values
Low, Medium, or High.

3. Open the **Save as type** drop-down list and choose **XML Document (*.xml)**.

4. Type a name for the file in the **File name** text box.

5. Ensure the **Save data only** check box in the Save As dialog box is checked.

6. Choose **Save**.

7. In the Microsoft Office Word Warning box, select **Continue**. Figure 17.8 shows the saved XML data file opened in Internet Explorer. This simple text file now fully represents the data extracted from the original Word document.

If the marked XML data to be saved conforms to the attached Schema, the warning dialog box in step 7 should note only that document features such as formatting, pictures, and objects will be lost. This is fine when you only want to save marked XML data from the document.

If, however, the warning dialog states that the document cannot be saved as XML because its structure violates the rules set by the schema, you will need to check for errors. Look in the Elements in the document section of the XML Structure task pane for entries with symbols next to them. Right-click on the symbol for help with the error.

Working with XML files is an advanced concept, so there is a lot more to learn. See Que Publishing's *Special Edition Using Microsoft Office Word 2003* by Bill Camarda (ISBN: 0-7897-2859-X) for more details.

FIGURE 17.8

The saved XML data, conforming to the XML schema used, is now ready to share and is available for use in other applications that support XML.

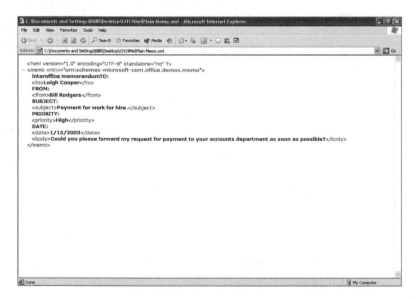

THE ABSOLUTE MINIMUM

After reading this chapter, you now know how to

- Grasp the basics of the XML format so you have a better idea of why it is used.

- Open an XML document so you can work with it just like any other document.

- Save a document in XML format so it can be used in other applications.

This is the last chapter. You made it all the way through! Congratulations! You now have a good understanding of Word 2003 and its features. For more information about other Office 2003 books, visit us online at www.quepublishing.com.

PART VI

ON THE WEB
(www.quepublishing.com)

Index

C

    revision marks, Track
        Changes feature, 309-310
    text, 67

**Colors and Lines tab,
    PDF:371**

column markers, 172

Column tab, 181

columns
    formatting, 144
    newspaper, 143, 234
    parallel, 234
    setting up, 143-144
    tables, 169
        adding, 174
        copying, 176
        deleting, 175-176
        formatting, 181-182
        moving, 176
        selecting, 173-174
        widths, 172-173
    tabular, converting to
        tables, 194-195

Columns button, 143

**Columns command (Format
    menu), 144**

**Columns dialog box,
    143-144**

commands
    context menu, Delete Cells,
        175
    Edit menu
        Copy, 42
        Cut, 42
        Find, 90, 93-94
        Office Clipboard, 42,
            250
        Paste, 42
        Paste Special, 253, 256

        Redo, 44
        Replace, 91
        Undo, 44, 148
    File menu
        New, 292, 295-297,
            301, PDF:376
        Open, 26, 303, 345,
            PDF:394
        Page Setup, 69, 132-134
        Print, 54-55, 133, 316
        Print Preview, 53, 148
        Print, Properties, 55
        Save, 21
        Save as, 23, 299, 346,
            351
        Send To, 58
        Send To, Mail Recipient,
            58
        Send To: Mail Recipient
            (for Review), 308
        Send To, Recipient Using
            a Fax Modem, 56
        Send To, Recipient Using
            Internet Fax, 57
        Versions, 326
    Format menu
        AutoFormat, 126
        Background, Printed
            Watermark, 141
        Borders and Shading,
            145-147, 185, 188,
            218-219
        Bullets and Numbering,
            201-202, 207-209
        Columns, 144
        Font, 66-67
        Paragraph, 115-118,
            121-122
        Reveal Formatting, 76
        Styles and Formatting,
            152, 303

        Tabs, 112-113
        Text box, 231
        Text Direction, 184
    Help menu
        About Microsoft Office
            Word, PDF:400
        Check for Updates,
            PDF:400
        Detect and Repair,
            PDF:401-402
        Equation Editor Help
            Topics, PDF:373
        Help Topics, 56
        Microsoft Word Help, 14
    Insert menu
        AutoText, AutoText,
            98-99
        AutoText, New, 99
        Break, 130
        Comment, 312
        Diagram, PDF:368
        Object, 254-256,
            PDF:358-360,
            PDF:371-372
        Page Numbers, 135
        Picture, Chart, PDF:358
        Picture, Clip Art, 220
        Picture, From File,
            223-225
        Picture, From Scanner or
            Camera, 224
        Picture, WordArt, 245
        Symbol, 74
        Text Box, 229, 231
    Layout menu, Fit Diagram
        to Contents, PDF:369
    New menu, Folder, 34
    Reinstall or Repair Office
        (Setup application),
        PDF:402-403

Text Form Field Options,
PDF:383
Versions, 326-327
WordArt Gallery, 245
Zoom, 48

dictionaries
bilingual, 88-89
custom, 84

digital signatures, 342

division formula, 191

document identification footer macros, recording, 335

document lists, sorting, 28-29

Document Map view, 50

documents
blank, 10
Change access, 325
comparing, 317-319
conversion files, 23
converting, 37-38
copying, 35-36
creating
templates, 292-295
wizards, 294-295
deleting, 36-37
emailing, 57-58, 308
faxing, 55-57
icons, 26
inserting, 287-288
main (Mail Merge),
265-266
modifying. *See* formatting
moving, 35-36
multiple, 45-46
opening, 26-28
previous versions, 325-327

protecting, 158
available styles, 322-323
comments, 320-322
document parts,
321-322
IRM (Information Rights Management), 325
passwords, 323-324
read-only setting,
319-320
Track Changes feature,
320-322
Read access, 325
recently accessed, opening,
26
recovered, opening,
PDF:391-394
renaming, 36
saving
alternate formats, 23
older Word versions,
259-260
Word formats, 21-22
searching, 31-32
settings, changing globally,
291
switching, 46
templates
creating, 301
items, transferring to,
304-305
viewing, 47-48
XML (Extensible Markup
Language)
opening, 344-345
question mark (?), 351
saving, 351-352
saving to WordML
formats, 345-346
squiggly vertical lines,
351
XML Schemas, attaching to,
347-349

downloading templates, Office Online Web site, 297-300

drag-and-drop, text, 43

drawing canvas, 228
diagrams, PDF:369
text boxes, 229-231

drawing objects, drawing canvas, 228

Drawing toolbar, 229

drives
adding to My Places bar, 30
navigating, 30-31

drop-down fields (form fields)
adding, PDF:380-382
help text, PDF:384

Drop-Down Form Field Options dialog box, PDF:381

E

Edit menu commands
Copy, 42
Cut, 42
Find, 90, 93-94
Office Clipboard, 42, 250
Paste, 42
Paste Special, 253, 256
Redo, 44
Replace, 91
Undo, 44, 148

Edit WordArt Text dialog box, 245-246

emailing files, 57-58, 308

How can we make this index more useful? Email us at indexes@quepublishing.com

How can we make this index more useful? Email us at indexes@quepublishing.com

informIT

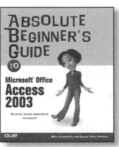